Koehler, Jack H. 1936-
The science of pocket billiards.
1. Sport 2. Billiards 3. Pool (Game) I. Title

Published by:
SPORTOLOGY PUBLICATIONS
N2689 Spring Lane
Marinette, WI 54143

Library of Congress Catalog Card Number: 88-62401
International Standard Book Number: 0-9622890-2-7 (paper)

Second Edition, 1995
3 - 4 - 5 - 6 - 7 –8 -9
Printed in the United States of America

THE SCIENCE OF POCKET BILLIARDS

BY
Jack H. Koehler

SPORTOLOGY PUBLICATIONS
Marinette, WI

Jack H. Koehler

DEDICATION
This book is dedicated to the pool players of the world,
those of the past, present, and future.

CONTENTS

PREFACE

Is it "*pocket billiards*" or is it "*pool*?" In this book these terms are considered synonymous and are used interchangeably. Life is too short to worry about semantics just for the sake of semantics.

Pool is a unique game. To be a great pool player requires the knowledge of a physicist, the strategy of a chess player, and the precision of a brain surgeon. However, pool can be played and enjoyed by anyone regardless of sex, physical stature, age, or intelligence. A person can participate competitively for decades. Willie Hoppe won his first world billiards championship at the age of 18 and his last one 46 years later at the age of 65.

There are similarities among all serious pool players. They enjoy the challenge, the adventure, and the fulfillment that the game offers. Every player who has ever executed a shot shares the thought processes of players a century ago and those who will play centuries into the future. Consider what may go through a person's mind while shooting a simple shot: "Aim a little more to the left; no, that's too far; a trifle to the right; OK, that's perfect; check the striking point on the cue ball, that's OK; check aim again; everything feels perfect--now shoot!" That could be you making that shot, the great Willie Mosconi, or any other pool player from the past or future.

Fundamentals as well as the advanced aspects of pocket billiards are presented in this book. The beginner may not be able to (or want to) comprehend all of the technical aspects the first time through. As one gains experience, the technical aspects will become more intuitive and less academic. Keep in mind, **FACTS ARE FACTS WHETHER YOU'RE AWARE OF THEM OR NOT**. The beginner should concentrate on the fundamentals and not be too concerned about the technical analysis the first time through. As the player becomes progressively more accomplished, he/she can go back and fill in the technical gaps.

There are two major components that combine to make up a player's competence. They are *knowledge* and *ability*. Every shot of every game has a knowledge component and an ability component. To separate the two; ask yourself, "Do I know (knowledge) where to hit this ball?" and "Am I able (ability) to hit it there?" Only the knowledge component can be learned from this book (or for that matter, any other book, person, or source). The ability component can only be attained through practice and repetitive execution. Usually, knowledge lags behind ability. However, that should not be the case after carefully reading and absorbing the material in this book.

Many players have become very good at pool without having a great deal of technical knowledge. But then, birds can fly without knowing the principles of aerodynamics. Technical knowledge enables one to progress faster and further.

Pool knowledge is passed most effectively from one person to another by technical explanation. For example, a pool instructor may point to the proper banking point for a particular bank shot; the student makes the shot and "that's it" there is no residual knowledge. If instead, the instructor indicates exactly how the banking point can be determined; describes all the variables and how each affects the shot; the student is then able to apply this technical knowledge to all subsequent bank shots.

Shooting a shot in pool is much like operating a computer. In operating a computer, information or data is fed in. The program within the computer manipulates the information then returns a response. Similarly, in shooting a pool shot, information is fed in (striking the cue ball); the program (laws of physics) causes the information to be manipulated (movement of balls); then returns a response (new position of balls). If all the relevant information is fed in accurately, the proper response will occur; if not, something unexpected will happen. The information given the cue ball can be thought of as a simple three-part code. The elements of the code are: (1) The *speed* with which the cue ball is struck. (2) The *aim* of the stick as the cue ball is struck. And (3) the *point* at which the cue ball is struck. This code can whimsically be referred to as the "**SAP**" code (**S**peed, **A**im, and **P**oint of contact). Learn the SAP code and you will never miss a shot or lose a game.

Many examples of shots are used in this book to explain various concepts. The reader is encouraged to make up two or three additional examples depicting the same concept. Doing so will help solidify the concept in the mind.

INTRODUCTION

CONTROLLED EXPERIMENTATION

Much of the information presented in this book was determined from controlled experiments. It's difficult to predict exactly what happens when one ball collides with another ball or cushion unless its direction and speed are precisely controlled. Equipment was designed and built specifically to control these variables. The following describes some of the equipment and techniques used in conducting the experiments:

Speed control--Several types of ramps (photo 0-1) were used to assure ball speed control. The position on the ramp, from which the ball is released, determines the speed of the ball. Using the ramp, a specific ball speed could be duplicated as often as desired.

Directional control--An alignment box (photo 0-2) was designed to control ball direction. Inside the box are two metal blades that are set one ball diameter, plus 3-thousandths of an inch, apart. Rolling a ball through the box assures directional control to precise tolerances. Using the ramp and alignment box in conjunction, both ball speed and direction can be controlled with great precision. Photo 0-3 shows various types of

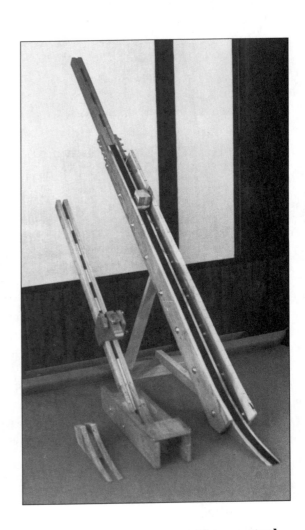

PHOTO 0-1. Ramps used to control ball speed.

jigs (and other equipment) used to position the object ball (or target) at the end of the alignment box so that it could be struck at different angles.

PHOTO 0-2. Alignment box.

PHOTO 0-4. Alignment sight.

PHOTO 0-3. Jigs and other equipment.

PHOTO 0-5. Targets.

Alignment sight--The alignment sight (photo 0-4) was used to align the desired trajectory of the object ball prior to being struck by the impacting ball.

Targets--Targets (photo 0-5) were used to determine where the balls struck the cushion. Knowing this point, the path of each ball and the various associated angles were able to be determined. The targets consist of a strip of mylar over carbon paper taped onto a formica backing. A black mark is left on the mylar at the point where it is struck by the ball.

Balls--Each ball was carefully weighed; only those balls that were within a few tenths of a gram of each other were used in the collision experiments. The surface of each ball was clean but without wax or polish. Each ball was wiped clean of dirt, dust, and fingerprints prior to each collision experiment.

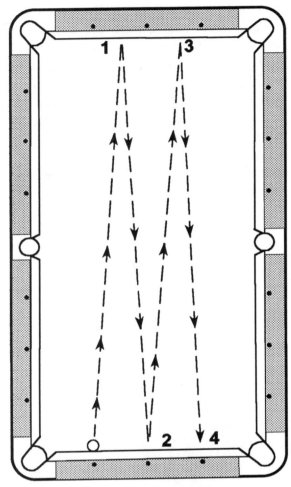

FIGURE 0-1. Ball-speed terminology relative to travel distance.

MEASUREMENT UNITS

Both English and metric units of measurement are used in this book. A precedent for this confusion has already been established. For example, in describing the dimensions of a pool cue, the length is always given in inches and the diameter of the shaft is always given in millimeters. Conventional usage was used whenever possible.

BALL SPEED TERMINOLOGY

Cue ball speed is described relative to how many lengths of the table it will travel (figure 0-1). The terms either describe speed (slow, fast, etc.) or cue stick striking force (soft, hard, etc.). The following terms were used:

Table lengths	Speed	Striking force
1	Very slow	Very soft
2	Slow	Soft
3	Medium	Medium
4	Fast	Hard
4+	Very fast	Very hard

ESTIMATING ANGLES

Angles are a very *important* part of pool. Many people are only able to describe angles as being big, little, or medium. This may be good enough for the masses but it's not good

enough for the pool player. In order to discuss any shot one must be able to describe the angles involved. The precision in which one can estimate angles plays a large part in how well that person retains shot information in the mind. Without an intimate acquaintance with angles the information presented in this book will be perceived and retained in only vague generalities.

To become better aquatinted with angles try this exercise: With a straight edge, draw a random series of crossing lines on a sheet of paper. Estimate the number of degrees in each of the acute (less than 90°) angles made by the crossing lines. Now measure each angle with a protractor. Keep repeating this exercise until you're sure you can estimate angles better than your pool competitors.

If you were to start at a point and draw two 57-inch lines such that they were one inch apart at the end, you would have drawn an angle of one degree. This makes it easy to estimate angles on a pool table. It just so happens that most pool cues are 57 or 58 inches long. Therefor, you can create precise angles by holding the butt end at a point and moving the tip through an ark. For each inch that the tip is moved an angle of one degree is created.

CHAPTER 1

EQUIPMENT

POOL CUE

A pool cue is generally referred to as a *cue, cue stick,* or *stick.* Serious pool players should have their own personal cue stick. Most people play better and more confidently when they use only one familiar stick. Having one's own pool cue may even eliminate some behavioral problems; a person is less likely to bang it on the table, throw it, or otherwise subject it to an abusive tantrum.

Most house sticks (in pool rooms and bars) are one piece; most personal sticks are made in two pieces. Figure 1-1 shows a two-piece cue stick and its component parts. Each of these parts will be examined in detail.

Tip--Most tips are made of leather; other materials have been tried but none have gained wide acceptance. Leather suits the purpose because it resists slipping off the cue ball and lacks resiliency. When the cue tip strikes the cue ball, the leather compresses and conforms to the curvature of the cue ball. The leather does not try to resume its original shape until after the cue ball has been propelled on its course and is no longer in contact with the tip.

Leather for the tip can be from elk hide, cowhide, water-buffalo hide, or practically any other type of hide. The texture of the leather may vary somewhat depending on its source, but this has little overall effect on its function. Some players have a preference for certain types of leather but this preference probably has more of a psychological than functional basis.

Hardness is the most important characteristic of a cue tip. Unfortunately, there is no standard by which cue-tip hardness can be measured. Hardness can be approximated by pressing the thumb nail into the tip and releasing; the deeper the indentation, the softer the tip. Usually, the thicker the tip, the softer it is.

Characteristics of a soft tip relative to that of a hard tip are:

1. The collision between the soft tip and cue ball is cushioned and thus requires slightly greater striking force to achieve the

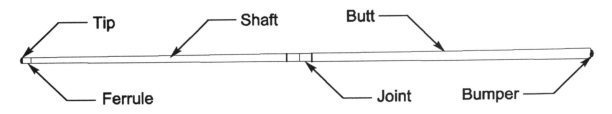

FIGURE 1-1. Two-piece cue stick and its component parts.

desired ball speed.

2. The soft tip has larger surface contact with the cue ball and therefore is less likely to miscue (slip off) when the cue ball is struck off-center.

3. The soft tip has a tendency to become more compacted with use and thus becomes progressively harder.

4. The soft tip has a tendency to lose its shape and become flattened with minimal use.

5. The soft tip maintains chalk better than the hard tip.

Experienced pool players generally prefer the harder tips because their playing characteristics remain constant longer. When a soft tip is used its playing characteristics will gradually change from soft to hard as it becomes more compact. In order to maintain the soft-tip characteristics it must be replaced frequently. The compaction of a tip is accelerated if the stick is used for the power break shot (maximum power stroke). Therefore, to extend the life of the tip on your playing cue, it is suggested that a different stick be used for the power break shot. Even under normal usage the tip will become progressively more compacted due to the repeated battering against the cue ball. Cue tips also wear down and become thinner due to repeated chalking, thus requiring eventual replacement.

Serious players may find it challenging and rewarding to replace the tip themselves when it becomes too worn or compacted. Only quality brands of tips should be used. Cheap tips found in some department stores will crack, flatten, or otherwise deform with minimal use.

Tip replacement may be done using the following procedure:

1. Cut off the old tip with a razor blade or sharp knife.

2. Scrape the remaining glue off the end of the shaft being careful not to round off the edge.

3. Sand the bottom of the new tip so that it's flat and scuffed.

4. Apply glue to shaft and tip. Glue made for this purpose is recommended but several other types of fast drying, flexible-setting glue can be used.

5. Press tip onto shaft making sure all air bubbles are squeezed out.

6. Hold or clamp in place until the glue has set.

The specialist usually installs an oversized tip then cuts it down to ferrule size on a lathe. The amateur must be sure that the tip is the same size as the ferrule before installation. Sanding it down to ferrule size may result in unwanted sanding of the ferrule. After the new tip has been installed it must be shaped to the desired curvature. The tip is generally shaped to the same curvature as a dime (0.70-inch diameter) or a nickel (0.85-inch diameter). There are advantages to both. A tip with the curvature of a nickel will maintain its shape longer because it starts out a little flatter. A tip with the curvature of a dime is less likely to slip off the cue ball when it is struck off-center. Figure 1-2 shows an example of two tips, with different curvature, striking a cue ball the same distance off-center. Note that with the flat tip of stick "B", very little of the tip comes in contact with the cue ball. The contact area of the tip of stick "A" is larger, and thus, is less likely to slip off. For practical reasons, most players play with a tip that is slightly flattened in the center. After shaping, the center flattens first. If the tip were reshaped each time it starts to flatten it would be ground completely off with only minimal use.

The shape of the leather tip (to some degree) determines how much english is applied to the cue ball when it is struck off-

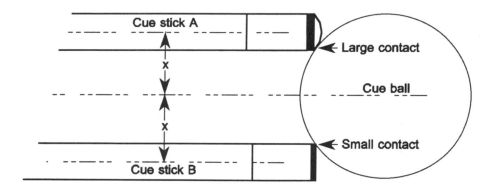

FIGURE 1-2. Cue tip contact area.

center. Tip shape relative to english will be discussed in Chapter 6.

The side of the leather tip should be conditioned. This can be done by wetting a finger then transferring the moisture to the side of the tip. While the tip is still moist, rub it with the dark ink side of a dollar bill. This procedure serves two purposes; the dark ink causes the side of the tip to turn black making it easier to see with peripheral vision; and the moisture tends to harden the side of the tip. The hardening effect is similar to that of getting a pair of leather shoes wet; when they dry out they become hard and stiff. The hardening of the edge of the tip helps prevent it from mushrooming as it compacts.

A tip that works well on one stick may not work well on another. The tip functions in combination with cue weight and shaft flexibility. When the perfect tip for your stick is found, go back and buy several more tips from the same batch for posterity. Serious players should avoid screw-on tips. The inadequacies of these tips will be discussed in relation to ferrules.

Ferrule--Ferrules can be made of ivory or other exotic material but most commonly they are made of a hard, impact-resistant plastic compound. A plastic ferrule is as functional as any other type of ferrule.

One function of the ferrule is to spread the shock of impact over the entire end of the stick so that the wooden shaft doesn't crack or otherwise deform. The ferrule also serves as a visual reference while aiming and aligning a shot. The ferrule requires no special maintenance except for occasional cleaning. Care should be taken to avoid scratching and discoloring the ferrule from contact with the chalk.

Ferrules used to facilitate a screw-on tip are constructed different than the normal ferrule. Figure 1-3 shows the construction of both types of ferrules. With the standard ferrule, the leather tip rests solidly on the ferrule and the tenon (wooden extension of the shaft). The shock of impact is distributed over the ferrule and tenon allowing for a solid hit. With the screw-on tip the tenon does not support the central part of the tip; all of the shock of impact must be absorbed by the ferrule alone. This is likely to cause the ferrule to crack, loosen, or even deform the wood where it butts against the ferrule.

Shaft--The shaft of a cue stick is generally made of some type of hardwood such as ash or birch but maple is by far the most

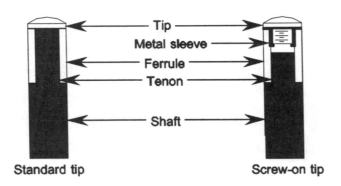

FIGURE 1-3. Standard tip and screw-on tip.

common. The shafts of some cheap sticks are made of softwood which is less expensive and easier to mill.

A good shaft should have a straight grain; the less prominent or obvious the grain is -- the better. If the grain is too obvious there may be a subconscious tendency to aim along the grain rather than along the shaft when aligning a shot. Crooked grain or knots also increase the likelihood of eventual warping.

Expensive shafts are milled down to final size in several stages to help insure against warping. With each milling a thin layer of wood is shaved off. This changes the internal stresses and the shaft may warp slightly. After several months another thin layer is milled off which straightens the shaft and again changes the internal stresses. Each time this is done the warpage is less; when it's milled down to its final size future warpage is very unlikely. The shafts of cheaper sticks are taken down to final size in one milling. These shafts may or may not remain straight. When purchasing a stick, make certain that the shaft is absolutely straight; a slight warp may worsen with time.

Typical shafts range in thickness (diameter at ferrule) from about 12 mm (millimeters) to 13.5 mm. (For reference: a 1/2-inch shaft is 12.7 mm.) The size of the shaft, with any given type of wood, determines the flexibility

and consequent playing characteristics of the stick. The thickness of the shaft also affects the balance point; the thicker the shaft, the farther forward the balance point will be. Most professional players use a 13-mm shaft, and a beginner is well advised to start with a 13-mm shaft. As skill and finesse develop, one can experiment with different size shafts and particularly with shafts of different flexibility.

The taper of some shafts starts at the ferrule and uniformly becomes larger toward the joint. This is referred to as a *standard taper*. The taper on other shafts begins about eight to ten inches from the tip. This is known as a *professional taper*. As the name implies, most professional players prefer this type of taper. A shaft with a professional taper is slightly more flexible and its balance point is farther from the tip than a comparable shaft with a standard taper.

The proper procedure for conditioning a new shaft depends on its original condition. Some of the cheaper shafts have a sealer of varnish or shellac to keep out moisture. The sealer prevents smooth sliding on the bridge hand and should be removed with a fine grade steel wool or scouring pad. After the sealer has been removed, the shaft should be sanded with progressively finer sandpaper. Start with extra fine (220 grit) and progress to ultra fine

(600 grit). Expensive sticks usually don't have a sealer. If necessary, ultra-fine sandpaper can be used to remove any foreign material that may have gotten on the shaft during manufacturing or shipping.

Most players occasionally sand the shaft with ultra-fine sandpaper to remove chalk, talc, or other foreign substances. One should avoid removing too much wood from the shaft thereby reducing its diameter. Frequent sanding may also cause the shaft to become out-of-round due to differential wood loss caused by grain orientation.

The following test was conducted on a maple shaft to determine wood loss from sanding:

Sandpaper--Ultra fine. A total of 4.5 sheets measuring 9 by 11 inches were used. Each sheet was cut into quarters and each quarter was used for 200 strokes.

Sanding strokes--The sandpaper was held on two sides of the shaft with thumb and two fingers. Each stroke consisted of a back and forth motion from the tip to a distance 12 inches back. The shaft was slowly rotated while being sanded.

Wood loss--After 3,600 sanding strokes the diameter of the shaft was reduced an average of 0.43 mm. In other words, one sheet of sandpaper and 800 strokes reduced the shaft diameter about 0.1 mm.

In order to maintain the shooting characteristics of a stick, wood loss should be kept to less than 0.2 mm over the life of the stick. If sanding is limited to a few strokes before each tournament, the stick should last a lifetime.

Once the shaft has been sanded smooth, it should be conditioned to make it slippery. The following are some of the conditioning techniques used by professionals in the past:

1. Rub in cigarette lighter fluid with a piece of cloth.
2. Rub with soft leather or chammy.
3. Polish with furniture polish or oil.
4. Polish with carnauba wax.
5. Rub with a dollar bill.

There are several commercial products available today to condition the shaft. The new products not only make the shaft slippery but they also seal the wood pores as a guard against moisture. These products were developed specifically for conditioning cue shafts and therefor are much better than the products previously used.

No matter how carefully the stick is treated, it may eventually become dinged or dented. Small dings can sometimes be removed using the following technique:

1. Sand the indented area with ultra-fine sandpaper to remove foreign matter and expose the wood pores.
2. Apply a drop of water directly into the indentation. The water will cause the wood to swell thus removing the dent.
3. Allow the area to dry thoroughly, then sand and condition.

Serious players should get two shafts when purchasing a new stick. Both shafts should be as nearly identical as possible. With a high quality stick, both shafts are made from the same piece of wood thereby insuring that their playing characteristics are identical. If a tip comes off, or if one shaft gets dinged beyond repair, the other shaft can be used without having to adjust to its playing characteristics.

Joint--The joint facilitates the screwing together of a two-piece stick. The joint can be made of metal, plastic, wood, or any combination thereof. The type of material used has little bearing on the playing characteristics of the stick except that it may affect the balance point. A stick with a heavy metal joint will have a balance point farther forward than a comparable stick with a light plastic joint. A short person, who holds the stick nearer the center, or someone who prefers the open bridge, would probably prefer a balance point that is relatively farther forward. Those players should choose a stick with a heavy metal joint.

Many mystical playing qualities have been attributed to the various types of joints. If you hear a particularly convincing argument for any specific type of joint -- then use that type of joint. If nothing else it will give you a psychological boost and, in that way, it may help your game.

Butt--A pool cue butt and its component parts are shown in figure 1-4.

The forearm is the part of the butt between the joint and the wrap (see figure 1-4). The forearm can be made of any kind of wood. Generally, wood type is based on appearance rather than function. Strips of various colored woods may be laminated into the forearm to form a vee shape. These laminates are called *prongs* or *points*. The appearance of the butt may be further enhanced by inlays of mother-of-pearl, ivory, or other ornamental material. Prongs and inlays serve little functional purpose but they do increase price and enhance pride of ownership.

Most personal cue sticks have some type of covering over the wood where the butt is held, this covering is called a *wrap*. Friction between the hand and the butt of the stick allows it to be moved back and forth. If the friction is low, the grip must be tighter in order to achieve the same movement. This is similar to picking up a greasy drinking glass; it must be held much tighter than a clean dry glass. As will be discussed in a later chapter, the stick should be held loosely, therefore hand-butt friction should be high.

The most common types of wraps are made of nylon, linen, naugahyde, or leather. The type of wrap determines the friction characteristics between the hand and cue stick. Hand-stick friction of some of the more popular wraps increases in this order (least friction first): (1) nylon or linen, (2) leather, (3) naugahyde, and (4) urethane or varathane finish on plain wood. The friction characteristics of each of these wraps are examined in more detail:

Nylon and linen: Nylon and linen are considered together because friction is about the same for both. The hand-wrap friction is less for nylon-linen than for any other wrap material considered here. It's about one-half that of a plain urethane finish. The positive aspect of nylon-linen is that friction remains the same even if the hand is sweaty and clammy.

Leather: Friction of leather wraps varies considerably depending on the dryness and texture of the leather. If the leather is very dry and hard, friction will be less than with nylon-linen. However, properly cared for and conditioned, the friction characteristics of

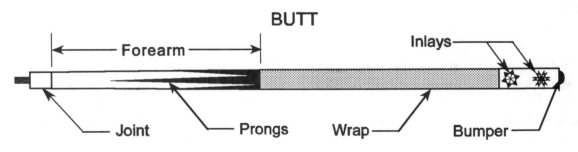

FIGURE 1-4. Pool-cue butt and its component parts.

leather are about 1.3 times greater than nylon-linen. The unique thing about leather is that hand-wrap friction becomes slightly greater when the hand becomes sweaty. Leather probably deteriorates faster than any other type of wrap. Similar to leather steering wheel covers and leather gloves, the leather deteriorates much faster for some people than for others due to the quantity and chemistry of their sweat.

Naugahyde: Friction between the hand and a naugahyde wrap is about 1.6 times greater than nylon-linen. The problem with naugahyde is that friction drops to that of nylon-linen when the hand becomes sweaty. This variation in friction is undesirable.

Urethane: (A plane urethane finish over wood isn't technically considered a wrap but will be considered here for the sake of comparison.) Urethane over wood has about twice the hand-stick friction as does nylon-linen. However, when the hand becomes sweaty it drops to about 1.4 times that of nylon-linen. Friction characteristics of a urethane finish can be altered considerably by waxing or polishing. With a proper wax finish, friction will remain high even when the hand is sweaty.

As indicated, the hand-wrap friction of nylon-linen is the poorest of all the wraps examined here and is far inferior to a plain urethane finish on wood. However, nylon and linen are the most popular wraps because they remain consistent regardless of hand condition, and -- they look attractive.

Bumper--The bumper is made of rubber and serves to protect the stick when set on the floor or other hard surface. In the olden days, players removed the bumper so that the stick would make a loud noise when taped on the floor. Tapping on the floor was used as means of expressing approval when someone made an especially good shot.

Stick length--In the past the standard pool cue was 57 inches long. For people that are small to average in height and arm span, a 57-inch stick will suffice. A tall person or a person with a long arm span should consider using a longer stick. Most cue stick manufacturers today have 58-inch and sometimes 59-inch cues in their standard line. Anything longer may have to be custom ordered. One should not have to compromise a comfortable stance to accommodate stick length -- remember, **THE EQUIPMENT SHOULD CONFORM TO YOUR NEEDS, NOT VICE VERSA**.

Special attention should be given to stick length when selecting a cue stick for a small person or child. When a small person assumes the proper stance he/she may have to hold the butt end at or in front of the balance point. This causes the tip to wave about uncontrollably. For this reason, a shorter stick that has its balance point farther forward should be used. This is particularly important in selecting a stick for a child; stance, stroke, and form could be compromised for life if an improper stick length is used.

Stick weight--Cue sticks commonly range in weight from 16 ounces to 23 ounces. Professionals generally use sticks ranging from 19 to 21 ounces. Some authorities advise using a stick weight that *feels good*. If bowlers were given the same advice they would probably select a very light ball because it feels good. However, it wouldn't take long to discover that the light ball, as good as it feels, doesn't knock the pins down. The fact is that a heavier ball does a better job of knocking the pins down. With this in mind, the selection of stick weight should be based upon what *works best*; not what *feels best*.

The weight of the stick affects aim, the distance the cue ball rolls, and the amount of english (spin) imparted to the cue ball.

In order to understand how stick weight affects aim and cue ball roll, it's necessary to understand something about *kinetic energy*. Kinetic energy is the energy contained in a moving object (stick). The amount of energy the moving stick has depends on the weight of the stick and its velocity. A light stick must have greater velocity in order to contain the same kinetic energy as a heavier stick. A freight train moving at 10 mph (miles per hour) has much more kinetic energy than a car moving at 10 mph. But, if the speed of the car is increased, at some point the kinetic energy of the car would equal that of the train. The same principle applies to cue sticks. A light stick must be stroked faster than a heavy stick in order to propel the cue ball a given distance. The slower stroke of a heavy stick allows more accurate directional control. Therefore, *the heavier the stick, the more accurate the aim*. Since the heavier stick is stroked slower than the light stick, it's more speed sensitive (like putting downhill). A greater percentage of stick speed error is tolerable with a lighter stick (like putting uphill). Therefore, *cue ball speed control is easier with a lighter stick*.

A beginner would be well advised to start with a 20-ounce stick. After a degree of proficiency is attained, one can move up an ounce to improve aim accuracy or down an ounce to improve cue ball speed control. However, be advised that by changing stick weight, one aspect of your game may improve to the detriment of another.

A heavy stick is not slowed down as much as a light stick when it contacts the cue ball. The tendency of the stick to keep moving forward (inertia) causes it to remain in contact with the cue ball longer. The effects of any torsional force applied to the cue ball will be increased due to longer contact time.

Therefore, *a heavier stick will enhance english*. This can be a two-bladed sword; if the cue ball is inadvertently struck off-center with a heavy stick, the resulting english will have a greater detrimental effect on the shot.

The same analytical justification for the selection of cue stick weight applies to women as well as men. A woman can handle a 20- or 22-ounce stick as easily as a man can. It's not unusual to see a lady shopping or otherwise going about her business with a 20-*pound* kid under her arm.

The effects of stick weight are small and subtle, especially with slow to medium speed shots. The subtle differences can only be detected over a period of time, so don't expect to see big functional differences the first few shots after changing cue weight. To those casual players that only play infrequently -- choose a stick weight that *FEELS GOOD*.

Balance--Balance is one of those illusive qualities that everyone hears about but rarely is it adequately described. Generally, balance is described in terms of value judgments *good* balance or *poor* balance. Here, balance will be examined in terms of two physical characteristics; *balance point* and *weight distribution*.

The balance point is that point, along the length of the stick, at which the total weight of the stick is equally distributed. The location of the balance point can be described in relation to its distance from the tip. The balance point is usually not designated by the manufacturer because it's dependent on total stick weight. For example, a 17-ounce stick may have a balance point 37 inches from the tip. An identical stick weighing 22 ounces will have a balance point several inches farther from the tip. This is because most manufacturers increase stick weight by adding weight to the butt end of the stick.

NOTE: Some authorities describe balance point in relation to the distance from the butt end of the stick. This can be misleading and deceptive. For example, assume a person is down in a shooting stance; now add a 4-inch styrofoam extension to his stick. He probably won't even know the difference and yet you have changed the balance point nearly 4 inches (measured from the butt end of the stick). Changing the balance point 4 inches (measured from the tip of the stick) would be clearly noticed. In other words, balance point must be described in relation to the distance from the tip for it to have any functional meaning.

The type of joint affects the location of the balance point. A stick with a metal joint will have a balance point farther forward than a similar stick with a plastic joint even if the total weight is the same.

The location of the balance point determines how much of the total weight is supported by the bridge hand. Short people who hold a 17-ounce stick at or near the balance point must modify their entire stance to accommodate a 22-ounce stick with its balance point farther back. If these players assumed their normal stance, they would have to hold the stick at or forward of the balance point. This means there would be no weight on the bridge hand and an open bridge could not be used even if the situation called for it. Consequently, short people and people that always use an open bridge, should use a stick with the balance point relatively far forward.

The second consideration regarding balance is weight distribution. If a spear had most of its weight in the rear, it would be difficult to keep the front end pointed forward so that it would stick into a target. Weight distribution affects torsional stability. If a pool cue were of uniform size and density throughout, it would be torsionally stable. However, cue sticks are tapered so that most of the weight is near the butt end causing

them to be torsionally unstable. Fortunately, in pool we use two hands. The bridge hand helps keep the stick pointed in the proper direction and thus negating the need for torsional stability. With regard to function, weight distribution and consequent torsional stability is not a high consideration and is only important in that it affects balance point.

Workmanship--The workmanship of pool cues, even from the same manufacturer, may vary considerably. Keep in mind, the higher the price, the less tolerable are the imperfections. All the pieces should fit together properly. The ferrule should butt tightly against the shaft without a perceptible space or glue line. If the ferrule and shaft aren't perfectly butted together, the stress of repeatedly hitting the cue ball will cause the glue to fail and the ferrule to loosen. The union of shaft to joint and joint to butt should be smooth and without visible cracks or glue lines. One should not be able to feel the crack between the two parts of the joint when screwed together. All prongs and inlays should be smooth and without visible glue lines.

Roll the shaft on a flat surface. If the space between the shaft and surface varies more than about 0.05 inch (about the thickness of a dime), it's warped; don't buy it at any price. Assemble the stick and again roll it on a flat surface. If it wobbles, and the shaft is straight, it probably has a crooked joint. A slightly crooked joint is excusable on an inexpensive stick but intolerable on an expensive one.

The finish should look and feel smooth and be void of bubbles or blemishes. The finish doesn't affect the stick's function but does reflect *pride of ownership* which may in turn affect one's game.

Cue care--When buying a cue stick, one should also invest in a cue case. The case should be hard enough to absorb bumps and bruises without damaging the stick. The case should also protect the stick against moisture and temperature extremes. This is not always possible, especially in very humid or dry climates. However, a sealed case can help average-out moisture extremes for short periods of time.

The worst thing for a stick, aside from physical abuse, is exposure to extreme temperature changes. The difference in the coefficient of thermal expansion between the ferrule, wood, joint, glue, etc. causes the individual parts to expand and contract at different rates. This creates extreme internal stresses. Eventually, the material may crack or the glue joints may fail. A good case will help stabilize short-term temperature variations. Temperature extremes can be avoided by keeping the stick in an inhabited area where the temperature is controlled.

A cue stick should not be left *leaning* up against a wall. The bending force, although small, will tend to warp the stick over a long period of time.

TABLE

Figure 1-5 shows the surface of a pool table and its component parts.

Dimensions--The playing surface of all tables is twice as long as it is wide (measured between cushions). The most common size tables are referred to as 7, 8, or 9-foot tables. This description is vague and erroneous because most tables don't measure 7, 8, or 9 feet. A 7-foot table (bar table) is actually 40 inches wide; an 8-foot table (home or commercial table) is either 44 or 46 inches wide; and a 9-foot table (regulation size) is 50 inches wide. The 56-inch table was common in the past but is rarely seen or used today. Please note, one need only give the shortest dimension to describe the size of the table.

Most players find it easy to adjust to the various size tables. The balls generally must travel a little farther on a big table but there is less ball congestion which means that fewer shots are blocked by intervening balls.

Pockets--The opening of the pockets varies in size from table to table. The corner pockets are usually 4½ to 5 inches wide (measured between the tips of the jaws). The side pockets are about ½ inch larger than the corner pockets. Large tables with small pockets are usually used for top professional tournaments. Pocket characteristics are discussed in detail in Chapter 4.

Height--According to the *Billiard Congress of America*, the table bed, or playing surface, must be 29¼ inches (plus or minus ¼ inch) above the floor.

Structure--A good table is heavy and well braced. One should be able to bump it with the hip without moving the balls. The playing surface is usually made of slate (some cheaper tables use a less expensive substitute) covered with cloth. The thickness of the slate generally ranges from ¾ inch to 1.0 inch. The slate can consist of one single piece, or three interlocking pieces.

Cushions--The terms *cushion* and *rail* are generally used interchangeably. Technically speaking, the cushion is the triangular strip of rubber that is attached to the rail and covered with cloth. The term "rail" refers to the cushion and its supporting structure. The rebound efficiency of the cushions depends on the thickness of the rubber, type of rubber, and sturdiness of the table. Cheap, light tables generally have less efficient cushions. Players must adjust to the rebound efficiency of each individual table.

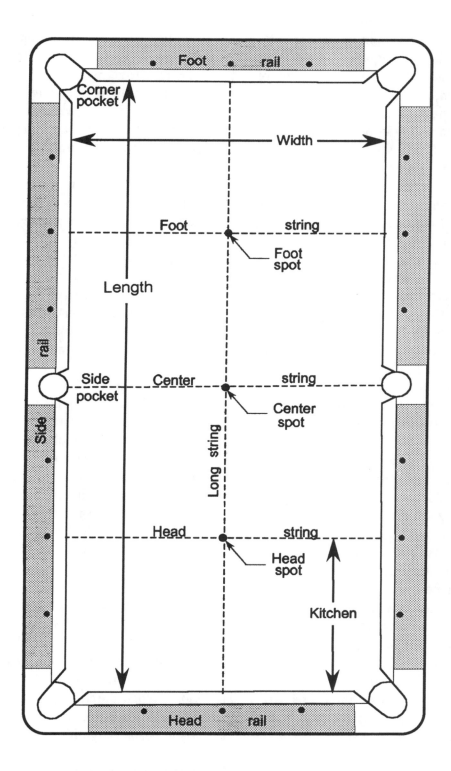

FIGURE 1-5. Pool table and its component parts.

Cloth--Cloth comes in various colors and types. Green or greenish blue is the color of choice for most serious pool players; not because it's superior but because it's traditional. Chalk and powder marks that inevitably get on the cloth may be more noticeable on some colors than on others.

The cloth material consists of wool or a wool-nylon blend and may or may not have a rubber backing. Cloth with rubber backing tends to stick to the slate bed better and doesn't move or wrinkle when pushed with the hand or ball. The cloth material and weave have an effect on ball speed. Generally, the shorter the nap the faster the cloth. Old, worn cloth is usually smooth, yet ball speed is slow. This is due to an accumulation of dirt, chalk, powder, etc. in and under the cloth. On a dirty table the balls encounter rolling resistance similar to that of a bicycle going through sand. The amount of cloth stretch and uniformity of stretch, both on the bed and on the cushions, affect the playing characteristics of the table. Recovering a table should be left to the experienced specialist.

Buying a table--There are several things that should be considered when buying a table. If you're a serious player it's imperative that you buy a good quality table. Balls don't roll straight or bank properly on a poor quality table. This results in frustration rather than fun. Practicing on a poor quality table can do your game more harm than good. Be sure it has a slate bed, is heavy, and well braced. Bump it with your hip or give it a sharp push with your hands; the balls should stay in place and the table should not noticeably move. Check the resiliency of the cushions; set the cue ball on the center string between the center spot and the side pocket. Shoot it very hard into a side rail (on the same side of the table) near a corner pocket. The ball should strike seven rails before coming to rest.

If the table is to be moved frequently there are several pertinent aspects that should be considered: A three-piece slate bed is easier to move than a one-piece slate. All the major component parts of the table should be doweled together so that it can be reassembled in perfect alignment. The table should be constructed with nuts and bolts rather than with self-treading lag bolts. Lag bolts tend to cross tread and become loose with repeated use.

A decision must be made as to the preferred pocket size. Serious players often prefer small pockets because it forces them to shoot more accurately. If the prime reason for having a table is to entertain friends and neighbors, then get large pockets. Small pockets tend to frustrate casual players. If the table is to serve primarily as a practice table, the pockets should be the same size as on the table in which you compete.

Decide whether you want a ball return or regular pockets. The pool *purest* generally prefers regular pockets (for nostalgic reasons) but a ball return is a little more efficient when the balls have to be racked.

The maximum size of the home table may be dictated by the available space. To determine the minimum space required for a particular table: Take the width or length of the table, add 12 inches for the rails (6 inches each); then add twice the length of the cue stick (57 x 2) or 114 inches. For example, a 44-inch table would require a space 44 + 12 + 114 = 170 inches or 14.2 feet wide, by 88 + 12 + 114 = 214 or 17.8 feet long.

A person that can afford it should buy a new table. However, the best value for the money can often be gotten by buying a used table. When purchasing a used table it is not advisable to get one with new or near new cloth, especially if it has to be totally disassembled to move. The price will be at a premium because it looks good but there's always a chance that the cloth may be damaged during disassembling or assembling. A table with a worn or ripped cloth is not only cheaper but: (1) the cloth can be cut off and the slate examined, (2) misaligned cushions are not a major concern, (3) it can be recovered in any color, and (4) it will be fast because dust and dirt under the cloth can be removed prior to recovering. But first, check the cost of recovering so that a proper cost comparison can be made when evaluating various tables.

Care of table--The first thing that must be done with a new table is leveling. If it's being set up on carpet or other soft material it is advisable to set the legs on plywood supports and let it settle in for a few weeks before final leveling. Some tables can be leveled by turning a support at the bottom of each leg but most tables require placement of shims (ordinary playing cards are often used as shims) under the appropriate leg or legs. If it's a multiple slate table, always lift the side, never the end. Lifting from the end will cause the slates to be forced into each other which may result in chipping or cracking along the upper edge as shown in figure 1-6. Occasionally, it's impossible to level a table over its entire surface indicating that the individual slates are not flat. This can be corrected by propping up the low spots with thin shims inserted between the slate and the table frame. In some cases the table may require partial disassembly in order to insert the shims. In these cases calling an expert

should be considered.

Sweeping the cloth occasionally with a soft brush will remove chips of chalk and other foreign material from the surface and rejuvenate the nap. Vacuuming will suck up the ground-in chalk, talc, and dirt that accumulates in and under the cloth. The accumulation of chalk can be minimized by avoiding chalking the stick over the table and by avoiding over chalking. Remember, all of the chalk that's put on the cue tip eventually ends up in the cloth or on the floor. Talcum powder is another problem. If traces of powder can be seen on the cloth someone is using too much. Chalk and talc in and on the cloth not only make the table slow but also change the friction characteristics between ball and cloth. These friction characteristics are very important and will be explored in later chapters. Some other *no-nos* regarding table care are: Don't sit, stand, or lay on it; don't lift it up and bounce it on the floor; don't drop balls on it; don't pound balls into the cloth; and, don't flip coins on it. When not in use the table should be covered to avoid the accumulation of dirt and dust in the cloth. It's good practice to remove the balls from the table surface when play is finished. The balls settle into the nap and leave an indentation much like furniture does to a carpet.

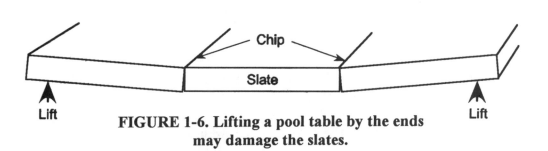

FIGURE 1-6. Lifting a pool table by the ends may damage the slates.

BALLS

In the beginning, billiard balls were made of wood. Knots from the roots of hardwood trees were aged then turned on a lathe. This process of aging and turning was repeated until the proper size was attained. Wooden balls had several shortcomings. They shrank differentially thus losing sphericity; they cracked upon severe impact; weight of the balls varied considerably; and, because of density variations, they were usually out of balance. Later, ivory balls were introduced. They were more expensive but far superior to the wooden balls because of their greater resiliency. They made a beautiful clicking sound as they caromed off each other and lost little energy in the collision. But, like wooden balls, they were prone to differential shrinking and loss of sphericity. Ivory balls also had a tendency to crack, discolor, and were sensitive to temperature and humidity changes. In addition to these problems, ivory was expensive which prompted the search for other materials. Clay compound, celluloid, and even metal balls were used until the introduction of the modern day phenolic plastic balls. Plastic balls are far superior to all the balls of the past, including ivory.

The modern-day ball is 2¼ inches in diameter and weighs about 6 ounces. Some coin-operated tables require an oversize cue ball (so that it returns) which is ¹/₈ inch larger and one ounce heavier. The larger, heavier cue ball reacts differently than the normal cue ball. These differences will be discussed in Chapter 14.

There are many grades of plastic balls. The more expensive balls will generally have a smooth shiny surface. The numbers on some of the cheaper balls are not flush with the ball surface. Before buying a set of balls be sure to inspect every ball individually, look for air bubbles, irregular surface, and color imperfections

Balls should be kept clean by wiping with a clean towel or cloth. It's not advisable to polish or wax the balls because it changes the friction between ball and ball, ball and cloth, and between ball and cushion. These friction characteristics are extremely important as will be discussed in later chapters. Avoid striking the numbered balls with the cue stick because it may leave a permanent scratch.

Balls generally come in sets of sixteen; a cue ball and fifteen numbered balls. Balls 1 through 8 have a solid color and are referred to as *solids* or *small ones*; balls 9 through 15 are white with a band of color and are referred to as *stripes* or *big ones*. The color of each ball is standardized so the number can be recognized without looking at the digit printed on it. The color code is: 1-yellow, 2-blue, 3-red, 4-purple, 5-orange, 6-green, 7-maroon, and 8-black. The striped balls are colored in the same sequence, the 9 is yellow, 10 blue etc. Add eight to the number of the solid ball to determine the color of the striped ball. For example; the 3-ball is red, eight added to three is eleven; therefore, the 11-ball must have a red stripe.

CHALK

There is very little friction between a leather cue tip and the cue ball. The lack of friction causes the tip to slide off the cue ball when it is struck off-center; this is called a *miscue*. When a miscue occurs the cue ball goes in some unpredictable direction, not in the direction the cue stick was pointed. To increase friction and prevent a miscue, chalk must be applied to the leather tip.

Chalk is made of a very fine grained gritty substance and generally comes in the shape of a cube slightly less than an inch on a side. The main differences between brands are hardness, color, and grit. Soft chalk results in a thicker layer being applied to the tip. It's prudent to note that every bit of chalk that is used eventually ends up on the table or on the floor. For cosmetic reasons, the chalk should be the same color as the cloth.

Some brands of chalk contain hard grainy particles. These grainy particles cause minute scratches which helps the chalk adhere to the tip. On the negative side, the scratching causes the tip to wear more rapidly requiring more frequent tip replacement. Some brands of chalk tend to absorb more moisture from the air than other brands. The moisture causes the chalk to *cake* on the tip and on the cue ball. Chalk is generally provided with the table but many experienced players prefer to use their own chalk with the qualities they personally prefer.

Chalk should be applied often but sparingly. To apply, first put the cue tip into the recessed cavity of the chalk cube (figure 1-7a) then rotate the stick; touch it up with several gentle perpendicular scraping motions while turning the stick (figure 1-7b). Avoid heavy handed grinding of the tip into the chalk cube. This results in excessive tip wear, chalk consumption, and may cause scratching and discoloring of the ferrule. Theoretically, the center of the tip doesn't need chalk because it makes contact with the cue ball

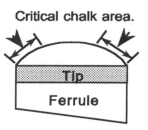

FIGURE 1-8. Chalking the critical area will help prevent a miscue.

only when it's struck dead-center. When the cue ball is struck dead-center there's no chance of the tip slipping off and thus, no need for chalk. The outer one-third of the rounded part of the tip (figure 1-8) is the critical chalk area. When a miscue occurs examine the cue tip. A dark mark will be left where it slipped off the cue ball. Make a special effort to cover the mark with fresh chalk.

After prolonged use the surface of the tip becomes hard and smooth and will not retain chalk properly. To rectify this problem the tip must be roughened either with a *tip taper* or scuffed with sandpaper. A tip taper is similar to a coarse, cross-hatched metal file. Tapping the cue tip with this instrument creates small dimples and loosens up the surface. It's advisable to apply a generous layer of chalk on the tip before using the tip taper so that chalk is forced into the dimples. Scuffing the tip by scraping it with medium to coarse sandpaper creates scratch marks which help to retain chalk. Tapping and scuffing accelerate tip wear and therefore should be done sparingly.

TALCUM POWDER

Talcum powder is used to decrease friction between the cue shaft and bridge hand. Talcum powder can cause as many problems as it cures. It can get on the balls and change

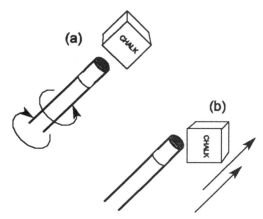

FIGURE 1-7. Proper chalking technique. (a) Rock chalk back and forth while rotating stick. (b) Finish by scraping edge of chalk on critical area of tip.

the ball-to-ball friction coefficient which changes the direction they carom off each other. When it gets on the cloth it changes the ball-to-cloth friction which affects the path of the cue ball after contact with the object ball. The use of powder should be avoided whenever possible. If it must be used, apply it sparingly and only to the parts of the bridge hand that make contact with the stick. If you have your own table, don't provide powder. If you must provide powder, be sure to advise the user on its proper application.

GLOVE

The pool glove is made with two fingers and a thumb. It is worn on the bridge hand to allow the shaft to slip smoothly through the bridge hand. (If everyone wore a glove there would be no need for talcum power.)

There are several advantages in wearing a pool glove. (1) The shaft need not be super smooth for it to feel comfortable in the bridge hand. For that reason it doesn't ever have to be sanded. (2) The shaft can be conditioned with many different substances and still slip well in the bridge hand. For example, it could be coated with polyurethane or wax, both of which would offer superior wood protection, and still slip better than in the bare hand. (3) The shaft slips equally good regardless of humidity. (4) Many people play well for most of a session or tournament. But, when it gets to the finals they get nerves and start to perspire. Their hands get a little sticky and they start shooting at less than one hundred percent. They may lose the tournament and blame it on choking when it was actually just sticky hands. (5) Consider this scenario: A person powders his bridge hand then plays until he has to powder again. What actually happened here is that his hand went from

slippery (after powdering) too sticky (just before powdering again). This variable has to deteriorate his game to some extent. This changing friction can be avoided by using a glove; the bridge hand remains equally slippery at all times.

If you choose to wear a glove, it is best to always wear it regardless of whether you're playing serious pool or just practicing. Even if you chose not to wear a glove, it's good policy to carry one with you for those extra humid days. There's nothing like taking advantage of the weather.

BALL RACK

The standard ball rack is shaped like a triangle and is capable of containing all fifteen object balls. Specialty racks for games such as NINE-BALL are shaped differently. The cheaper racks are made of plastic; wooden racks are superior because they are less flexible and more durable. Many new wooden ball racks haven't been sanded sufficiently smooth which causes them to catch onto, and rip the threads of the cloth. A new rack should be sanded until it can be rubbed on a piece of test cloth without snagging.

When racking, the balls must be pushed forward into the apex of the rack to insure that they are properly aligned and in contact with each other. The front ball must be directly on the foot spot (figure 1-5) and all succeeding rows perfectly parallel to the end rail. The center ball of the rear row can't be easily reached while pushing the outer balls forward. To move the center ball forward simply rotate the two adjacent balls with the thumbs as shown in figure 1-9. Another common technique is to place the fingers down between the rack and the last row of balls forcing the balls forward.

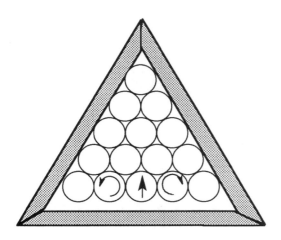

FIGURE 1-9. Rotate balls with thumbs to force the middle ball forward.

Special care must be taken to insure that all balls remain in contact with each other when the rack is removed. Occasionally, there may be one or more balls that simply will not stay in place when the rack is removed. When this occurs, the nap of the cloth under the rack should be reconstituted by rubbing with the hands, table brush, or towel. If this doesn't work, there may be something under the cloth. Try placing the fingers on the cloth over the offending area and pushing to cause a wrinkle in the cloth. If these techniques don't work, then the offending ball or balls should be tapped lightly with another ball while being held in place. Do not tap the ball any harder than you would dare tap your own finger without causing pain or disfigurement. Tapping any harder may crush the threads in the cloth which will eventually result in a hole or permanent indentation.

MECHANICAL BRIDGE

When a shot can't be reached in the normal manner, the mechanical bridge (also called a crutch or rake) can be used in place of the hand bridge. The larger the table, or the shorter the player, the more often the mechanical bridge must be used. Most advanced players learn to shoot with their opposite hand thereby reducing the need for the mechanical bridge in some situations.

The mechanical bridge is usually made of wood, aluminum, or plastic. It has notches at various heights in which the cue shaft can rest. The selection of the proper notch depends on the position of any obstructing balls and the type of english to be employed. Photos 1-1 and 1-2 show the proper technique for using the mechanical bridge. Whenever possible, the bridge handle should

PHOTO 1-1. Use of the mechanical bridge.

**PHOTO 1-2. Using the mechanical
bridge to shoot over a ball.**

rest solidly on the table and be gripped so that
it won't move while shooting and can be
removed quickly after the shot is executed.

Most players dislike using the mechanical
bridge because it requires a completely
different stance and shooting technique. The
only way to become accurate and comfortable
with it is to practice with it.

CHAPTER 2
SHOOTING STANCE AND TECHNIQUE

Shooting stance and technique must be practical as well as functional. Learning and using proper stance and technique is the most critical aspect of a person's early pool career. How well these fundamentals are learned will affect every shot that you ever execute. This means that even a small improvement in stance and technique will translate into making thousands of balls during your pool career that you would otherwise have missed.

Keep in mind that your stance must serve you when you are practicing as well as when you're playing competitively. For example, assume that you adopted a stance that has both knees together and bent. This stance would probably be adequate for a few shots or even a few games. But, could you maintain this stance after practicing alone for two or six hours. After an extended period your knees would become less and less bent as they became more and more fatigued. This means that you would end up practicing with a stance that you don't even use in a game; or even worse, you would simply become tired and quit practicing. You may not even know that your stance has caused you to want to quit. Meanwhile, your opponent down the street, with a less taxing stance, is practicing twice as much as you.

STANCE

The objective of a proper stance is to provide a solid foundation that minimizes unintentional movement while the shot is being executed. A proper stance must allow the stick to be held as level as possible (for most shots) as it is being stroked. Pool players come in various sizes and shapes; therefore, stance may vary somewhat from person to person while still meeting this objective. The descriptions and illustrations that follow assume a right-handed player. A left-handed player would have everything reversed.

Foot position--The proper foot position is shown in figure 2-1. The right foot should be positioned in line with the shot and turned out about 45 degrees. The left foot should be to the left of the line of aim at an angle of about 35 degrees. The distance between the feet depends on the person's height. Tall people must place their feet farther apart than short people. As with a tripod or any other type of structure, stability is greatest with the broadest possible foundation (spread of feet). Therefore, the feet should be as far apart as possible while still being comfortable.

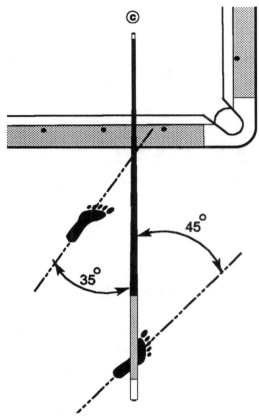

FIGURE 2-1. Ideal foot position.

PHOTO 2-1. Proper leg position.

Leg position--The left knee should be bent slightly while the right knee is kept straight (or nearly so) as shown in photo 2-1. Photo 2-2 shows some common mistakes; the feet are too close together and both knees are bent (fatigue prone).

Grip-arm position--The grip arm is the arm that holds the butt of the cue stick. The forearm should be vertical when the tip of the cue is addressing (nearly touching) the cue ball (photos 2-3a and b). A common mistake is shown in photo 2-4. The cue is held such that the forearm is past vertical when the cue ball is addressed, this hinders follow-through. The entire body would have to be raised in order to get the necessary follow-through. Raising the body during the stroke causes errors.

PHOTO 2-2. Improper stance.

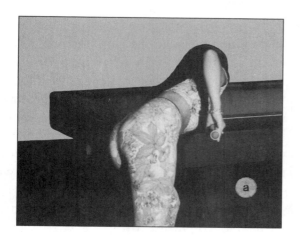

**PHOTO 2-5. Butt arm is too far
from body.**

**PHOTO 2-3. Forearm should be
vertical when cue ball
is addressed.**

PHOTO 2-6. Incorrect wrist position.

Photo 2-5 shows another common mistake; the stick is held too far from the body.

Grip position--Many instructors start by advising the student where to hold the stick in relation to the balance point. This means that the entire stance must accommodate this grip position. A better technique is to assume a

PHOTO 2-4. Arm is passed vertical.

proper stance then grip the stick wherever the stance dictates. The grip on the stick must be light enough to allow a smooth stroke without lifting the shaft off the bridge hand. If the shaft can be lifted off the bridge hand, the stick is being gripped too tightly. Bending the wrist (photo 2-6) is a common problem, the wrist should be in line with the forearm.

Head position--The cue stick should be held as level as possible; the body should be bent so that the chin is no more than a few inches above the stick (photo 2-7). The closer the line of sight is to the stick, the more accurate the aim. A person shooting a rifle gets the line of sight as close to the gun barrel as possible. Pool players must be able to stroke the stick while aiming, therefore some concessions must be made. Holding the chin immediately above the stick is as close as one can get and still manage a smooth stroke.

Many top professionals, both pool and snooker, hold their chin so close to the stick that they touch during the stroke. This allows for consistency; when the chin is normally held this close to the stick, it's immediately obvious when the head is out of position. If a person normally holds the chin 12 inches above the stick, one could get into a shooting

PHOTO 2-7. Chin should be just above stick.

slump by unknowingly changing this distance to 10 or 14 inches. Or worse, a person could inadvertently change the chin position an inch or so to either side in relation to the stick. This would present an entirely different aiming perspective that could result in a severe shooting slump and the problem would be very difficult to detect and rectify. If the chin is normally positioned immediately above the stick, any deviation from this position will be eminently obvious.

Certain types of shots require the chin to be positioned farther from the stick, power shots and some judgment shots are examples. Power shots are those that require extreme stick acceleration; power break shots and long draw shots are examples. A more vertical body position allows greater stick acceleration but does so at the expense of aim accuracy. A judgment shot is one in which judgment as to where to strike the object ball is more difficult than aim accuracy. An example of a typical judgment shot is one in which the cue ball is an inch or less away from the object ball that must be cut more than 30 degrees. In this case it's easier to judge where the cue ball must strike the object ball if it is viewed from a higher perspective.

We spend our whole lives looking at things, judging distances and angles, with our eyes level. Since we have practiced this way every waking hour of our lives it seems reasonable that we should use the same viewing technique on the pool table. **When shooting a shot THE HEAD SHOULD BE HELD SUCH THAT THE EYES ARE LEVEL** (photo 2-8). Perception becomes distorted when the head is cocked to either side. The importance of keeping the eyes level can be demonstrated by experiment. Set an object ball on the foot spot; position the cue ball near the corner pocket so that the shot is straight into the side pocket; shoot the shot with your head intentionally tilted to one

PHOTO 2-8. Eyes should be level.

side. The shot will quite likely be missed demonstrating distorted perception when the eyes are not kept horizontal. Cocking the head is a common cause of shooting slumps. The next time you get into a shooting slump, check your head position and eye orientation.

Upper body position--The upper body should be as close as possible to the stick while stroking and shooting. Joe Davis, one of the most accurate shooters of all time, went undefeated as the world's snooker champion for twenty years. Snooker requires a much greater accuracy than pool because the balls are smaller, the table is bigger, and the pockets are smaller. Joe Davis held the cue stick such that it rubbed against his chest as he shot. He considered this rubbing absolutely essential to his accuracy. When using this technique, once the stick is properly aligned, stick alignment will remain constant as long as the body is held steady. When this technique is mastered, one can make practically any shot, even with the eyes closed, just by keeping the upper body stable. As with the low chin position, this body position does not lend itself to power shots. The upper body must be in a more vertical

position to facilitate maximum stick acceleration.

Bridge hand--The purpose of the bridge is to provide a solid perch for the cue shaft so that it can be aimed and the cue ball struck at the proper point. The bridge must be solid but flexible enough to accommodate adjustments in striking position. Two general categories of bridges are commonly used; the *closed* or *looped* bridge and the *open* or *vee* bridge. There are many variations within each category.

Closed bridge: The construction of the basic closed bridge is shown in photo 2-9. To create a closed bridge: (a) lay the hand flat on table with the fingers spread, (b) arch hand at knuckles, and (c) loop the finger around the shaft so that it touches the tip of the thumb. The hole through which the shaft slides should be large enough to allow the shaft to slide without excessive friction. Most professional players hold the loop loose enough so that there is an open space above the stick.

To lower the shaft, reduce the arch of the knuckles (photo 2-10). To raise the shaft, twist the wrist so that the ball of the thumb rotates off the table (photo 2-11). If further elevation is required, rotate the hand forward (photo 2-12) so that only the fingertips are on the table. If still further elevation is required the open bridge must be used.

The advantages of the closed bridge are: (1) can be used by children and short people who hold the stick at or forward of the balance point, (2) the finger around shaft gives a more secure feeling of stick control, and (3) prevents raising the stick off the bridge during the stroke. The disadvantages are: (1) the looped finger obscures view of stick thereby reducing aim accuracy, (2) cannot be elevated sufficiently to facilitate shooting over another ball, and (3) cannot be consistently used for all shots.

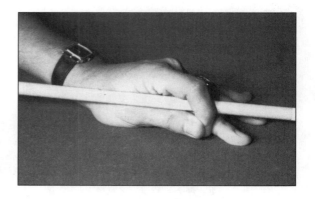

PHOTO 2-10. To lower bridge, reduce
arch of knuckles.

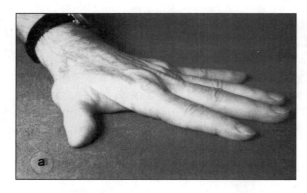

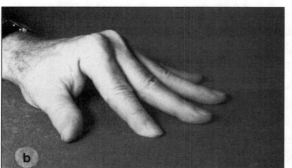

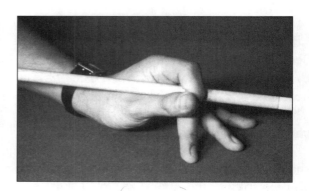

PHOTO 2-11. To raise bridge rotate
ball of thumb off table.

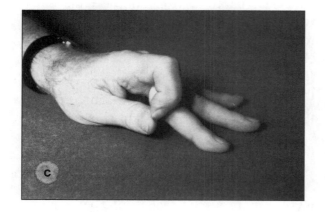

PHOTO 2-9. Forming a proper bridge.

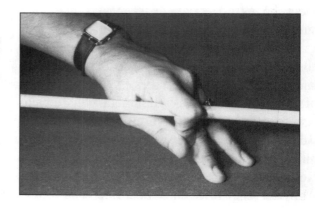

PHOTO 2-12. Hand is rotated forward
for greater elevation.

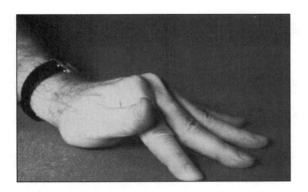

PHOTO 2-13. Basic open bridge.

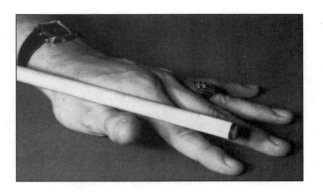

PHOTO 2-14. Stick should not rest on fleshy part of thumb.

Open bridge: The basic open bridge is shown in photo 2-13. It is constructed in the same way as the closed bridge except that the thumb is pressed against the first finger between the knuckle and joint. The stick should rest on the first joint of the thumb, not on the fleshy part (photo 2-14). Raising and lowering this bridge is done similar to that of the closed bridge.

The advantages of the open bridge are: (1) no part of the shaft is obscured from sight which allows accurate aim, (2) can be used for every shot allowing consistency, (3) can get maximum elevation for shooting over a ball while maintaining four stabilizing fingers on the table (the raised closed bridge has only three stabilizing fingers), (4) the bridge hand can be extended farther forward; therefore, more shots can be reached without using the mechanical bridge, and (5) if the hands sweet a lot, the open bridge offers a little less friction. The disadvantages of the open bridge are: (1) allows for the bad habit of lifting the stick off the bridge while shooting, and (2) can't be used if the butt hand is near or forward of the balance point.

A modified form of the closed or open bridge must be used when the rail interferes with normal bridge hand placement. They are generally referred to as *rail bridges* and can be formed from the basic closed bridge as

shown in photo 2-15, or from the basic open bridge as shown in photo 2-16. The modified closed bridges shown in photo 2-15c and 15d have the advantage of being more solid in the vertical plane when the stick is supported by the rail. But, because of the narrow width of the rail, the back stroke has to be limited to a few inches when the cue ball is near the rail. The open rail bridge allows for a near normal back stroke regardless of how close the cue ball is to the rail and thus it maintains the advantage of consistency.

Most professional pocket billiard players use the closed bridge, yet from the above analysis, the open bridge seems to have more advantages. My theory is that the top caliber pool players probably started playing when they were very young, and because they were small, they <u>had to</u> hold the stick at or forward of the balance point. Consequently, they had to use the closed bridge in order to keep the shaft on the bridge hand. As they grew older and bigger they continued to use the closed bridge. As these professionals teach or otherwise influence new players, use of the closed bridge is further perpetuated. Professional snooker players (whose accuracy is paramount) nearly all use the open bridge. This is probably due, in large part, to the influence of Joe Davis and those that emulated him.

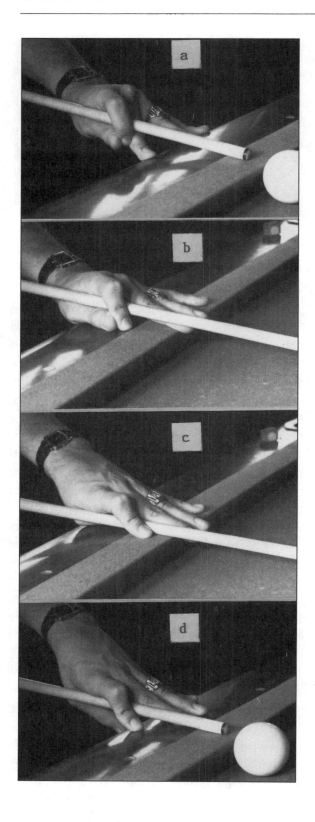

PHOTO 2-15. Rail bridges formed from a closed bridge.

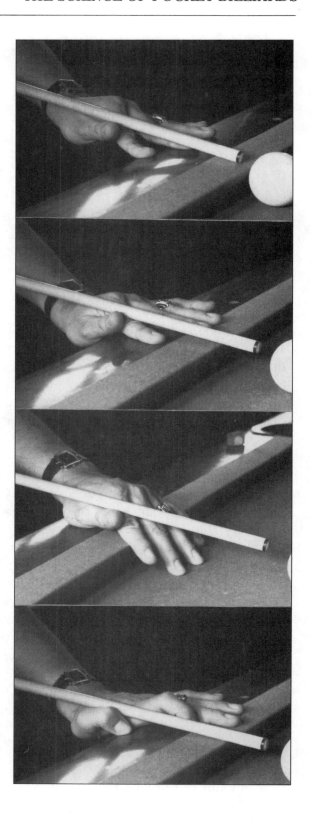

PHOTO 2-16. Rail bridges formed from an open bridge.

Bridge distance--Bridge distance refers to the distance between the cue ball and the point of support on the bridge hand. As with many other things, bridge distance must be a compromise. The closer the bridge is to the cue ball, the more accurately the cue ball can be struck. However, the stick must be stroked back and forth; the longer the bridge distance, the smoother the stroke, and the better the speed control. With a short bridge distance, the stick must be brought up to speed very quickly. In doing so, the sudden acceleration may cause the body and stick alignment to be jerked out of position. Another factor that must be considered is the bending of the shaft when the cue ball is struck off-center. The stick flexes less with a short bridge than with a long bridge. The amount that the stick flexes affects aim. This will be discussed in relation to english in Chapter 6.

A telephoto lens was used to photograph the bridge distance of 31 top-ranked professional NINE-BALL players. The only shots considered were those that were easy to reach, of medium speed, and required little or no english. The bridge distance (edge of cue ball to center of bridge support) was later measured. The average bridge distance of the 31 players was 11.4 inches. Most of the players shortened their bridge distance when the shot required slow speed and/or extreme finesse.

Beginners have difficulty striking the cue ball properly and should therefore use a short bridge (about 6 inches). As their stroke gains precision they should strive to extend the bridge distance to about 11 inches.

The most common mistake made by most players is that they don't use all of their bridge distance. It does absolutely no good to use an 11-inch bridge distance if you only use a 4-inch stroke. The advantage of the long bridge distance is muted while not even getting the advantages of a short bridge.

Stance summary--The individual's stance should be close to that described in this chapter. Beginners should take meticulous care to start with the proper stance. Experienced players should consider the benefits of correcting any gross deviation from proper stance. Changing one's stance will probably cause a temporary decrease in accuracy but will allow the player to eventually become better.

Any gross deviation from proper stance should be justified with logic. If it can't be justified with a convincing logical explanation then it should be changed. Most frequently, when one deviates from proper stance, it is done under the guise of efficiency of movement; but, efficiency of movement results in *instability*. If we use a bridge in which only the tips of the fingers rest on the table, it's easier (more efficient) to move it when making fine aim adjustments. If the hand is solidly on the table, it must be picked up and replaced (inefficient) in order to make aim adjustment. Therefore, the efficient bridge (allowing ease of movement) is not the best (solid) bridge. The same is true for the legs. If they are kept close together with both knees bent, it's easier (more efficient) to move the upper body. Spreading the legs and locking one or both knees makes it difficult (inefficient) to move the upper body. The fact that it is more difficult to move makes for a more stable and therefore more functional stance. The point is, **WE MUST FORFEIT OUR PROCLIVITY FOR EFFICIENCY FOR THE IMMOBILITY OF INEFFICIENCY**.

The optimum shooting stance cannot always be used because of interference by the table. If the stance is not too awkward, leaning against the table adds stability and prevents inadvertent movement. Occasionally when the shooting stance is assumed, the thigh, hip, or some other body part is very near the table but not touching. On these occasions, stance should be modified so that the table is used for added stability.

TECHNIQUE

Now that all the body parts are in the proper position it's time to develop technique. Technique is the method or manner in which an activity is executed.

Stance adjustment--Once a shot has been selected, the feet must be placed in the proper position, a bridge made, and the stick aimed. The average pool player cannot consistently place the feet and bridge hand in the exact optimum position before the aiming process begins. However, there is a tendency to accept the initial stance even though the feet and bridge hand are not in the optimum position. The upper body is leaned into position rather than moving the feet; the bridge hand is twisted and strained into position rather than picking it up and moving it. The best technique is to **HABITUALLY READJUST THE FEET AND BRIDGE POSITIONS AFTER THE INITIAL AIMING PROCESS BEGINS.** Ritualistically making these fine adjustments will insure that you're always in the proper shooting position. The added physical activity will also help reduce muscle *tension*. Observe professional golfers; they never accept their initial foot positions, they make adjustments many times before executing the shot.

Preliminary strokes--The stick should be stroked back and forth during the aiming process; these warm-up strokes are called *preliminary strokes*. Preliminary strokes should incorporate a full back stroke but stop short (1/2 inch) of striking the cue ball on the

forward stroke. These preliminary strokes serve several purposes:

1. They relieve muscle tension during the aiming process.
2. They help groove (ability to repeat with precision) the stroke. The stroke is trained and maintained by repetition; a person that takes five preliminary strokes gets five times more training than the player that takes only one preliminary stroke.
3. Allows fine turning of the bridge-hand position, back stroke, pace, and aim.
4. Alerts the proper muscles to the pending task.

Most players develop a shooting technique that incorporates a specific number of preliminary strokes. Any deviation from this specific number may result in reduced accuracy. If the shot is not executed after the normal number of preliminary strokes, the shooter should pause, perhaps make some stance adjustments, then begin the preliminary strokes all over again.

During the preliminary strokes, concentration must be on *Speed*, *Aim*, and striking *Point* on the cue ball (SAP code). The path of the object ball and cue ball must be visualized; when all elements seem proper; and, during the visualization, the shot is executed.

Back stroke--Some players tend to speed up the final back stroke. This is a common mistake made by golfers as well as pool players. When the back stroke is extremely fast it takes a greater effort to stop the stick then start the acceleration of the forward stroke. In the process, everything gets jerked out of position and the shot is consequently missed. The back stroke should be no faster on the final stroke than during the preliminary strokes. Some players avoid a hurried back stroke by deliberately hesitating after the final back stroke and before the final forward stroke.

Aim alignment--There are players that habitually align the stick in one direction during the preliminary strokes then change alignment during the final stroke. Most of these players aren't even aware that they're doing it and will never realize their full potential until this habit is corrected. As with any other bad habit, it's difficult but not impossible to correct. To help correct the problem, set up an easy straight-in shot; aim the cue ball while taking the normal preliminary strokes, then close the eyes, take a few more preliminary strokes, then shoot. The shot will probably be missed because there was no last moment correction. Keep repeating the shot until it can be made every time. If this is done repeatedly the old habit of moving will eventually disappear.

Some players make an aim adjustment on the final stroke only occasionally. They are usually aware of what they did as soon as the shot is missed. The habit can be corrected with the use of discipline; tell yourself that you will refuse to make that last second adjustment even if it means missing the shot. Many shots will be missed during this corrective period but eventually, your game will improve. Rubbing the stick on the chest while stroking will also help alleviate this bad habit.

During the aiming process, the path of the object ball must be visualized. Each time stick alignment is changed, the visualized path of the object ball must be changed; when aim is such that the projected object-ball path is directly into the pocket, the shot should be executed.

EACH SHOT SHOULD BE A LEARNING OR CONFIRMING EXPERIENCE. When a shot is missed, the error must be immediately diagnosed while the shot is fresh in your mind. Was the object ball cut too much or too little? Shot too fast or too slow? Why was the mistake made? Imagine shooting the shot again but this time incorporate all the necessary corrections. When a shot is made and the path of the object ball was exactly as imagined, you should consciously confirm that your aim was proper.

During the aiming process your visual focus should go back and forth from the cue ball, to the object ball, to the pocket. You're actually concerned about the direction that the stick is pointing, but that's registered in your peripheral vision. The moment the shot is executed, visual focus should be on the object ball. There are some exceptions to this rule. Obviously, with a kick shot (cue ball strikes cushion, then the object ball) the focus should be on the striking point on the cushion. If extreme english is to be used, or if the shot requires extreme power, visual focus should be on the cue ball during execution.

Follow-through--Follow-through refers to the continued forward motion of the stick after impact with the cue ball. Follow-through is recommended in every sport and practically every other imaginable activity. Everyone has heard of follow-through but rarely is it explained in logical terms, people are told to *"just do it and shut up!"* Any prudent person would surmise that once the ball leaves contact with the bat, golf club, or pool cue, it doesn't matter what you do with the propelling instrument -- it won't change the course of the ball. This is true, so why is follow-through necessary? **FOLLOW-THROUGH IS FOR THE MIND AS WELL AS THE MECHANICS**.

If we tell our conscious mind that we can stop the stroke (or swing) immediately after impact with the ball, our subconscious mind will be concentrating on stopping the stroke while it is still in progress. It won't be concentrating on speed and accuracy when it's needed most. Some people not only don't follow-through, but instead, they jerk the stick back or lift it up. **The muscles were obviously instructed to do so**, with all these extraneous messages in the mind, there is no room for the essentials. Follow-through is natural (inertia), it will occur without conscious effort; therefore, one need only to allow it to occur.

Normally, the cue tip remains in contact with the cue ball for only an instant; with follow-through it remains in contact slightly longer; and, if the stick is accelerating, contact time will be even longer. The longer a force is applied (cue stick to cue ball) the greater the transfer of energy. Thus, with follow-through, a deliberate smooth stroke will transfer more energy than a hard stroke with no follow-through. Professional pool players seem to exert only half the effort that the lesser player does to accomplish the same result. This is due to proper follow-through.

Follow-through is as much an effect as it is a cause. Some shots require that the stick be accelerating at the moment of impact with the cue ball. It's difficult (if not impossible) not to have follow-through on these shots. Therefore, one can conclude that if there was no follow-through, the stick was not accelerating at the moment of impact.

The proper length of the follow-through depends mostly on the speed of the shot. For slow shots, follow-through of an inch or so is adequate; when the cue ball is shot very hard, follow-through of 6 or 8 inches is required. If the shot requires that the stick be accelerating at impact, follow-through should be even longer. Actual follow-through distance will vary somewhat depending on stance, the size of the player, and stick weight.

Post-shot-stance--Post-shot-stance refers to the stance after the stroke has been executed and before the balls come to rest. There's a tendency to pick up the cue stick

and stand up _during_ the execution of a shot. Here again is our proclivity for efficiency; as long as we must stand up, efficiency of movement dictates that we do it in one smooth motion in conjunction with shot execution. And again, efficiency of motion is detrimental to the shot. Stay down in the shooting stance until the balls stop moving, or at least until the object ball either does or does not go into the pocket. There are two compelling reasons for staying down: First, it prevents extraneous body movement during shot execution. If movement is allowed immediately after the stroke, the subconscious mind will, at times, anticipate the stroke and allow movement during the shot. When the mind starts to anticipate moving, it has less time and capacity to concentrate on the essential elements. And second, in order to aim properly, the path of the object ball must be visualized while in the shooting stance. If the path of the object ball is never observed from a shooting stance, then it will be difficult or impossible to visualize from this position. The more observations of ball movement that are made from the shooting stance, the easier it becomes to aim properly. The necessity of visualizing the shot will be examined in detail in Chapter 15.

CHAPTER 3

POCKETING THE OBJECT BALL

BASIC SHOTS

In pocket billiards, the most common types of shots are straight-in shots (1-ball in figure 3-1) and cut shots (2-ball in figure 3-1). The straight-in shot is the most fundamental of all shots and requires the *least* accuracy and judgment. The object ball lies directly between the cue ball and pocket. The cue ball must be shot directly at the center of

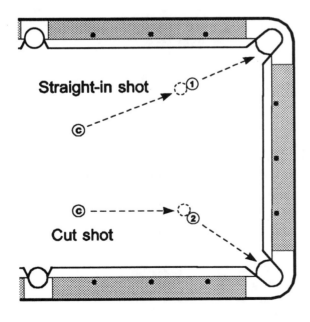

FIGURE 3-1. The two most common types of shots in pool.

the object ball. The *line-of-aim* goes through the center of the object ball. The point at which the cue ball makes contact with the object ball is called the *point-of-contact* or *contact point*. As shown in figure 3-2a, the contact point is directly in line with the line-of-aim. The straight-in shot is the easiest shot in pool because it requires the least amount of judgment. All that is required is the ability to shoot the cue ball directly at the center of the object ball.

With a cut shot, the object ball must be struck to one side of center. As shown in figure 3-2b, the line-of-aim is not through the contact point; therefore, judgment must be used to determine what aim alignment would yield the proper contact point. The acute angle between the line-of-aim and the path of the object ball is referred to as the *cut angle*. The cut angle can be anywhere from zero degrees to slightly less than ninety degrees.

🎱　　　🎱　　　🎱

AIMING TECHNIQUE

An imaginary ball (or phantom ball) can be used to determine the proper cue ball line-of-aim. The imaginary ball is positioned in contact with the object ball such that their centers are aligned with the intended path of

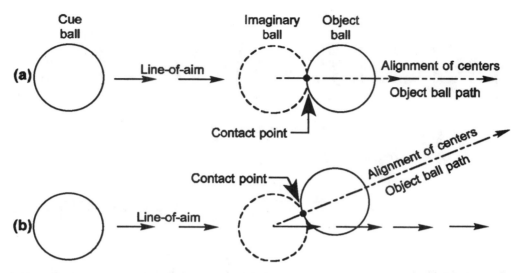

FIGURE 3-2. Line-of-aim goes through contact point on a straight-in shot but not on a cut shot.

the object ball (figure 3-3). The cue ball must be shot directly at the center of the imaginary ball (from any direction) to achieve the desired object ball path. This aiming technique is accurate and simple enough for beginners but must be modified slightly to achieve absolute accuracy.

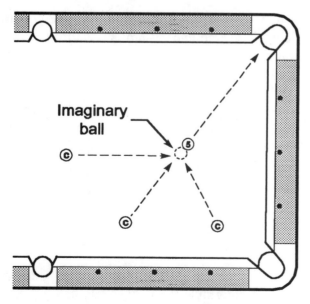

FIGURE 3-3. An imaginary ball can be used to determine line-of-aim.

The aforementioned aiming technique assumes that the path of the object ball is exactly opposite the point-of-contact. This is not absolutely true because there is friction between the two balls. The friction causes the object ball to be propelled at a cut angle slightly less than expected. The deviation caused by friction is called *collision-induced throw*. The concept of collision-induced throw is not well known; for this reason, it will be examined in detail.

COLLISION-INDUCED THROW

It's difficult to visualize how friction causes collision-induced throw. The concept may be best explained by a comparison to a known high friction collision; namely, cue tip on cue ball. Figure 3-4 shows an object ball being struck at the same point with a cue stick and with a cue ball both traveling in the same direction. When struck with the cue stick the object ball moves away along path "A" which is nearly the same direction the stick is moving. This is because friction between the

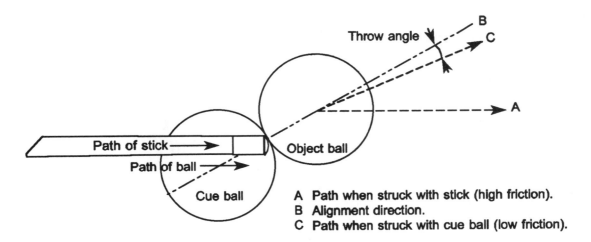

FIGURE 3-4. Collision-induced throw resulting from friction at contact point.

stick and ball is very high. If there were no friction between the propelling force and the object ball, it would take path "B" directly opposite the point-of-contact. If there is any friction between the propelling force and the object ball, the path of the object ball will be between these two extremes. As it turns out there is very little, but some, friction between balls; therefore, the path of the object ball, when propelled by the cue ball, is very near "B" as shown by path "C". The angle between path "B" and path "C" is the collision-induced throw angle.

The magnitude of collision-induced throw depends on cut angle and the amount of friction between the balls. The amount of friction depends on the material from which the balls are made, surfacing (polished, oiled, waxed, etc.), and foreign substances on the surface of the ball (chalk, talcum powder, oil from hands, etc.). In the collision-induced throw experiments that were conducted, the speed of the cue ball did not seem to discernibly effect the throw angle.

Figure 3-5 shows the magnitude of collision-induced throw at various cut angles for clean plastic balls and for balls with various surface impurities. To use the throw chart: Find the cut angle at bottom of chart;

draw a vertical line from that point through the curved lines. From the point of intersection of the vertical and curved lines read the throw from the left side of the chart. For example, the throw for a 60 degree cut shot would be 3½ degrees for a clean ball.

If either ball has talcum powder or palm prints on its surface where the balls make contact, friction is less; consequently, throw is less. When there is chalk on the contact point, friction is greatly increased and so is collision-induced throw.

When the cue ball is struck with a cue tip that has a generous amount of chalk, some of the chalk comes off onto the cue ball. If contact with the object ball occurs at this point, the shot could very likely be missed due to excessive throw. As the cue ball rolls over the cloth, the chalk generally comes off. However, when the cue ball is struck to the side of center, it doesn't roll on the chalk mark so it stays on the cue ball. Different types of chalk and/or humidity conditions affect the amount of chalk that stays on the cue ball. At times, the cue ball can be nearly covered with chalk marks, in which case, cut shots are very unpredictable. Occasionally, players put talcum powder on their hands before racking the balls or handling the cue

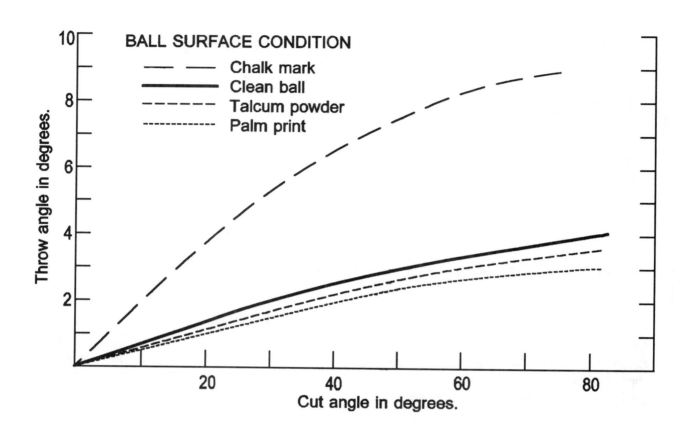

FIGURE 3- 5. Collision-induced throw with different ball surface conditions.

ball; the powder comes off onto the balls causing ball-to-ball friction to become less; and consequently, throw is less. The same is true for palm or finger prints; the oil from the hand acts as a lubricant, thus reducing ball-to-ball friction. High humidity can cause moisture to form on the balls which also acts as a lubricant to reduce friction.

Figure 3-6 shows a typical cut shot; the object ball is 60 inches from the pocket and requires a 45-degree cut angle. Collision-induced throw for a clean ball at a 45-degree cut angle is 2.7 degrees (from figure 3-5). This translates to a distance of 2.8 inches off-center at the pocket. If no allowance is made for throw, the center of the pocket would be missed by 2.8 inches to the right. An expert player shooting this same shot automatically

allows for throw and the clean ball goes into the pocket dead center. Let the expert shoot the same shot again but this time assume that the balls make contact on a chalk mark. The difference in throw between clean balls (2.7 degrees) and chalked balls (7 degrees) is 4.3 degrees. This translates to a net error of 4.5 inches to the right of center pocket. If the balls make contact on talcum powder, the error would be 0.3 inch to the left of center pocket; if the balls make contact on a palm print the error would be 0.6 inch to the left of center pocket. Now you have an *excuse* for missing those long cut shots.

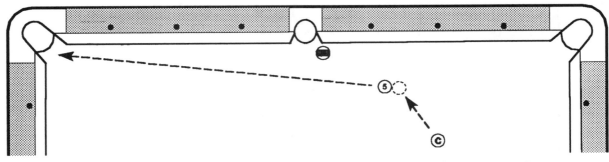

Surface condition	Collision-induced throw (degrees)	Error at pocket (inches)
Clean ball	2.7	2.8
Talcum powder	2.2	2.5
Palm print	2.1	2.2
Chalk mark	7.0	7.3

FIGURE 3-6. Effects of throw on a 45 degree cut shot with the object ball 60 inches from pocket.

Most people learn to shoot cut shots by trial-and-error thereby allowing for throw without even knowing anything about the concept. But generally, the learning process is speeded up and broadened by having this knowledge. Knowing about collision-induced throw may offer an explanation for why a person starts missing shots right after the balls have been polished. And, recognizing the possible problems of practicing with a set of old balls and playing with a set of new balls may help save a few bucks. And that's not all, this knowledge may help resolve other questions. For example: Why do you suppose the guy in the black hat secretly polishes all of his even numbered balls with polish that leaves an oily residue and all of the odd numbered balls with a sticky wax?

CHAPTER 4

SHOT SELECTION

One of the first things a beginner must learn is proper shot selection. Usually one develops this capability by trial-and-error; those shots that are tried and made are considered easier than those that are tried and missed. The beginner is concerned mainly with selecting the shot that has the highest probability of being made. The probability aspects are the main consideration in this chapter. As the player's skill develops, cue ball positioning, strategy, etc. must also be considered.

PERMISSIBLE ERROR

The difficulty of every shot depends largely on how accurate the cue ball's path must be in order to pocket the object ball. The object ball is usually aimed for the center of the pocket. If it succeeds in going into the exact center, the cue ball path was perfect and there was no error. If the object ball does not go into the center of the pocket there was an error in the path of the cue ball. The maximum allowable error, while still pocketing the object ball, is called *permissible error*. The permissible error is the angle, expressed in degrees, in which the cue ball path can deviate and still pocket the object ball. Figure 4-1 shows a diagrammatic example of permissible error for a short, straight-in shot. The cue ball could be shot anywhere between direction "A" and "B" and it would still pocket the object ball. The angle formed by "A" - cue ball - "B" is the

permissible error angle of this shot; in this case it's about 25 degrees. The smaller the permissible error, the more difficult the shot.

There are several factors that affect permissible error. Most significant are; effective pocket size, cut angle, and distance (cue ball to object ball and object ball to pocket).

Effective pocket size--The term *effective pocket size* refers to the limits of the target area of a pocket from the perspective of the object ball. The object ball will go into the pocket if its center is anywhere within the target area. Generally, aim should be at the center of the target area (target point) in order to allow for the greatest error in either direction.

The shape and size of the pockets influence effective pocket size. Before a thorough analysis of effective pocket size is made, some of the pocket variables will be examined. Figure 4-2 shows the critical parts of a corner pocket and a side pocket.

The effective pocket size depends mainly on the width of the pocket (dimension x) which is measured from lip to lip. The width of a corner pocket is generally from 4.5 to 5.0 inches; the side pockets are always about 0.5 inch larger. On the corner pockets, the hole (drop) is set back from the lips (dimension z) about 1.25 inches; the greater this distance, the more difficult it is to pocket a ball. The radius of the hole (dimension y) is generally about 3 inches for the corner pockets and 2 inches for the side pockets. The larger the hole radius the easier it

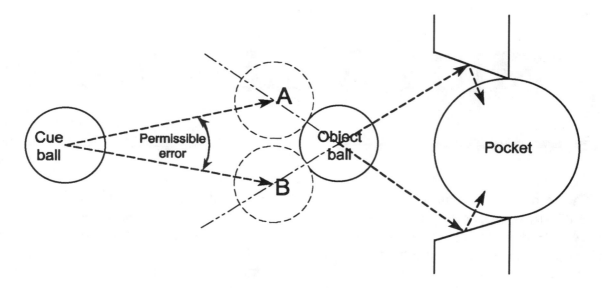

FIGURE 4-1. Cue ball can be shot in any direction from "A" to "B" and still pocket the object ball.

is to pocket a ball. Angle "a" is generally about 140 degrees for the corner pockets, and about 105 degrees for the side pockets. The smaller this angle is, the easier it is to pocket a ball. Irregularities such as wrinkled or worn cloth in the pocket area will alter the characteristics of a pocket.

Effective pocket size differs between side pockets and corner pockets. Each will be examined individually.

<u>Side pockets</u>: Before playing on an unfamiliar table the limits of the target area should be determined. To do so, shoot straight at the pocket as shown in figure 4-3. Shoot farther and farther from the center of the

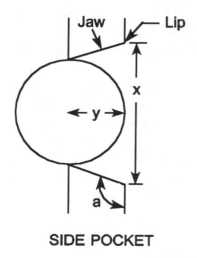

SIDE POCKET

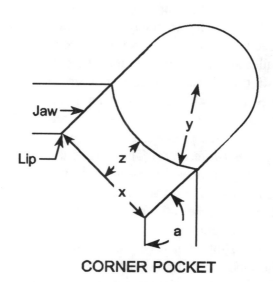

CORNER POCKET

FIGURE 4-2. Pocket dimensions that determine effective pocket size.

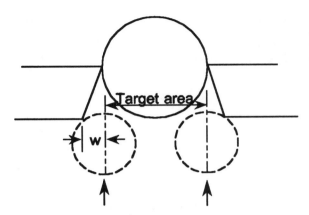

**FIGURE 4-3. The target area of a
side pocket when the object
ball approaches at 90 degrees.**

pocket until the ball fails to go in. Remember the distance (distance w) where the ball just barely goes into the pocket. This distance is generally between 0.5 and 0.6 inch for most pockets. The length of the target area is the effective pocket size. As shown in figure 4-4, when the object ball approaches the pocket at an angle less than 90 degrees, the effective pocket size becomes smaller. The smaller the approach angle, the smaller the effective pocket size. At approach angles of less than

about 20 degrees, effective pocket size becomes zero and the ball can't be made.

Defining the target area, for shots that have an approach angle of less than 90 degrees, is a little bit complicated. Consider the shot shown in figure 4-4 that has an approach angle of 55 degrees. Assume that it has been previously determined that a straight-in shot must be shot 0.5 inch (or more) inside the lip in order to make the ball. The extent of the target area on the far side of the pocket remains 0.5 inch regardless of approach angle. To determine the extent of the target area on the near side of the pocket, imagine a ball touching the lip with its center 0.5 inch inside the lip as shown. The center of the imaginary ball defines the extent of the target area on the near side of the pocket. In general, if the approach angle is less than about 45 degrees the ball must barely touch the pocket lip on the near side. At approach angles between 45 and 90 degrees the distance from the lip varies from 1.12 inches (1/2 ball diameter) to 0.5 inch.

Many players have difficulty with side pocket shots when the approach angle is less than 90 degrees. This is generally because the

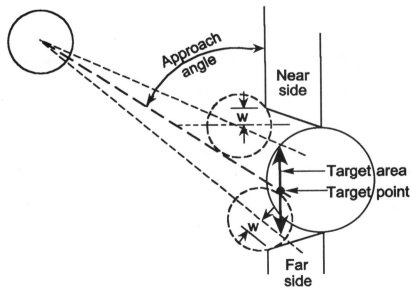

**FIGURE 4-4. The target area of a side pocket when object
ball approach angle is less than 90 degrees.**

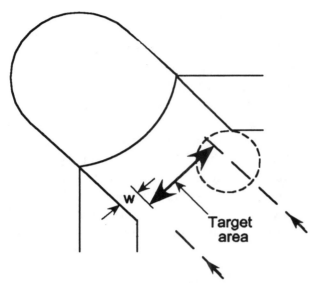

**FIGURE 4-5. The target area of
a corner pocket.**

about 80 percent of the missed shots strike the lip on the near side of the pocket then rebound away. This tendency can be overcome by consciously delineating the target area and target point before the aiming process begins.

Corner pockets: As with the side pockets, the corner pockets must be tested to determine the extent of the target area. Figure 4-5 shows the target area when shooting straight into the pocket. The unique thing about corner pockets is that *the effective pocket size remains the same **regardless** of approach angle*. The target area shifts so that it is always perpendicular to the path of the object ball. This means that a ball can strike a cushion adjacent to the pocket and still go in. Figure 4-6 shows how to determine where the target area is regardless of approach angle. Imagine that the pocket is rotated so that it faces the object ball using the far lip as the pivot point. Figure 4-6 shows that the target area remains the same size but has shifted to

target area and target point are not clearly envisioned prior to shot execution. There is a subconscious tendency to shoot for the center of the hole in the pocket. Consequently,

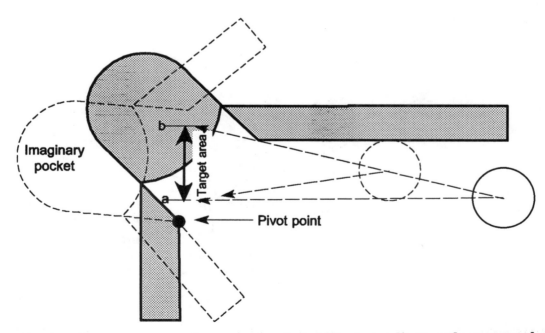

**FIGURE 4-6. The target area of a corner pocket shifts depending on the approach angle
of the object ball. An imaginary pocket can be rotated (to face the object ball)
to determine the target area.**

the right. The ball can be shot in any direction between "a" and "b" and still go in. If shot in direction "b" it would strike the cushion and rebound toward "a" but still go in. In order to have the largest possible permissible error, the center of the object ball must be aimed at the center of the target area of the imaginary pocket.

Cut angle--Permissible error is greatest for straight-in shots. As the cut angle increases, the permissible error becomes smaller until the cut angle is about 85 degrees, at which point, the shot becomes impossible.

Small cut angles have very little affect on permissible error; this is partially because collision-induced throw increases permissible error of straight-in shots and shots that have a small cut angle. Figure 4-7 shows a straight-in shot with and without collision-induced throw. The object ball can travel in any direction between "A" and "B" (target area) and still go into the pocket. This means that the cue ball could be shot anywhere between

"a'" and "b'" and the object ball would be made. If there were no throw and the cue ball were shot to point "a'" or "b'" the object ball to go toward "a" and "b" respectively and would consequently be missed. Therefor, on a straight-in shot, throw allows for a larger permissible error.

Figure 4-8 shows why throw has little effect on shots with larger cut angles. Without throw, shooting the cue ball in directions "a'" and "b'" would cause the object ball to go toward "a" and "b" respectively; with throw, the object ball goes toward "A" or "B". The path of the object ball has shifted but permissible error has not been affected significantly.

Distance--There are two distance variables; the distance between the object ball and pocket, and the distance between the cue ball and object ball. Both have a crucial influence on permissible error. Double either distance and the shot will require about twice the accuracy. Table 4-1 shows the permissible

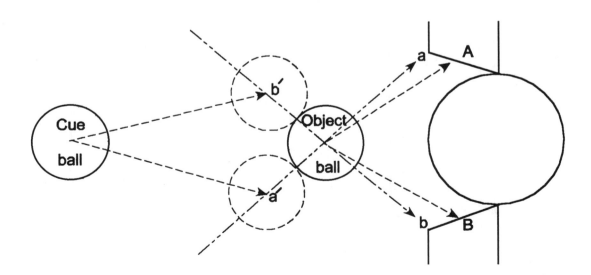

FIGURE 4-7. If the cue ball were shot in direction a' the alignment would indicate that the object ball would go in direction "a" and would consequently be missed. With throw, the object ball will go in direction "A" and be made.

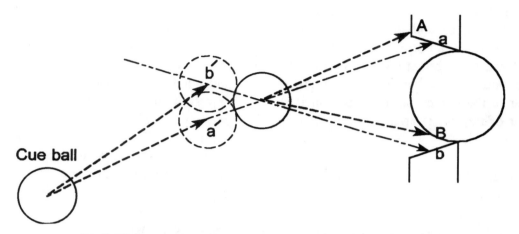

FIGURE 4-8. Collision-induced throw does not affect permissible error on a cut shot.

Distance from object ball to pocket in inches.

	6	12	18	24	30	36	42	48	60	72	84	96
6	14	7.7	5.2	3.9	3.1	2.6	2.2	2.0	1.6	1.3	1.1	.99
12	7.3	3.8	2.6	1.9	1.6	1.3	1.1	.97	.78	.65	.56	.49
18	4.8	2.5	1.7	1.3	1.0	.86	.74	.64	.52	.43	.37	.32
24	3.6	1.9	1.3	.96	.77	.64	.55	.48	.39	.32	.28	
30	2.9	1.5	1.0	.77	.62	.52	.44	.39	.31	.26	.22	
36	2.4	1.3	.85	.64	.51	.43	.37	.32	.26	.21		
42	2.1	1.1	.73	.55	.44	.37	.32	.28	.22	.18		
48	1.8	.95	.64	.48	.38	.32	.28	.24	.19			
60	1.4	.76	.51	.38	.31	.26	.22	.19				
72	1.2	.63	.42	.32	.26	.21						
84	1.0	.54	.36	.27								
96	.91	.47	.32									

Distance from cue ball to object ball in inches.

Distance
object ball to pocket

Distance
cue ball to object ball

TABLE 4-1. Permissible error (in degrees) for straight-in corner pocket shots. To determine permissible error for straight-in side pocket shots, multiply by 1.12.

error for straight-in corner pocket shots of varying distances. For example, if an object ball is 12 inches from a corner pocket and the cue ball must travel 12 inches, the permissible error is 3.8 degrees. If the cue ball is twice the distance from the object ball (24 inches) the permissible error becomes 1.9 degrees. The permissible error for any straight-in corner pocket shot can be interpolated from this table.

It is interesting to note that permissible error is smallest when the object ball is halfway between the cue ball and pocket. As the object ball is moved closer to the pocket, or to the cue ball, the shot becomes easier. For example, assume the cue ball is 48 inches from the pocket; with the object ball directly between the cue ball and pocket, the permissible error is 0.96 degree; if the object ball was 12 inches from the pocket, the permissible error would be 1.3 degrees; if the object ball was 12 inches from the cue ball, the permissible error would be 1.3 degrees.

CALCULATING SHOT DIFFICULTY

Experienced players judge the relative difficulty of shots by using the trial-and-error data they have stored in their memories. Inexperienced players make the wrong choice and miss many shots in the process of developing their data banks. A lot of time can be saved, and experience gained, by practicing determining the relative difficulty of shots on paper.

Mathematically calculating the permissible error of a shot is a long and arduous task. If one has a thorough knowledge of geometry, trigonometry, and computer programming, a computer can be made to do the calculations. Or -- table 4-1 can be used; with a few adjustments for angles, a close approximation of permissible error for cut shots can also be determined.

Table 4-1 gives the permissible error for straight-in corner pocket shots. To determine

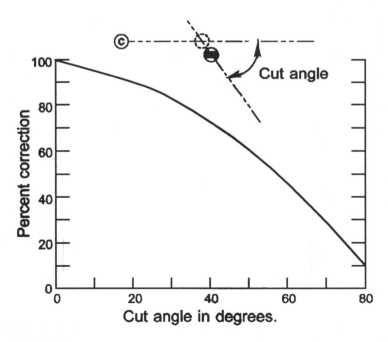

FIGURE 4-9. The permissible error calculated for a straight-in shot must be reduced if a cut angle is involved. This chart shows the correction required.

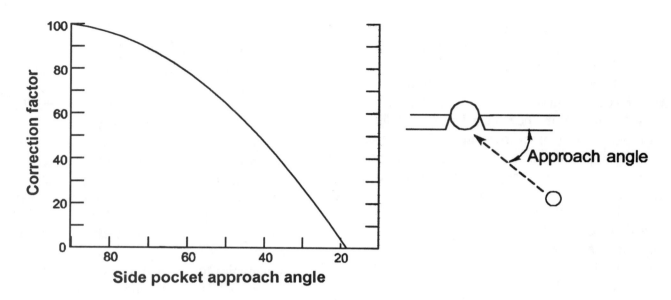

FIGURE 4-10. Permissible error must be reduced for approach angles less than 90 degrees. This chart shows the required reduction.

permissible error of a shot one must measure or estimate the distances from the pocket to object ball and from object ball to cue ball. For example, assume it is 36 inches from the pocket to object ball and 24 inches from object ball to the cue ball. Find 36 at the top of the chart to determine the proper column and 24 at left side of chart to determine row. The permissible error (0.64 degree) is the number at the junction of column 36 and row 24.

Cut shots are more difficult; therefore, the permissible error must be reduced by some factor. Figure 4-9 shows how much the permissible error must be reduced due to cut angle. As an example, assume a 30-degree cut shot with the object ball 24 inches from the corner pocket and a cue ball travel distance of 18 inches. For these distances, table 4-1 indicates a permissible error of 1.3 degrees for a straight-in shot. Figure 4-10 shows that at a 30-degree cut angle the permissible error is 85 percent of the straight-in shot; therefore, the adjusted permissible error is 1.1 degrees (0.85 x 1.3 = 1.1). Computer analysis indicates a permissible error of 1.07 degrees.

Table 4-1 can also be used to determine the permissible error for side pocket shots. However, permissible error must be adjusted higher (because the pockets are larger) by multiplying by the factor 1.12 and, must be adjusted lower for approach angles less than 90 degrees. Figure 4-10 shows the correction factor for approach angles less than 90 degrees. As an example, assume an object ball is 12 inches from the side pocket; an approach angle of 60 degrees; a cue ball travel distance of 18 inches; and, no cut angle. The permissible error from table 4-1 is 2.5 degrees; multiplied by the factor 1.12 to correct for pocket size yields 2.8

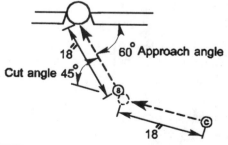

FIGURE 4-11. Angles and distances required to calculate permissible error for a cut shot into a side pocket.

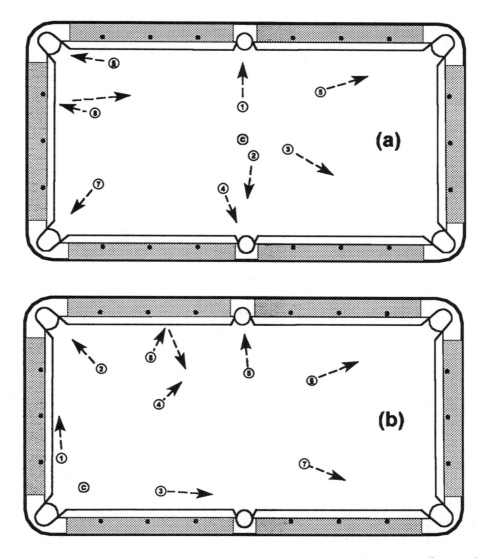

**FIGURE 4-12. A series of typical shots. The permissible error for each
shot is shown in Table 4-2.**

degrees; multiplying by 0.80 (determined from figure 4-10) to correct for approach angle gives a permissible error of 2.24 degrees. The permissible error for this shot determined by computer is 2.28 degrees.

Consider the shot shown in figure 4-11. The object ball is 18 inches from the side pocket with an approach angle of 60 degrees; the cue ball is 18 inches from the object ball requiring a 45-degree cut angle. Permissible error for a corner pocket shot at these distances is 1.7 degrees (from table 4.1). Corrected for a side pocket shot, the permissible error is 1.9

degrees (1.12 x 1.7 = 1.9). The approach angle of 60 degrees reduces the permissible error to 1.5 degrees (0.80 x 1.9 = 1.5). Figure 4-9 shows that for a cut angle of 45 degrees the permissible error must be reduced by a factor of 0.70; 0.70 x 1.5 = 1.0 degree permissible error. Computer analysis indicates a permissible error of 0.95 degree for this shot.

Figure 4-12 shows a number of possible shots; table 4-2 shows the computer calculated permissible error for each.

Figure 4-12 (a)		Figure 4-12 (b)	
Ball number	Permissible error	Ball number	Permissible error
1	10.3	1	2.3
2	2.1	2	0.51
3	1.7	3	0.52
4	2.0	4	0.46
5	1.1	5	0.36
6	1.1	6	0.32
7	0.83	7	0.31
8	0.18	8	0.29

**Table 4-2. Computer calculated permissible error
for shots shown in Figure 4-12.**

JUDGMENT AND SKILL

All shots require *judgment* (application of knowledge) and physical *skill* (ability) but not necessarily in the same proportions. Compare the 1-ball and 3-ball shots in figure 4-12b. The 3-ball requires about four times as much accuracy as the 1-ball yet many good shooters would select the 3-ball as the easier shot. It's pretty obvious that the 3-ball is straight-in. Since it must be struck head-on, little or no judgment is needed to determine where to aim the cue ball. In shooting the 1-ball judgment must be used to determine where to aim during the aiming process. There lies the difference. The 3-ball requires physical skill and practically no judgment; the 1-ball requires less physical skill but more judgment. In figure 4-12a the 5-ball requires twice the accuracy as does the 2-ball, yet most people would elect to shoot the 5-ball for the same reason. Shots can be subjectively categorized by the relative proportion of judgment and skill required for each. Those shots that require a greater proportion of judgment (the 2-ball in figure 4-12a) are referred to as *judgment shots*, and those that require a larger proportion of skill (3-ball in figure 4-12b) are referred to as *skill shots*.

CHAPTER 5

CUE-BALL DEFLECTION PATH

Any player that intends to advance beyond a novice must be able to predict where the cue ball will go after it collides with another ball. When the cue ball strikes another ball at an angle, it is deflected from its original path. The path it takes after striking another ball is called the *cue-ball deflection path*. There are three main factors that influence cue-ball deflection path: (1) the resiliency of the material from which the balls are made, (2) the amount of rotational energy contained in the cue ball at the moment of impact, and (3) the coefficient of friction between the ball and cloth.

BALL RESILIENCY

The *coefficient of restitution* of a material is a measure of its resiliency. If billiard balls were made of a material that had perfect resiliency, the coefficient of restitution would be equal to one and the balls would carom off each other at 90 degrees. Fortunately, the coefficient of restitution of modern billiard balls is very nearly equal to one. Therefore, billiard balls carom off each other at nearly 90 degrees; for all practical purposes it can be assumed to be 90 degrees. This means that if the path of the object ball can be predicted, the deflection path of the cue ball can also be predicted. However, cue ball roll must also be taken into consideration.

NORMAL ROLL

A moving ball is said to have *normal roll* when there is no slippage between ball and cloth. With normal roll, a ball makes one full revolution as it travels the distance of its circumference. As shown in figure 5-1, when a ball is struck in the center with a cue stick, or another ball, it starts its lateral movement with no rotation. Friction between the cloth and ball causes the ball to accumulate forward rotation as it moves forward. At some point it attains normal roll and continues with normal roll until it strikes something, or stops. Normal roll is an important concept because it plays a significant role in determining how the cue ball reacts after impact with another ball. The roll or rotation of the cue ball must be considered before executing each and every shot in order to accurately predict the cue ball's path after contact with the other ball.

In order to understand the significance of normal roll, the concept of energy (the ability to do work or cause something to happen) must be understood. When a ball is rolling on a table, it possesses kinetic energy which is

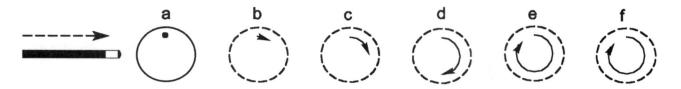

a - Ball at rest, no rotation.
b - Begins to accumulate roll as soon as it is struck.
c - Slips on cloth but roll is accelerating.
d - Only slight slippage between ball and cloth.
e - No slippage, ball has normal roll.
f - Continues with normal roll until it stops or strikes something.

FIGURE 5-1. Cue ball accumulating normal roll.

the energy contained in its motion. The kinetic energy of a rolling ball is of two types, linear energy (energy of translation), and rotational (angular) energy. Linear energy is the energy contained in the ball's movement from one point to another on the table; this is much like the energy contained in a shuffle board or hockey puck. Linear energy is passed from one ball to another when they collide. When a moving ball runs head-on into a stationary ball, the moving ball transfers all of its linear energy to the stationary ball. (There is a slight loss of energy to other sources). If the collision is not head-on, only a portion of the linear energy is passed from the moving ball to the stationary ball. As the angle of collision (cut angle) increases, less and less energy is transferred to the stationary ball.

The rotational energy of a ball with normal roll (28.6 percent of its total kinetic energy) is contained in the circular motion of the ball. Rotational energy is similar to the energy contained in a spinning top or flywheel. The rotational energy, as such, is not of concern to the pool player; but, at times it changes into linear energy which does concern the pool player. The change in energy type is

what causes the balls to curve and do all sorts of strange things.

Not only can the rotational energy be converted into linear energy but the opposite is also true. If a stationary ball is struck with a cue stick, or another ball, it starts out having only linear energy. Friction between the ball and cloth causes some of this energy to be converted to rotational energy. Rotational energy continues to accumulate until there is no slippage between ball and cloth which means it has reached the state of normal roll.

The distance that a ball must travel before it attains normal roll depends mainly on how hard it is struck. Figure 5-2 shows the approximate distance required to attain normal roll on an average table. The required distance varies somewhat depending on friction between the ball and cloth. The friction is generally highest with old, dirty cloth that has a heavy accumulation of chalk.

CUE BALL RESPONSE TO ROLL

When a ball with normal roll collides head-on into a stationary ball it transfers all of its

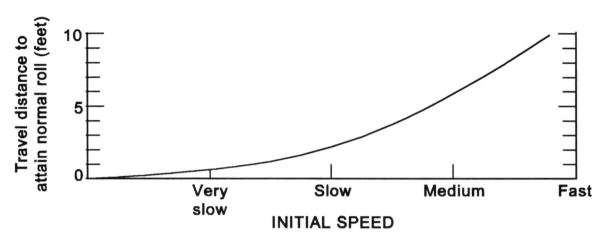

FIGURE 5-2. The approximate distance required for a ball to attain normal roll.

linear energy to the stationary ball but retains practically all of its rotational energy. Figure 5-3 shows what happens. Upon striking an object ball, the cue ball's linear motion is stopped but it continues to rotate. As it rotates, friction between ball and cloth causes the rotational energy to be converted to linear energy and the cue ball begins to move forward. The cue ball accelerates forward until normal roll is attained; and, at that point it starts to slow down.

Figure 5-4 shows what happens when a cue ball with normal roll collides with an object ball at an angle. If the cue ball had no rotation at the moment of collision, it would take the path shown as the resiliency force which is 90 degrees from the path of the object ball. The rotational force is in the direction of its original path. The cue ball's actual path is somewhere between the resiliency force and rotational force. The cue ball path is actually curved. It starts out in the direction of the resiliency force, then curves in the direction of the rotational force. When the original rotational force has dissipated the cue ball assumes a straight path.

CUE BALL PATH WITH NORMAL ROLL

It would be of great value to be able to predict the path of the cue ball (with normal roll), after impact with the object ball at various angles. Its path is difficult to describe because of the slight curve after impact with

SIDE VIEW

Moving cue ball (normal roll)

Cue ball stops momentarily after collision

Object ball

Cue ball moves forward

FIGURE 5-3. Normal roll causes the cue ball to accelerate forward after striking an object ball head-on.

TOP VIEW

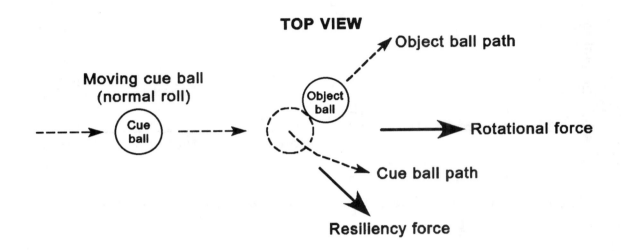

**FIGURE 5-4. The rotation of the cue ball causes it to curve
as it caroms off an object ball.**

the object ball. Its path is also affected by speed; the curve has a small arc at slow speeds and a large arc at high speeds. Even with these complications the cue ball path, after collision, can be closely approximated.

Figure 5-5 shows the approximate cue-ball deflection angle for all cut angles at slow to medium speed. The deflection angle denotes the cue ball's position after it has traveled 24 inches from the point of impact. Keep in mind that the cue ball actually had to curve in getting to that point. If cue ball speed is very slow the effective deflection angle will be slightly smaller than indicated; if it's moving faster than medium speed it will be slightly larger than indicated.

As shown, when the cut angle is zero, the deflection angle is zero. The deflection angle increases rapidly as the cut angle increases to about 20 degrees; it levels off between 20 and 30 degrees then it gradually declines. To be of any practical value, this chart must be committed to memory. It's not as difficult as it would seem if the cut angles are put into three groups. For cut shots between 0 and 10 degrees, the deflection angle increases rapidly from 0 to 30 degrees. For cut shots between 10 and 45 degrees (about 70 percent of your shots), the deflection angle is between 30 and 40 degrees. For cut shots over 45 degrees, it may be easier to memorize the total angle between cue ball path and object ball path. This angle increases from 75 degrees at a cut angle of 45 degrees to 90 degrees on very thin cut shots.

ESTIMATING CUE BALL PATH

In order to estimate the cue ball's path after impact with the object ball, one must know how much rotation it has at the moment of impact. Assuming the cue ball is struck in the center, it will have anywhere from no roll to normal roll at the moment of impact depending on how hard it is struck and its travel distance. The harder the cue ball

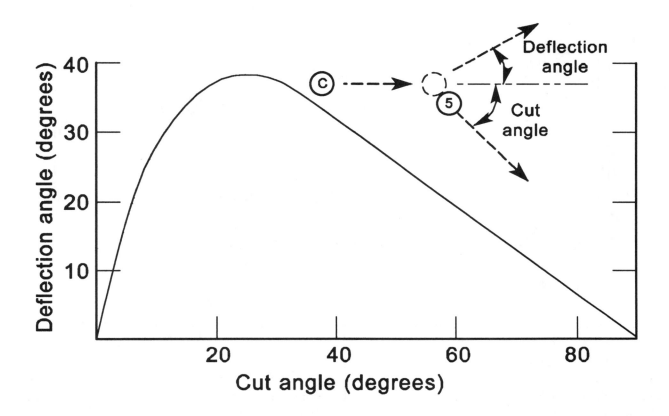

FIGURE 5-5. Cue-ball deflection angle with normal roll.

is struck, the greater the distance required to attain normal roll.

Cue ball at "A" Consider the situation shown in figure 5-6. With the cue ball at position "A" the 1-ball requires a 30-degree cut into the corner pocket. The cue ball is 5.5 feet away from the 1-ball. If it's propelled at medium speed it will have normal roll (from figure 5-2) when it strikes the 1-ball. With normal roll the cue-ball deflection angle is about 40 degrees (from figure 5-5) and the cue ball will go in direction "e". If the cue ball is propelled at a slow speed it will still have normal roll at the time of impact and will again go in direction "e".

Cue ball at "B" Assume the cue ball is at position "B" and is struck slowly. The distance between the cue ball and object ball is 33 inches, and it requires only 24 inches to attain normal roll. Therefore, cue-ball deflection angle will again be 40 degrees (direction "e"). If the cue ball is struck at medium speed it will require about 66 inches to attain normal roll. The cue ball will have about one-half normal roll (between no roll and normal roll) at the moment of impact. If the cue ball had no roll its deflection angle would be 60 degrees (90 - 30 = 60); with normal roll it would be 40 degrees; having one-half normal roll the cue-ball deflection

57

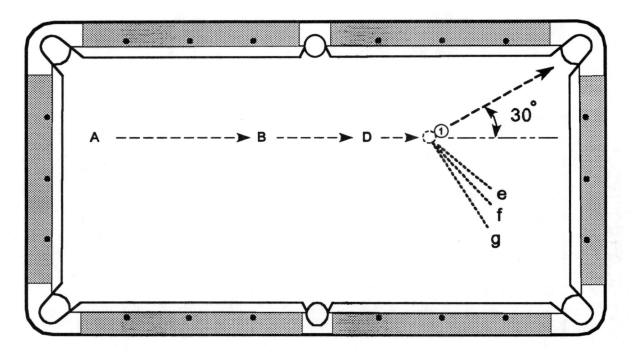

FIGURE 5-6. The path of the cue ball, after impact with an object ball, depends on its state of roll which in turn depends on how hard it was struck and its travel distance.

angle will be between 60 and 40 or 50 degrees as shown by direction "f".

Cue ball at "D" If the cue ball is at position "D" (about 12 inches from the object ball) and is struck slowly, it will have only one-half normal roll when it strikes the object ball and again will go in direction "f". If it's struck medium or hard it will have very little roll at impact; therefore, its path will be nearly perpendicular to the path of the object ball (direction "g").

Having to integrate cue ball speed and travel distance to determine its state of roll is a little complicated. It is actually easier to think in terms of *travel time*. Travel time combines speed and distance into one entity. Assume that it takes 0.8 second for the cue ball to attain normal roll. The cue ball will have normal roll for any shot that requires 0.8 second, or more, travel time to get to the

object ball. If travel time is less, due either to distance or speed, the cue ball will have less than normal roll at impact. All good players subconsciously use this travel time system to predict and control the cue-ball deflection angle. As a person's internal clock gains accuracy, timing and rhythm improve resulting in better cue ball control.

Question: How does talcum powder on the cloth affect cue ball deflection path?

CHAPTER 6

ENGLISH

Players that are just beginning to learn pool should concentrate on pocketing the object ball while striking the cue ball in the center. When they can pocket the object ball with relative regularity they must begin learning how to position the cue ball for the next shot. At first, positioning should be done by controlling the speed of the cue ball; when speed control has been mastered, positioning can be further enhanced with the use of english.

The term *english*, as used in this book, is defined as any spin or rotation of a ball that is not a manifestation of normal roll. English is applied to the cue ball by striking it off-center with the cue stick.

There are three basic types of english; they are described in relation to where the cue ball is struck: *bottom english* (also referred to as *draw*), *top english* (also referred to as *follow*), and *side english* (either left or right; *running* or *reverse*). Bottom or top english can be used in combination with side as in *bottom left*, or *top right*, etc.

Be cautioned; some authorities define english as side spin only. They don't consider top or bottom as being english. However, common usage dictates the broader definition which includes top and bottom. Before getting into any in-depth discussions about english, be sure the word is well defined.

As a rule, ***bottom and top english affects the angle at which the cue ball <u>rebounds off an object ball</u>***, and ***side* english** *affects the angle at which the cue ball <u>rebounds off a*</u>* *cushion*. The extent that the path of the cue ball is altered is determined by how much english the cue ball has when it contacts the object ball and/or cushion. The farther the cue ball is struck off-center, the more english it will have. But, there is a limit to how far from center the cue ball can be struck.

When the cue ball is struck too far from center the cue tip will slip off the ball. This is called a *miscue*. When a miscue occurs the cue ball rolls off in some unexpected direction without any english. The maximum distance from center that the cue ball can be struck, with a chalked cue stick, is about 0.6 inch. As shown in figure 6-1, when the contact point is 0.6 inch from center, the center of the stick is actually more than 0.6 inch off-center. It's generally easier to note the distance from the edge of the stick to the edge of the ball (distance "x" in figure 6-1) when a miscue occurs; when playing, be sure this distance is greater than "x". Any player that experiments with english will soon know intuitively how far from center the cue ball can be struck.

The shape of the cue tip affects the contact point on the cue ball. Figure 6-2 shows two sticks, both aligned with their centers "x" distance from the center of the cue ball. The stick with the rounded tip strikes the cue ball farther from center (distance "z") than the stick with the flat tip (distance "y"). Therefore, in order to be consistent in the amount of english given to the cue ball, ***the curvature of the tip must be kept constant***.

59

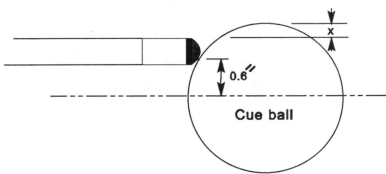

FIGURE 6-1. As a reference in judging maximum english, that can be applied before a miscue occurs, one must use either the distance from the contact point to the center of the cue ball, or the distance from the edge of the tip to the edge of the cue ball.

Shots that require maximum english require a slightly modified shooting technique. With most shots the visual focus shifts back and forth from the pocket -- to the object ball -- to the cue ball. The instant the shot is executed, focus should be on the object ball. When using maximum english, focus should be on the cue ball at the moment of execution. This shifting of focus helps to avoid a miscue but does so at the expense of aim accuracy.

BOTTOM ENGLISH

Bottom english is used more than any other type of english. It is applied to the cue ball by striking it below center causing it to rotate backwards. Bottom english does not affect aim alignment and therefore is easily learned and utilized by the novice. Bottom english, when used with speed control, offers a large variety of cue ball position possibilities. Players and nonplayers alike marvel at the sight of a cue ball backing up after it strikes an object ball.

To properly apply bottom english the cue stick must be held as level as possible. Care must be taken to assure ample cue stick **follow-through** after contact with the cue ball. That's the standard advice given to all novice players and indeed it's absolutely correct. However, the expert is able to draw the cue ball back a table length, or more, seemingly without effort while the average player struggles to draw it back a few inches.

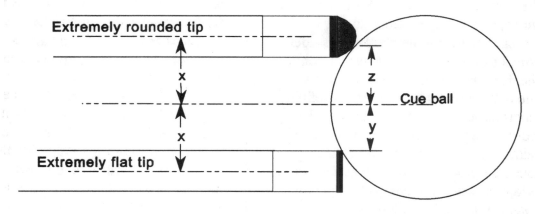

FIGURE 6-2. The rounded tip contacts the cue ball farther from the center than the flat tip.

60

The secret of maximum bottom is; THE CUE STICK MUST <u>ACCELERATE</u> THROUGH THE CUE BALL. If the stick is gaining speed as it strikes the cue ball it remains in contact longer. A law of physics states that the reaction to a force depends not only on the amount of the force but also on the duration of the force. Consequently, the longer the stick remains in contact with the cue ball, the greater the acceleration of reverse rotation. In order to accelerate through the cue ball, there must be greater than normal follow-through. Generally, the acceleration and longer follow-through, are made easier by moving the bridge hand closer to the cue ball. Imagine that the cue ball is made out of lead and must be pushed in order to get it to move. Hold the cue stick a little tighter than usual and keep applying forward pressure after contact with the cue ball.

A soft tip also enhances maximum bottom english. This is due, in part, to the added surface area in contact with the cue ball which allows it to be struck farther below center without miscuing. Also, the tip indents farther which means that it remains in contact with the cue ball longer, thus producing more english.

A heavy stick will produce more english than a light stick. The light stick has a greater tendency to stop when it strikes the cue ball; the added inertia of a heavy stick causes it to keep on driving forward. Because it drives forward it remains in contact with the cue ball longer and thereby transmits more energy resulting in greater backward spin.

The cue stick bends down when it contacts the cue ball. If the shaft is very flexible the tip will contact the table and slip off the cue ball (miscue). A stiff shaft will not bend as much; this allows the cue ball to be struck lower without miscuing. If a flexible shaft is used, the bridge hand must be moved closer to the cue ball to limit bending (reduces fulcrum lever).

The most common mistake in applying bottom english, is elevating the butt end of the stick and shooting down at the cue ball. (Special circumstances that require an elevated butt will be discussed later.) There are three major reasons why shooting down at the cue ball is not a good technique: First, it forces the cue ball down into the table which increases the friction between ball and table. By increasing the friction it's more difficult to cause backward rotation on the cue ball because it's momentarily pinned between the stick and table. Second, it's more difficult to aim. When shooting downward the cue ball and object ball, are farther from the line of vision. The shooter must either focus on the cue ball or on the object ball and rely on memory to determine where the other is. And third, shooting down at the cue ball will cause it to bounce. If the cue ball is not on the table when it strikes the object ball, the cut angle will be affected (more on this in Chapter 11). A bouncing cue ball also has a tendency to jump off the table.

As stated earlier, the effects of bottom english occur when the cue ball strikes the object ball. How the cue ball reacts depends on: (1) how much bottom is applied, (2) the speed of the cue ball, (3) the distance between cue ball and object ball, and (4) the angle at which the object ball is struck. Friction between the ball and cloth causes the backspin to start dissipating the moment the ball leaves contact with the cue tip. The longer the friction force works on the cue ball, the less backspin that will remain when it strikes the object ball. The harder the cue ball is struck, the faster it gets to the object ball and therefore it retains more of its backspin. The distance the cue ball is struck below center must be integrated with the speed of the shot so that the proper amount of backspin will remain when it makes contact with the object ball.

Straight-in shots--Bottom english on a straight-in shot facilitates a multitude of cue ball positions. Consider the shot shown in figure 6-3. Using the proper combination of bottom english and speed, the cue ball can be stopped at "A", "B", "D", "E", or anywhere between these positions.

To stop the cue ball at position "A", it must not have any forward or backward rotation at the moment it contacts the object ball. All the kinetic energy contained in the cue ball is transferred to the object ball at impact; then, having no energy left, it stops. If the cue ball does not have any rotation at the moment it strikes the object ball, it's called a *stun stroke*. When the stun stroke is used on a straight-in shot it's called a *stop shot*. **THE STUN STROKE CONCEPT IS BY FAR THE MOST IMPORTANT CONCEPT IN POOL. Not only is it used time and time again on straight-in shots but it's also used as a reference in judging the cue-ball deflection path on all cut shots**. More on this later.

The execution of a stun stroke requires the proper blend of velocity and striking point on the cue ball. Figure 6-3 shows some of the combinations that can be used to stop the cue ball at position "A". If the cue ball is struck very softly, it must be struck farther below center because the friction forces have a long time to dissipate the backspin. The harder it's

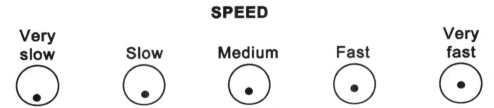

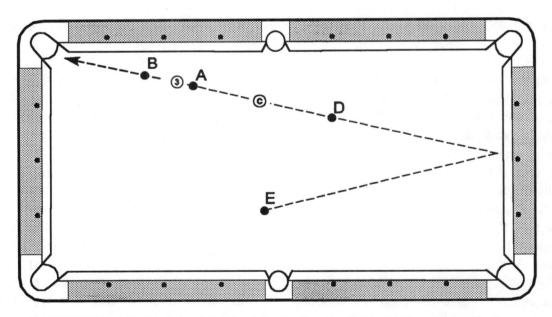

FIGURE 6-3. In shooting the 3-ball, the cue ball can be stopped at any point along the dashed line by using the proper mix of speed and striking point.

struck, the less bottom that is initially required. If the cue ball were at position "D", more bottom would be required to stop it at "A" because of the greater distance between cue ball and object ball.

In order to judge how far below center the cue ball must be struck to properly execute a stun stroke, both distance and speed must be considered. As with normal roll, the easiest way to integrate these two variables is to think in terms of *travel time.* The longer the travel time, the farther below center the cue ball must be struck. Judging travel time and the proper application of bottom english to produce a stun stroke is best learned by practicing the stop shot at various speeds and distances.

Assume you want to stop the cue ball at position "B". In order to allow the cue ball to move slightly forward, it must have a little forward rotation at impact. This requires that the cue ball be struck with a little less bottom than the stun stroke at any given speed. The cue ball should be struck low enough so that all of the backward rotation dissipates in about three fourths of the travel time. Thus, it will have some time to pick up a little forward rotation before it gets to the object ball. With the cue ball positioned close to the object ball, as shown in figure 6-3, little or no bottom is required when the cue ball is struck medium to hard. The best way to execute these shots is to imagine that the object ball is closer to the cue ball than it actually is, then shoot a stun stroke at the imaginary ball. Positioning of the imaginary ball depends on how far forward the cue ball is to roll after impact.

Assume you want the cue ball to back up to position "D". In order to make the cue ball back up after impact, it must be rotating backwards at the time of impact. The impact causes the cue ball to stop at "A", then the backspin causes it to accelerate backwards. Again, as with the previous shots, the cue ball

must initially have the proper combination of bottom english and velocity. If the cue ball is struck very low with a slow velocity it won't have enough backward spin to cause it to move to "D". Therefore, it has to be struck with a medium or faster velocity and with medium or more bottom english.

Assume you want the cue ball to stop at position "E". The cue ball must be struck very low, so that it has maximum backspin; and very hard, so that the friction forces have only a short time to dissipate the backspin. The cue stick must be accelerating when it strikes the cue ball and it must follow-through after impact. Care must be taken to strike the cue ball directly below center. Striking to one side while giving maximum bottom may result in a miscue or cause the cue ball to rebound off the cushion in some direction other than toward "E".

Cut shots--The effect of bottom english on cut shots depends on how far below center the cue ball is struck, cue ball velocity, and cut angle. As the cut angle increases, the effect of bottom english diminishes. On very thin cut shots (high cut angle), bottom english has no perceptible effect on the cue ball's path.

Figure 6-4 shows a 25-degree cut shot. If the cue ball has normal roll it will deflect about 40 degrees from its original path and go in direction "A". If the cue ball is struck in the center with medium speed it will have some forward rotation, but not normal roll, and will go in direction "B". If enough bottom english is used to result in a stun stroke, the cue ball's path will be 90 degrees from the path of the object ball as shown by direction "D". **WHEN A STUN STROKE IS USED, THE CUE BALL PATH WILL ALWAYS BE PERPENDICULAR TO THE PATH OF THE OBJECT BALL REGARDLESS OF CUT ANGLE.** For this reason, **the stun stroke concept can be used**

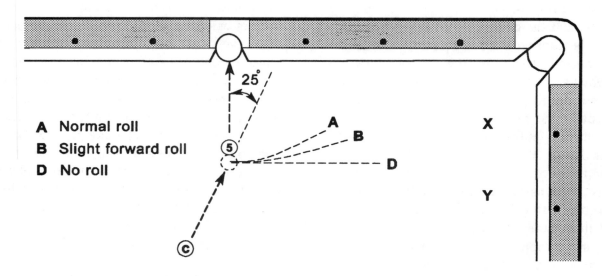

FIGURE 6-4. Example of how cue-ball rotation affects its deflection path.

as <u>**a reference for every cut shot**</u>. For example, if you want the cue ball to go toward "X" after impact, you must first determine where it will go with a stun stroke (direction "D"). Obviously, a stun stroke would deflect the cue ball a little too much, therefore it should be shot with a little less bottom than a stun stroke. If you want the cue ball to go toward "Y", the stun stroke direction can again be used as a reference. Obviously, a little more deflection is required, therefore the shot should be executed with a little more bottom than a stun stroke.

The cue ball's path *ALWAYS* starts out perpendicular to the path of the object ball, then curves as a result of rotation. The actual path, or circumference of the curve, depends on the amount of bottom in combination with cue ball speed. Figure 6-5 shows the approximate cue ball path at slow and fast speeds using the same amount of bottom english. The harder the cue ball is struck, the farther the curve is from the impact point.

Elevated cue stick--As previously stated, the cue stick should be held as level as

possible when applying bottom english. However, there are two exceptions to this rule; when the cue ball is very near the object ball, and when cue ball velocity must be kept to a minimum.

When the cue ball is very near the object ball there's no room for follow-through. If

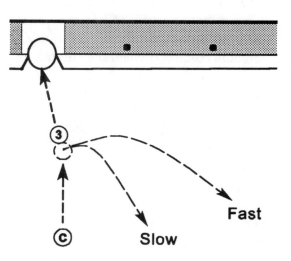

**FIGURE 6-5. An example of how
the cue ball's path is affected
by speed when bottom english is used.**

follow-through is used the stick will strike the cue ball a second time which is an illegal shot. To avoid fouling, the butt of the stick must be raised and the cue ball struck with a downward stroke. The eyes should be focused on the cue ball at the moment of execution to help avoid a miscue.

The cue ball must always be struck hard enough so that the desired amount of english will carry to the point of collision with the object ball. This means that if a lot of english is to be carried a long distance, the cue ball must be struck very low and very hard. There are occasions when a lot of bottom english is desired but with minimum cue ball speed. To accomplish this, the butt of the stick must be elevated. The higher the elevation, the less linear (translational) energy is imparted to the cue ball while still applying maximum backspin.

The drag shot--Occasionally, the object ball is at one end of the table, the cue ball is near the other end and you want to shoot the shot very slowly. When a long shot is executed very slowly, there's a chance that the cue ball's path will not be straight due to imperfections in the table. The greater the cue ball velocity, the less affect table imperfections have on its path. Therefore, it is desirable to shoot the shot as fast as possible.

A *drag shot* is a shot that allows the initial cue ball speed to be greater than desired (so that it won't curve), and yet it slows down to the desired speed before reaching the object ball. The drag shot is executed by putting bottom english on the cue ball and striking it with a little excess velocity. The backspin causes the cue ball to slow down faster than it normally would, thus allowing a greater initial velocity. If executed properly, the bottom english will dissipate before the cue ball reaches the object ball and won't affect the cue-ball deflection angle.

TOP ENGLISH

Top english is imparted to the cue ball by striking it above center. As with most other shots, the stick should be held as level as possible. Top english causes the cue ball to start out with forward rotation. It must be recalled that when the cue stick strikes the cue ball dead-center, the cue ball starts out with no rotation and slowly picks up rotation until it attains normal roll. If the cue ball is struck 0.45 inch above center, as shown in figure 6-6, it will have normal roll immediately upon being struck. If the cue ball is struck more than 0.45 inch above center, it will be rotating forward faster than it's

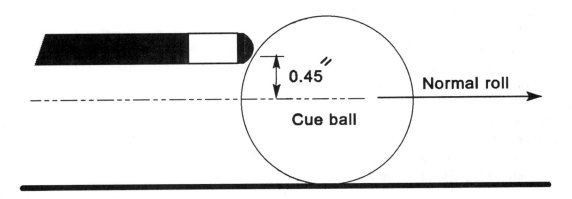

FIGURE 6-6. When the cue ball is struck 0.45 inch above center it will immediately have normal roll.

moving forward and thus will be spinning on the cloth. The excess forward rotation is converted to linear energy causing the cue ball to momentarily gain speed. The excess forward spin dissipates fairly rapidly. Striking the cue ball anywhere between center and 0.45 inch above center causes it to attain normal roll faster. For example, if the cue ball is struck 0.22 inch above center, it will take only half the normal distance to attain normal roll at any given speed. With most shots where top english is used, the cue ball actually has normal roll when it strikes the object ball. For example, assume the cue ball is 3 feet away from an object ball; if it's struck 0.35 inch above center at medium speed, it will have less than normal roll to begin with but will pick up more forward roll so that by the time it gets to the object ball it will have normal roll. If the cue ball is struck 0.55 inch above center it will initially have excess forward rotation, but by the time it reaches the object ball it will have dissipated, and again it will have normal roll upon impact. Obviously, the path of the cue ball, after striking the object ball, will be the same for both of these shots even though a different amount of top english was applied.

Straight-in shots--When the cue ball is struck above center it will always have some forward rotation when it strikes the object ball. When it strikes the object ball it stops; the rotational energy is then converted to linear energy causing it to accelerate forward once again. The cue ball will accelerate forward until there is no slippage between ball and cloth, at which point, it will have normal roll and will then begin to slow down.

Top english must be used sparingly on straight-in shots to avoid having the cue ball follow the object ball into the pocket. When the cue ball and object ball are very close together it seems to most shooters, that an exaggerated amount of top must be given to the cue ball just to make it move a little forward after impact. This is because the cue ball doesn't have much distance to accumulate forward roll from table friction; the only rotation it has is that which is given to it by the cue stick.

Cut shots--As previously stated, if the cue ball has no rotation when it strikes the object ball (stun stroke) it will rebound at 90 degrees from the path of the object ball. If the cue ball has any forward rotation, either from

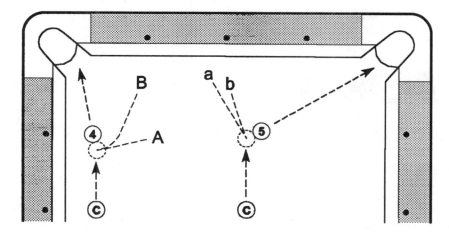

FIGURE 6-7. The smaller the cut angle the greater the effect rotation has on the path of the cue ball.

normal roll or top english, it will start out 90 degrees from the object ball's path, then curve to effectively reduce the cue-ball deflection angle.

The smaller the cut angle, the greater the affect forward rotation has on the cue ball's path. Figure 6-7 shows a 10 degree cut shot and a 60-degree cut shot. Directions "A" and "a" represent the path of the cue ball if it had no rotation at impact. Directions "B" and "b" represent the cue ball's path when struck at medium speed 0.5 inch above center. Note that the difference between paths "A" and "B", for the 10-degree cut shot, is much greater than the difference between paths "a" and "b" for the 60-degree cut shot.

When top english is used, there are two forces pulling in different directions. As diagrammed in figure 6-8, the resiliency force tries to make the cue ball go perpendicular to the path of the object ball, and the rotational force tries to make it go in its original direction. The resultant path is somewhere between these two forces and depends on the magnitude of each. A cue ball with top

english actually starts out in the direction of the resiliency force, then curves in the direction of the rotational force. As shown in figure 6-9, the arc of the curve depends mainly on cue ball speed. The slower it is moving, the smaller the radius of curvature and the closer it is to the point of impact.

Top english is sometimes used to maintain cue ball speed. Consider the situation shown in figure 6-10a. The 1-ball is shot into the corner pocket while trying to get shape (favorable shooting position) on the 2-ball at the other end of the table. With a center ball hit, the cue ball will go toward "A". In order to decrease the cue-ball deflection angle and cause the cue ball to strike the end cushion, top english must be applied. The cut angle on the 1-ball is fairly small, consequently most of the cue ball's speed will be transferred to the 1-ball on impact. Therefore, it is difficult to make the cue ball rebound far enough off the end cushion. Top english will again be beneficial because, after impact, the forward spinning cue ball will accelerate forward as it converts spin into linear acceleration. By the

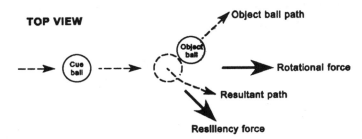

FIGURE 6-8. There are several forces acting on the cue ball that determine its actual path.

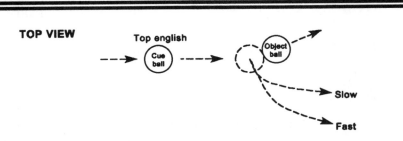

FIGURE 6-9. The ark of the cue-ball curve depends on its speed.

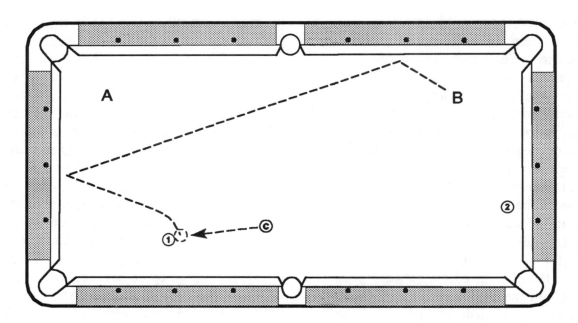

FIGURE 6-10a. Top english can be used to preserve cue ball speed when it has to travel a long distance after striking the object ball at a small cut angle.

time it reaches the cushion all of the excess forward spin will have been converted to linear velocity so it will be going fast enough to rebound all the way back to "B". It's important that all the excess forward spin be converted to linear velocity before the cue ball strikes the cushion. Consider the similar situation shown in figure 6-10b. The cut angle is about the same and the distance between

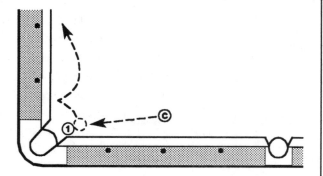

FIGURE 6-10b. If the top english hasn't all been converted to speed by the time the cue ball strikes the cushion, it will tend to curve back toward the cushion.

the cue ball and 1-ball is about the same. If the 1-ball is shot using the same speed and top english as used in the previous example, the path of the cue ball will be to the cushion, rebound, then curve back toward the cushion again as shown. The reason is that the cue ball did not have time to convert the excess forward rotation into linear velocity. As a result, it still had forward rotation after rebounding from the cushion. The rebound force is away from the cushion but the rotational force is toward the cushion which causes the cue ball to curve back toward the cushion.

Cue ball jump--When a cue ball with top english strikes an object ball at a small cut angle, it tends to climb up onto the object ball. This causes the cue ball to jump into the air upon impact. This jump is generally quite small and is usually insignificant (especially with polished balls). However, if the balls are dirty or scuffed (high ball-to-ball friction) the jump can be significant. If the object ball is near a cushion, the cue ball may be in the air when it strikes the cushion causing it to rebound higher or even off the table.

When a cue ball with top english strikes a cushion at a high angle of incidence, it has a tendency to climb up onto the cushion. As it rebounds it's pushed farther into the air, and in effect, jumps back off the cushion. Here again, the jump is greatly influenced by the surface condition of the cue ball. The higher the friction between ball and cushion, the greater the jump.

●   ●   ●

SIDE ENGLISH

Side english is imparted to the cue ball by hitting it to the right or left of center which causes it to rotate on a vertical axis. Actuality, the cue ball starts out rotating on a vertical axis but friction between cloth and ball causes the axis to tilt or the side as the ball starts moving forward. The tilting of the axis-of-rotation has little or no effect on the cue ball and so will be ignored in the ensuing examination of side english. As previously stated, *side english alters the cue ball rebound angle off the cushion.*

Side english is much more difficult to master than top or bottom english. For this reason, beginners should refrain from using side english until they have a good command of top and bottom english and can make shots of average difficulty with regularity. Inexperienced players should begin using side english only on short shots, and even then it should be used very sparingly (strike cue ball only slightly to the side of center).

There are three major reasons why side english is difficult to master: (1) aim, relative to stick alignment, is different when side english is used, (2) side english throws the object ball off-course, and (3) the cue ball may curve on its way to the object ball. Each of these elements will be examined individually.

Stick alignment--The cue ball does not go in the direction that the stick is pointed when side english is used. Figure 6-11 shows cue stick alignment in relation to the cue ball's path. When no side english is used, stick alignment is exactly the same as the path of the cue ball (figure 6-11a), and the stick is aimed directly at the target. Figure 6-11b shows stick alignment when side english (in this case right side) is used. The stick has to be aligned several degrees to the right of the target with the apex (or pivot point) about 20 inches from the cue ball.

The angle between cue ball path and stick alignment has been called *deflection* or *squirt.* Here it will be referred to as *cue-stick induced deflection.* Beginners generally have difficulty adjusting aim to compensate for cue-stick induced deflection. The following exercise can be used to help acquaint the beginner with the aim adjustment required when side english is used.

Place the cue ball on the center spot and a target ball at the center of the foot rail. The objective is to strike the target ball dead center, with the cue ball, using 0.5 inch right side english. Aim the stick somewhat to the right of the target, but before executing the shot, observe the exact alignment of the stick in relation to the target. Keep adjusting the stick alignment until you can consistently hit the target ball dead center. Keep in mind that the stick alignment will have to be change if distance, speed, or amount of english is changed.

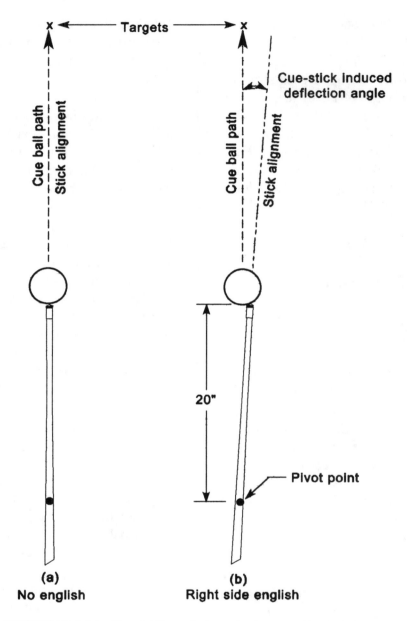

FIGURE 6-11. Cue ball path in relation to stick alignment when side english is used.

The actual alignment of the stick depends somewhat on the flexibility of the cue-stick shaft (in figure 6-11 the distance from cue ball to pivot point would vary). Consider the example of right side english shown in figure 6-12. Figure 6-12a shows the cue stick striking the cue ball distance "x" to the right of center. In figure 6-12b, the ball has been moved forward and rotated; the cue tip is still in contact at the same point (if it slips off, it's a miscue). In order that the tip remain in contact at this point, the stick must either bend; or, move to the right at the bridge. Actually, both occur.

Because the bending of the stick occurs so quickly it can't be observed directly. For this reason, many authorities don't think the stick bends outward when side english is used. The bending can be indirectly observed by a simple experiment. Stand a two inch nail, on its head, adjacent to the stick. Using side english and stroking as close to the nail as possible, shoot the shot. The nail will be knocked over.

Cue-stick induced deflection angle is **greater** with a <u>stiff</u> cue shaft than with a flexible shaft. In other words, if the stick doesn't bend to the right, the cue ball will go farther to the left. Shaft flexibility varies from stick to stick and consequently so does cue-stick induced deflection angle. This is a good reason to become familiar with a specific stick and use it exclusively. If playing with an unfamiliar stick is unavoidable, try to refrain from using side english; if you must constantly adjust aim to compensate for flexibility, your accuracy will suffer even when using your familiar stick. When

breaking in a new stick, concentrate your practice on shots that require side english and great accuracy; when these shots are mastered the others will be easy.

English-induced throw--When a cue ball with side english collides with an object ball, it throws the object ball off its normal path. This is called *english-induced throw*. If the cue ball has right english, the object ball is thrown to the left and vice versa. English-induced throw results from friction between the two balls when they collide. At the moment of collision, they are pressed together so tightly that they tend to act as one entity. Figure 6-13 shows the process:

(a) The cue ball is struck on the right side causing it to rotate counter clockwise.

(b) The cue ball collides with the object ball. Because the impact is confined to such a

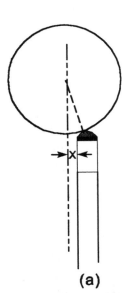

(a)

**Stick contacts ball
to right of center.**

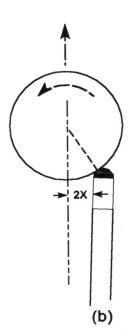

(b)

**Ball moves forward and rotates;
the stick must move to right.**

**FIGURE 6-12. The cue stick must move over or bend to the
side when side english is used.**

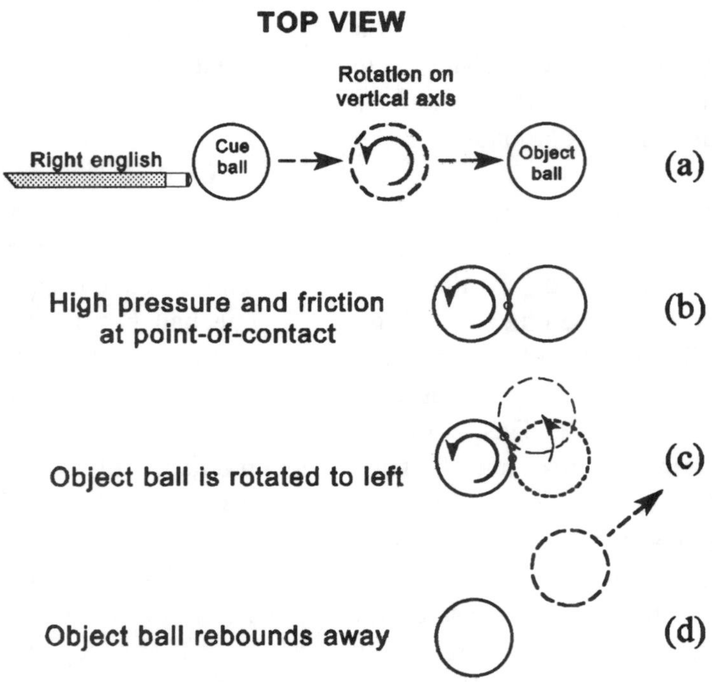

TOP VIEW

FIGURE 6-13. When side english is put on the cue ball, the object ball is thrown (english-induced throw) in the opposite direction.

small area there's a tremendous force between the two balls, at the point-of-contact, which causes them to stick together for an instant.

(c) Because the balls are stuck together, the rotation of the cue ball rotates the object ball to the left.

(d) The resiliency force now pushes the balls away from each other. Since the object ball is now aligned to the left of the original cue ball path it's propelled in that direction, not straight ahead.

The magnitude of english-induced throw depends on the cut angle and direction of the cut angle in relation to the side english. English-induced throw is greatest (up to about 5 degrees) in a head-on collision. As the cut angle increases, english-induced throw decreases; the rate at which it decreases depends on the direction of the cut angle in relation to the side english.

Side english, relative to the direction of cut angle, is referred to as being either *inside english* or *outside english*. Figure 6-14 shows examples of both inside and outside english. If the cut angle is to the same side as the english (left english - cut to left) then it's referred to as *inside* english. If english is opposite to the cut angle (left english - cut to right) it's referred to as *outside* english.

Figure 6-15 shows the magnitude of english-induced throw at all cut angles using maximum inside and outside english with average clean balls. The magnitude of throw will be different with balls that are polished, waxed, wet; or, have chalk, powder, or other contaminant on their surfaces. The line labeled <u>no english</u> represents collision-induced throw; the effect of english-induced throw should be evaluated in relation to this line.

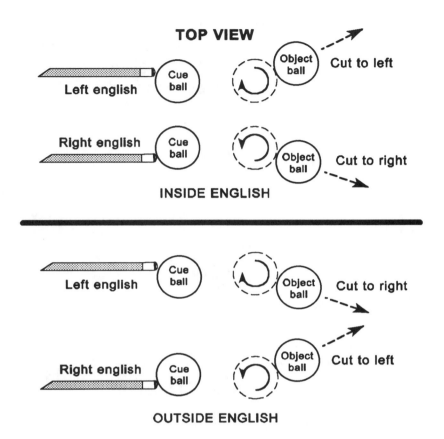

FIGURE 6-14. When side english and cut direction are the same it is termed *"inside english";* **when they are in opposite directions it is termed** *"outside english".*

A - Alignment direction.

B - Directional force caused by collision-induced english
and/or inside english.

C - Directional force caused by outside english.

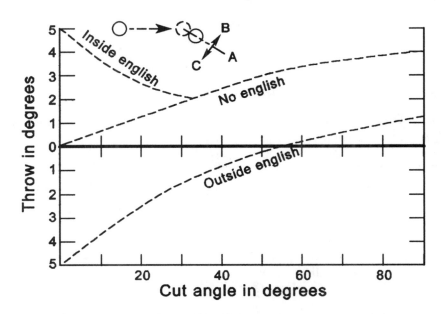

**FIGURE 6-15. The magnitude of english-induced throw depends
on the cut angle and whether it is inside or outside english.**

As indicated, inside english has no effect on cut shots over 35 degrees. For example, assume maximum inside english with a 50-degree cut shot; the object ball will be thrown 3 degrees, but that's due to collision-induced throw. Any amount of inside english will not change that. If maximum outside english is used, on a 50 degree cut shot, the object ball will not be thrown at all. But, this is still about 3 degrees from the direction it would have gone if it had no english. It is interesting that maximum outside english causes the path of the object ball to change about three degrees for any cut angle over about 30 degrees.

Figure 6-16 shows the effect of maximum inside and maximum outside english on four different shots. Keep in mind that the indicated effect is caused by english alone and therefore is measured in relation to collision-induced throw.

The error at the pocket (measured from center pocket), is greater for long shots. The error caused by outside english on the 4-ball is large (3.0 degrees) but the error at the pocket is small (.8 inch). This demonstrates that extreme side english, especially outside english, should be avoided whenever possible except with short shots.

It's impossible to make all of these throw calculations during a game. One must be able to make accurate estimates of how much aim adjustment is required when a specific amount of side english is used. One way to improve the accuracy of these estimates is to practice on paper. Draw a table with several object balls and a cue ball similar to figure 6-16. Make an estimate of the correction

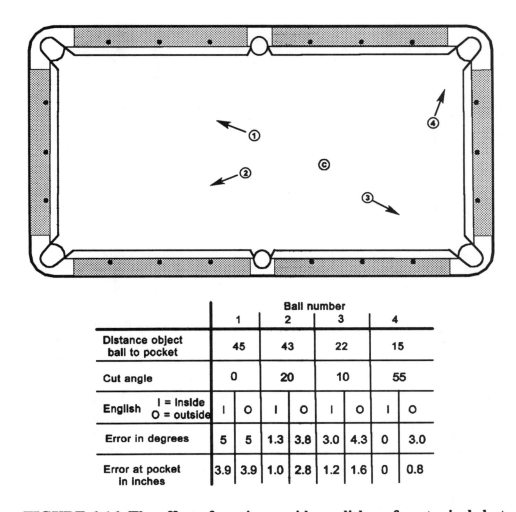

	Ball number			
	1	**2**	**3**	**4**
Distance object ball to pocket	45	43	22	15
Cut angle	0	20	10	55
English I = inside O = outside	I | O	I | O	I | O	I | O
Error in degrees	5 | 5	1.3 | 3.8	3.0 | 4.3	0 | 3.0
Error at pocket in inches	3.9 | 3.9	1.0 | 2.8	1.2 | 1.6	0 | 0.8

FIGURE 6-16. The effect of maximum side english on four typical shots.

required for each shot using both left and right english, then check the estimate using figure 6-15. After working out a few hundred of these shots on paper, your estimated corrections should be fairly accurate.

English-induced throw can aid in making a ball that otherwise could not be made. Figure 6-17 shows an example; the 9-ball is blocking the path of the cue ball preventing the 1-ball from being made. But, the 1-ball can be made by shooting a little to the right, to avoid hitting the 9-ball, and using maximum left side english. The outside english will throw the object ball about 4 degrees to the right allowing it to be made.

Many players have a tendency to use english-induced throw to help cut balls into a pocket when it's not necessary. This tendency most often occurs when the shot is nearly straight-in. It's tempting to aim for a center ball hit and throw the object ball into the pocket (with side english). The problem is that on some occasions you may throw it in and on other occasions you may cut it in. Some of these shots will inevitably be missed because your aim alignment will assume you're using throw when you aren't and vice versa. **Do not** become accustomed to using english-induced throw in place of cut angle. Use english-induced throw only when necessary, and when you do, make a mental

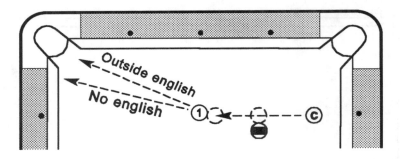

FIGURE 6-17. An example of using side english to throw the object ball into the pocket.

notation to that effect so that there is absolutely no question as to how you intend to make the ball.

Cue-ball curve--Since the beginning, people have been saying *"side english causes the cue ball to curve."* As with the tooth fairy, Easter rabbit, and snipe hunting, we have been deceived once again. It simply is not true; side english (by itself) does not cause the cue ball to curve. This can be demonstrated by spinning a ball like a top (with the fingers to simulate super side english) while gently throwing it laterally on the table. It will continue in the direction in which it was thrown. If side english would cause a ball to curve, then it should go in circles with super side. Why then does this fallacy perpetuate itself? Because, the curve *can* be demonstrated; but, when it's demonstrated the person always adds a little bottom by shooting down at the cue ball. The

more bottom that is used, in combination with side, the more pronounced the curve. With the butt of the stick elevated, the cue ball will curve to the right with right english, and to the left with left english. The cue ball can actually be made to curve in the opposite direction if great care is taken to make sure that the cue stick is kept level and the cue ball is struck with top side. With maximum top side and a level stick, the cue ball can be made to curve about 0.3 degree in the direction opposite to the applied english.

Some people shoot every shot with the butt of the cue elevated because it's part of their normal shooting stance. This causes the cue ball to curve on all shots where side english is used. Unintentional cue-ball curve greatly decreases accuracy, therefore it's important to develop a shooting stance that allows the cue stick to be held as level as possible.

Rebound angle--The principal use of side english is to change the angle in which the cue ball rebounds off a cushion. Figure 6-18 shows the terminology used in describing the various angles and effects of side english. The *angle of incidence* is the acute angle between the cushion and the ball's approach path. The *angle of rebound* is the angle between the cushion and the path of the ball as it leaves the cushion. If side english causes the angle of rebound to become smaller (right side english in figure 6-18b) it's called *running english*; if it causes the rebound angle to become larger (left side english in figure 6-18c) it's called *reverse english*.

The degree to which the rebound angle is affected by side english depends on how much english is used and the angle of incidence. When the angle of incidence is 90 degrees (perpendicular to cushion) maximum

deviation of the rebound angle will occur (about 30 degrees). As the angle of incidence becomes smaller, deviation becomes less. When the angle of incidence is less than about 20 degrees, side english has very little affect on the angle of rebound.

Note: The angle of rebound is affected by things other than side english. These factors will be examined in relation to bank shots in Chapter 10.

Figure 6-19 shows some examples in which side english is used to obtain favorable position (shape) for the next shot. Assume the 1- and 2-ball are to be made in succession; if the 1-ball is shot without english, the cue ball will go to the end cushion (position "A") and rebound nearly straight back. If it rolls to the center of the table, or farther, it will allow a shot at the 2-ball but not an easy one. If the cue ball is shot with left side english, it will

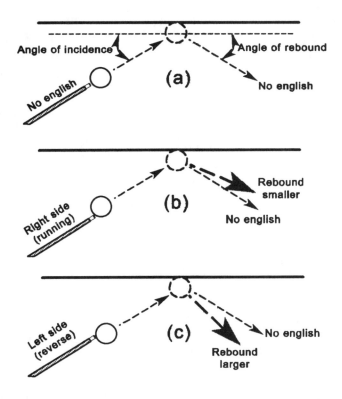

FIGURE 6-18. Side english changes rebound angle off cushion.

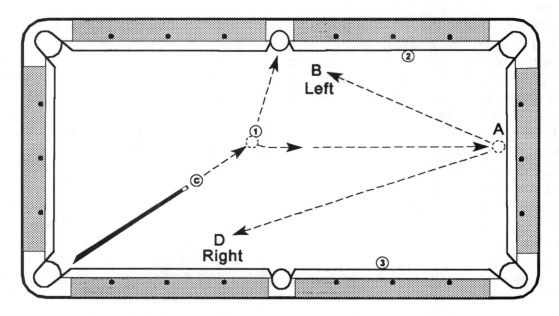

FIGURE 6-19. Examples of using side english to obtain favorable cue ball position for the next shot.

take the same path to point "A", but it will rebound to the left toward position "B" which will allow an easy shot at the 2-ball. To shoot the 1-ball, then the 3-ball, right side english should be used to cause the cue ball to rebound to the right toward position "D".

Assume the 4- and 7-ball in figure 6-20 are to be made in succession. With no english the cue ball will strike the cushion at "A", then rebound toward position "E". With left side english, the angle of rebound will be larger causing the cue ball to go toward position "F" for an easy shot at the 7-ball into the corner pocket. If the 6-ball is to be shot after the 4-ball, right side should be used causing the cue ball to go toward position "G" for an easy shot into the side pocket.

Ball speed off cushion--Cushions are not very efficient with regard to conserving the energy contained in a moving ball. When a ball with normal roll strikes a cushion at a 90-degree angle of incidence, about 60 percent of the ball's potential rolling distance is lost.

As the angle of incidence decreases, so does the energy loss. When running english is used, the cue ball doesn't lose as much speed when it strikes a cushion. If the cue ball is moving

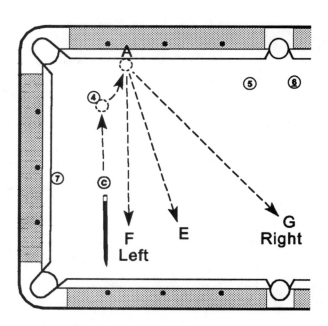

FIGURE 6-20. Examples of using side english for getting shape.

very slowly, and has considerable running english, it will actually *speed up* upon striking the cushion. If the cue ball has reverse english, it *slows down* upon striking the cushion regardless of its initial speed. The change in speed due to side english must be anticipated so that initial cue ball speed can be judged properly.

The loss of cue ball speed, due to reverse english, can be used to advantage in positioning the cue ball for the next shot. Consider the situation shown in figure 6-21. The 1-ball must be pocketed while getting position on the 2-ball. The cue ball must be shot hard enough to insure that the object ball reaches the pocket, therefore there is a minimum cue ball speed requirement. If the shot is made at minimum speed without english, the cue ball will rebound off the cushion to position "A", or farther, leaving a very difficult shot at the 2-ball. A similar situation exists with the 3- and 4-ball. However, if the 3-ball is shot with reverse english (right side) the cue ball will lose its speed when it contacts the cushion and will

rebound to position "B", leaving an easy shot at the 4-ball.

The increase in cue ball speed, caused by running english, can also be used to enhance positioning. With medium to thin cut shots the cue ball need only be struck harder to make it run farther. However, when the object ball is nearly straight-in, most of the cue ball's speed is transferred to the object ball at impact. If the cue ball has enough linear speed to make it to a cushion, the running english will increase its speed off the cushion causing it to travel farther. For example, assume the 4-ball in figure 6-21 is to be shot first while getting shape on the 5-ball. The 4-ball is nearly straight in, therefore most of the cue ball's speed will be lost on impact. If it is shot with top right, the top will help carry it to the first cushion at "D", the running english will cause it to speed up at "D" and at "E" so that it rolls all the way to "F".

Dissipation of side english--Top and bottom english dissipate very fast because

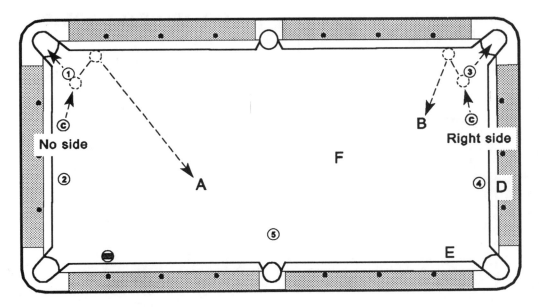

FIGURE 6-21. Reverse english can be used to control cue ball rolling distance.

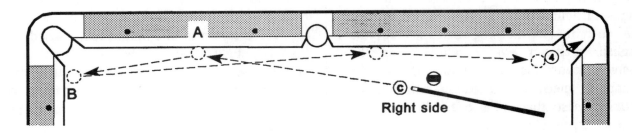

**FIGURE 6-22. Little side english is lost when the cue ball
contacts the cushion at a low angle of incidence.**

friction between ball and cloth is acting in direct opposition to the english. Therefore, the cue ball must be struck very crisply in order to maintain english over a long distance. Side english remains on the cue ball for long distances even when it's moving slowly. Very little side english is lost when the cue ball collides with another ball but considerable side english can be lost when it strikes a cushion. The amount that is lost at the cushion depends mainly on the angle of incidence. If the angle of incidence is high (approaching 90 degrees) most of the side english is lost. As the angle of incidence becomes smaller, less english is lost. If the angle of incidence is less than about 15 degrees, very little side english is lost on the first cushion.

The shot shown in figure 6-22

demonstrates the maintenance of side english at a low angle of incidence. Assume the cue ball is shot with maximum right side english to point "A" two diamonds from the corner pocket. The rebound angle at "A" is affected very little because of the low angle of incidence. The ball continues to point "B" on the end cushion. The angle of incidence at "B" is large, therefore the side english has a pronounced effect causing the rebound angle to be much larger than the angle of incidence. The ball rebounds from "B" back toward the side cushion from which it came.

COMBINED ENGLISH

Top or bottom english can be used in combination with side english. When they're

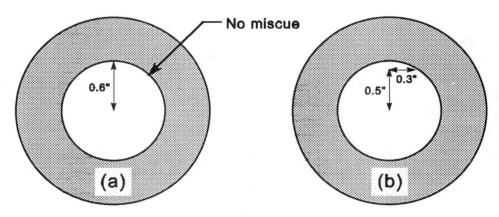

**FIGURE 6-23. When top or bottom english is used in combination with
side english, both must be less than maximum.**

used in combination, one or both must be used in moderation or a miscue will result. As shown in figure 6-23a, the cue ball can be struck a maximum of about 0.6 inch from the center without miscuing. As shown in figure 6-23b, if the cue ball is struck 0.5 inch above center it can only be struck a maximum of 0.3 inch to the right of center. Therefore, when top or bottom is used, it limits the amount of side that can be used and vice versa.

Before shooting any shot one must determine what, if any, english should be used. To make the determination:

(1) Determine where the cue ball will go with no english.
(2) If the cue-ball deflection angle must be altered, use top or bottom english.
(3) If the rebound angle off the cushion must be altered, use side english.
(4) If both deflection angle and rebound angle must be altered, use a combination of top

or bottom with side.

An example of a situation requiring a combination of english is shown in figure 6-24. Assume the 3-ball is to be made into the corner pocket while getting shape on the 4-ball. If the cue ball has normal roll, it will carom off the 3-ball into the cushion, then rebound into one of the other balls as shown in figure 6-25a. If it has bottom english, the carom angle off the 3-ball will be larger (figure 6-25b), and the ball will rebound off the cushion toward the opposite side pocket. This would be acceptable because if the cue ball stopped near the side pocket it would allow a shot, although a difficult one, at the 4-ball. If bottom right is used, the carom angle off the 3-ball will be about the same but the side english will cause the rebound angle to be smaller (figure 6-25c), and the cue ball will go toward the opposite corner pocket for an easy shot at the 4-ball.

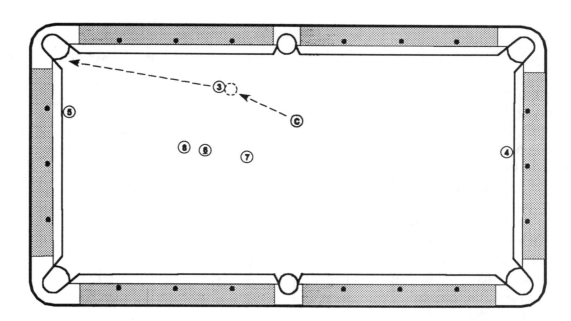

FIGURE 6-24. Typical table situation where english must be employed in order to get shape on the next ball.

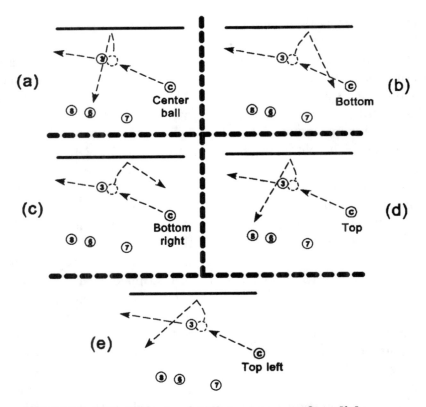

FIGURE 6-25. Effects of different types of english.

Assume the shooter would like to get shape on the 5-ball while pocketing the 3-ball. Top english (figure 6-25d) will cause the carom angle off the 3-ball to be smaller, but on rebounding from the cushion it may run into the 8-ball. With top left english (figure 6-25e) the cue ball will rebound farther to the left toward the opposite corner pocket avoiding the intervening balls and leaving an easy shot at the 5-ball.

Consider the situation shown in figure 6-26. The 1-ball is to be made into the corner pocket while getting shape on the 2-ball. First, consider what would happen if no english were used; the cue ball would strike the cushion at "a" then rebound toward "A". If right english were used, the cue ball would still strike the cushion at "a" but the side english would cause it to rebound toward "B". If top english were used, the cue ball would strike the cushion at "b" then rebound

toward "B". If a combination of top and right side were used, the top would cause the cue

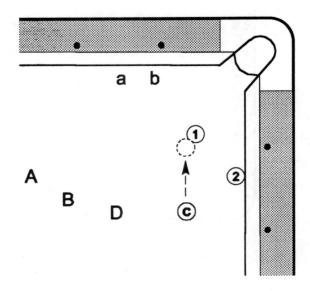

FIGURE 6-26. English must be used to get shape for the 2-ball.

ball to strike the cushion at "b", and the side would make the rebound angle larger causing the cue ball to go toward "D" which is the best of all options.

In figure 6-27, the 3-ball is to be made into the corner pocket while getting shape on the 4-ball. The 3-ball must be cut a few degrees to the left. Because of the angle, bottom english would cause the cue ball to go toward "A". The solution is to use bottom right. The 3-ball could be struck dead-center because the right side would throw it a few degrees to the left. The bottom would then cause the cue ball to back up toward "B".

In figure 6-28, the 5-ball is to be made into the corner pocket while getting shape on the 6-ball into the same pocket. If maximum bottom is used, the cue ball will back up to the cushion at "a" then rebound toward "A". If bottom right is used, the bottom will cause the cue ball to back up to "a", and the right english will reduce the rebound angle causing it to rebound to "B" for an easy shot at the 6-ball. As with the previous shot, the side

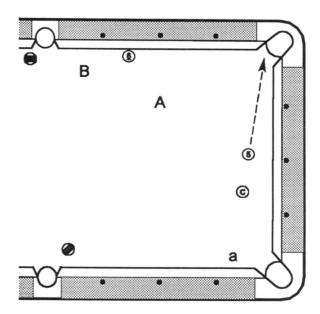

FIGURE 6-28. Bottom right is required to get shape on the 6-ball.

english will throw the object ball off-line which must be taken into consideration when aiming.

OTHER ENGLISH CONSIDERATIONS

Transfer of english--When a cue ball, with english, strikes an object ball, a small percentage of the english is transferred to the object ball. This is called *transfer of english*. The english that's transferred is opposite in direction to that of the cue ball. As shown in figure 6-29, right side english on the cue ball transfers to left side english on the object ball. Top english (or even normal roll) transfers as bottom english on the object ball. The amount of english that is transferred depends on the amount of english on the cue ball, cut angle, and the ball-to-ball friction. When the object ball is struck head-on the greatest amount of english is transferred, and even then it's very small and can usually be ignored. Bank shots

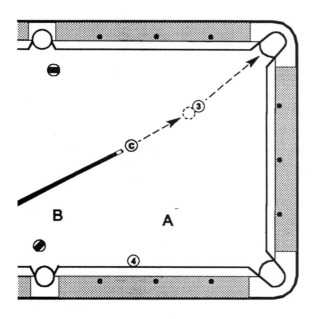

FIGURE 6-27. Bottom right is required to get shape on the 4-ball.

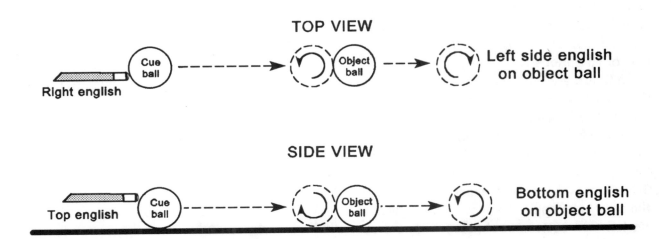

FIGURE 6-29. Some english is transferred from the cue ball to the object ball.

with a high angle of incidence are the only shots (assuming only two balls are involved) that functionally benefit from intentional transfer of english. And even then, only those bank shots that require very small cut angles are effected. Transfer of english is generally considered to be a hindrance that must be

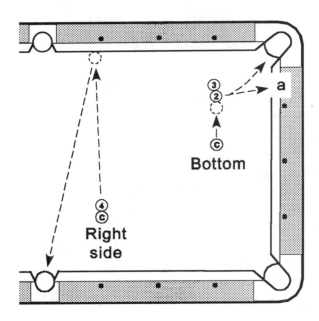

FIGURE 6-30. Two practical applications of transferred english.

allowed for rather than a functional tool; more on this in Chapter 10.

The amount of english that is transferred varies depending on the ball-to-ball friction. If contact is made on a chalk mark, friction will be high. If contact is made on talcum powder, oily polish, or moisture from humidity or other source, friction and subsequent transfer of english will be extremely small.

Transfer of english is generally small because the cue ball remains in contact with the object ball for such a short time. The rotational force of the cue ball doesn't have time to overcome the inertia of the object ball. If the object ball is pinned between the cue ball and another ball, so that it can't rebound away, then there is significantly more transfer of english. Figure 6-30 shows how this can be used to advantage. The 2-ball is in contact with the 3-ball. If the 2-ball is struck head-on, its path will be perpendicular to its alignment with the 3-ball (toward "a"). If the 2-ball is struck head-on with maximum bottom english, the english will be transferred as top english to the 2-ball. The 2-ball will start out toward "a" but the top english will cause it to curve into the pocket as shown. Top english doesn't function in this manner because the bottom that's transferred to the object ball causes it to run back into the cue ball.

Another situation in which an inordinate amount of english can be transferred is when the cue ball is frozen to (touching) the object ball. The 4-ball in figure 6-30 represents such an example. The cue ball is struck with right english which causes two things to happen; english-induced throw to the left, and the transfer of english (left side) to the object ball; both help the 4-ball bank into the opposite side pocket. The inordinate english-induced throw and transfer of english are caused by the extended duration of the actuating force. The cue ball remains in contact with the 4-ball longer than it normally would because the cue stick keeps it pinned there.

Cushion-induced english--When a ball strikes a cushion at an angle, the cushion imparts side spin on the ball. This type of english is called *cushion-induced english*. Figure 6-31 shows a graphic example of cushion-induced english. When the cushion is to the left, relative to the ball's path, the english will be equivalent to right side english and vice versa.

When the angle of incidence is small (0 to 10 degrees) cushion-induced english is small because friction between ball and cushion is small. At large angles of incidence, cushion-induced english is also small because the cushion is pushing back at the ball nearer to the center of its path. The amount of cushion-induced english is greatest with incidence angles between 30 and 45 degrees.

The relevance of cushion-induced english will be discussed in relation to rail shots, bank shots, and kick shots.

Collision-induced english--When a ball is struck at an angle by another ball, its reaction is somewhat similar to being struck at the same point, and direction, with a cue stick. However, there's a large difference in the amount of friction at the point-of-contact. The stick-ball friction is much greater than the ball-ball friction. Figure 6-32 shows a ball being struck at the same point with a stick and with a ball, both moving in the same direction. When struck with the stick, the ball's path is only a few degrees from the direction that the stick was moving, and considerable spin (english) is imparted to the ball. The spin is due to the high friction between the propelling stick and ball. When a ball is struck by another ball it does not move in the direction of the propelling ball, but instead, it goes in the direction nearly opposite the point-of-contact. Friction between the two balls is small but large enough to cause some throw and some side spin. This side spin is called *collision-induced english*.

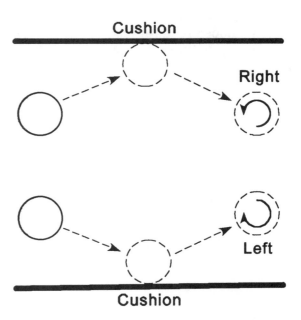

FIGURE 6-31. Side english can be picked up as a result of a collision with a cushion.

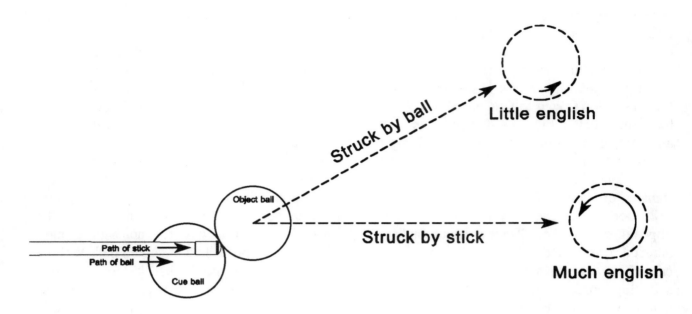

FIGURE 6-32. Collision-induced english is given to the object ball when struck, at an angle, by the cue ball.

Collision-induced english (as is the case with any other type of side english) affects the rebound angle when the ball strikes a cushion. Collision-induced english can generally be ignored except with bank shots which will be discussed in detail in Chapter 10.

CHAPTER 7
POSITIONING THE
CUE BALL

Except for safeties, the prime objective of each and every shot is to pocket an object ball. The second objective is to position the cue ball in an advantageous position for the next shot. Positioning the cue ball is generally called *getting position*, *getting shape* or *leave*, and refers to the cue ball's position relative to the difficulty of the next shot. The terms "shape," "position," or "leave" are generally used qualitatively. For example, "good shape" means the cue ball has come to rest in an advantageous position for the next shot. The terms "no shape," "bad shape," or "out of shape" mean that the cue ball is in a poor position for the next shot. The term "leave" generally refers to the difficulty of the shot that is left for the next player. The qualitative connotation is the opposite. "Good leave" means that the shooter has left the cue ball in a difficult position for the next player.

Many novice players quickly become good at pocketing the object ball but have little ability in controlling the cue ball's position. Pocketing skills of professional players are not much better than that of excellent barroom players; the main difference is in cue ball control. Pocketing skills can be learned in a relatively short time compared to the skills required in getting shape. If the object ball is pocketed, it can be concluded that no aim improvement is necessary; positioning skills are subjective and will forever require improvement.

PRE-SHOT ANALYSIS

Before selecting an object ball and a next ball, one must analyze the existing ball arrangement. This analysis depends somewhat on the type of game that's being played. In games such as NINE-BALL or ROTATION the balls must be pocketed in numerical order, therefore the selection of ball sequence is predetermined. In these cases the main concerns are; which pocket to use for the object ball, which pocket is best for the next ball, and how to go about getting the best possible shape.

In games such as EIGHT-BALL and STRAIGHT-POOL the sequence of balls must be selected from the remaining balls. Initially, each ball must be considered as a potential object ball and next ball. After tentatively selecting an object ball (usually the easiest shot) one must determine which ball will be next and how to get shape on it. If getting shape on the next ball is difficult or impossible, one must consider a different object ball and repeat the process for determining the next ball. Obviously, the mental processes are longer and more involved when the object ball and next ball are not predetermined by virtue of the game rules. On the other hand, the shots are usually easier because there's a greater selection of shots from which to choose.

After selecting the object ball and next ball, the total shot must be viewed from all perspectives. This can best be done by walking the long way around the table to get to shooting position. If you're already in shooting position, walk halfway around the table (in the direction where the action will be) then back to the shooting position. This is a good habit to get into because it allows time to think while getting a better perspective on the angles and distances involved in the shot.

Before executing a shot, always select *the exact spot* where you want the cue ball to stop for the next shot. This spot is called the *position spot*. The cue ball may not always end up exactly on the position spot, but by observing the error you're conditioning

yourself to do better next time. Conversely, if you select a large general area for the cue ball, you may never feel the need to improve. The *position spot concept*, if employed religiously, will improve your game dramatically by making every shot a learning process. Keep in mind, **YOUR IMPROVEMENT WILL BE DICTATED BY YOUR OWN EXACTING STANDARDS.**

In addition to selecting the position spot, you must also visualize a larger zone that, from within, you can still make the next ball without too much difficulty. This will be termed the *shape zone*. Figure 7-1 shows a typical shot. The 8-ball is shot into the side pocket while getting shape on the 9-ball into the corner pocket. The position spot is selected and the shape zone visualized. Now you must determine how to get the cue ball to the position spot, or at least stay within the shape zone. Bottom english could be used causing the cue ball to go directly to the

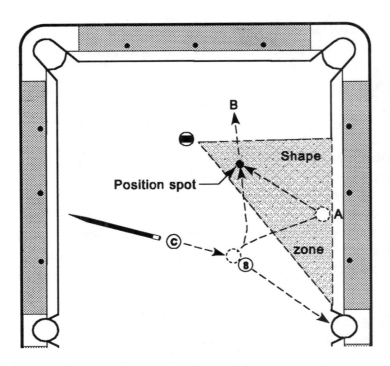

FIGURE 7-1. The cue ball should stay within the shape zone for as long as possible on its way to the position spot.

position spot, or top english could be used to cause the cue ball to go to the cushion at "A", then rebound toward the position spot. Using bottom english, the cue ball's path (path "B") remains in the shape zone for a distance of 8 inches. Using top english, the cue ball remains in the shape zone for about 30 inches. Obviously, top english allows a far greater (six times greater) error in cue ball travel distance and therefore is a safer shot. This example emphasizes an important point; if possible, **ALWAYS APPROACH THE POSITION SPOT FROM THE CENTER OF THE SHAPE ZONE.** Conversely, try to avoid approaching the position spot from the side of the shape zone because speed is more critical.

Before executing any shot, consideration must be given to what may go wrong. Become consciously aware of those areas on the table that must absolutely be avoided. Some may call this negative thinking but it's not; it's unbiased analytical reasoning. Figure 7-2 shows the shape zone for the 3-ball. Within the shape zone there's an area, behind an intervening ball, that must be avoided. This will be referred to as the *snooker zone* (the term "snookered" means the cue ball is behind an intervening ball). It's better to accept a larger cut angle on the object ball than to take a chance on being left in the snooker zone.

Don't try to get too close to your work. Figure 7-3 shows what can happen when trying to get the cue ball too close to the next ball. If the cue ball were to stop at position "A" or "B", the shot at the 4-ball would be very easy. However, as the cue ball moves to positions "C" and "D" the shot becomes progressively harder.

At times, it's desirable to get position such that the next ball is straight-in; however, a slight cut angle is usually more desirable. Consider the example shown in figure 7-4. The cue ball is in perfect position to pocket the 5-ball; the problem is getting shape on the 6-ball. If the cue ball were at positions "A" or "B" the cushions could be used to help get to the other side of the 6-ball. The potential problem of the straight-in shot must be anticipated and avoided.

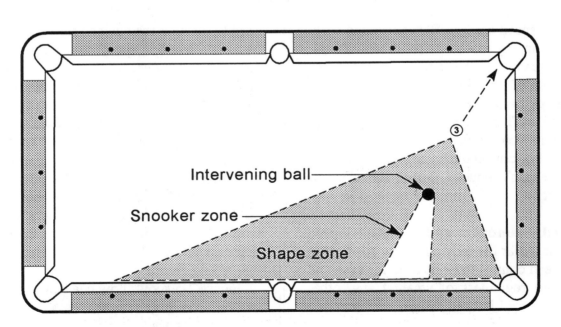

FIGURE 7-2. A snooker zone within a shape zone.

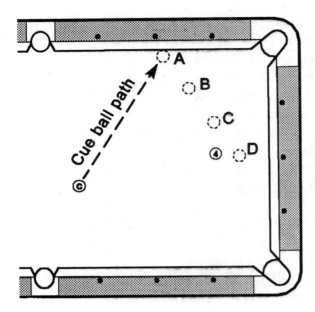

FIGURE 7-3. Trying to get too close to your next ball may result in problems.

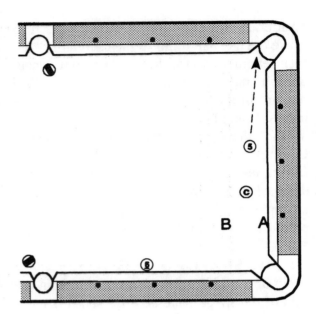

FIGURE 7-4. Having a slight cut angle on the object ball allows many more position options than a straight-in shot.

POSITIONING TOOLS

Learning how to get shape is the most difficult aspect of pool. A ball can be pocketed without knowing anything about english or speed control. But, pocketing a ball and winning a game are two different things. No one can win consistently without the proper use of positioning tools. Most of the tools used for positioning have already been discussed. This section will focus on application. Positioning tools include speed control, bottom english, top english, side english, english induced throw, and cheating the pocket.

Speed control and english--Speed control is by far the most effective positioning tool. Speed control must be used for each and every shot regardless of what, if any, other positioning tool is used. When amateurs and professionals alike fail to get good shape, it's

most often the result of improper cue ball speed.

Minimum cue ball speed is that which barely propels the object ball into the pocket. Any speed in excess of this minimum can be used to position the cue ball for the next shot. Minimum cue ball speed depends on the cut angle and the distance between object ball and pocket. When the object ball is struck head-on, the cue ball transfers all of its linear energy to the object ball. Therefore, the options for positioning with speed control are limited. If the cut angle is very thin, the cue ball retains most of its speed after impact with the object ball. Since the cue ball travels farther, it is harder to predict where it will stop. Ideally, a moderate cut angle (5 to 15 degrees) allows the greatest control of cue ball rolling distance.

Figure 7-5 shows how cue ball speed alone can be used in getting shape. Assume the 1-ball is to be pocketed in the corner pocket. If shape on the 2-ball is desired, minimum cue

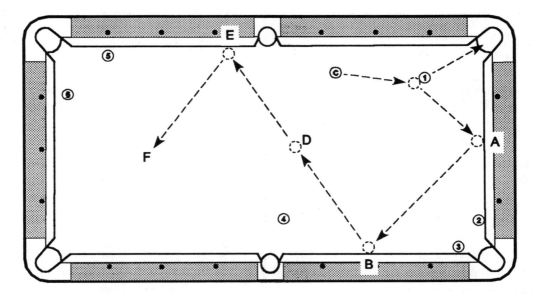

**FIGURE 7-5. In this example, speed alone can be used
to get shape on any ball on the table.**

ball speed could be used to cause the cue ball to stop near "A". If the cue ball were to be shot progressively harder it could be stopped at "B" for shape on the 3-ball; at "D" for shape on the 4-ball; at "E" for shape on the 5-ball; or at "F" for shape on the 6-ball.

The lack of cushion efficiency can be used advantageously in getting shape. Generally speaking, the more cushions that the cue ball strikes, the easier it is to judge where it will stop. The shot shown in figure 7-6 illustrates this point. The cue ball is shot from the center

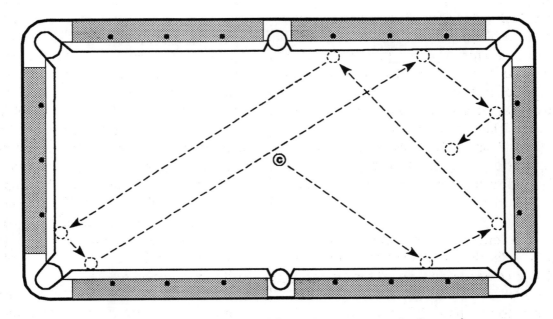

**FIGURE 7-6. The more cushions that are struck the easier
it is to control rolling distance.**

spot into the side cushion about one diamond from the corner pocket. It can be shot anywhere from fast to very fast and either way it will still stop within a few inches of the same spot after striking seven cushions.

A mathematical analysis of this shot yields the same result. Assume that 40 percent of the cue ball's rolling potential is lost each time it strikes a cushion. If its initial speed is the equivalent of traveling 200 feet, it will rebound 2.3 inches off the seventh cushion. If its initial speed is equivalent to traveling 300 feet, it will rebound 3.0 feet off the seventh cushion. An increase in initial speed, the equivalent of rolling 100 feet, only produces a 34-inch difference in the ball's final position.

Figure 7-7 shows another shot where several cushions can be used to help get shape. The objective is to pocket the 2-ball and get shape on the 3-ball. The cue ball can be shot with top left english causing it to go to the end cushion at "A", then rebound to "F". But it's difficult to judge speed and english with the precision required for this shot. A better technique would be to shoot the 2-ball much faster with top right english.

The cue ball would go to the end cushion at "B", side cushion at "D", and opposite side at "E". This shot can be executed at any speed between medium and fast while still getting good shape on the 3-ball. Obviously, increasing the number of cushions makes this shot less speed sensitive.

English-induced throw--English-induced throw is occasionally used for straight-in shots. The object ball can be thrown up to about 5 degrees, therefore it can be cut up to 5 degrees in either direction (brought back in line with throw). Being able to cut the object ball from 0 to 5 degrees results in a cue-ball deflection angle of between 0 and 20 degrees. A 20-degree variability in either direction allows many cue ball position possibilities. Conversely, if the object ball must be cut anywhere from 0 to 5 degrees, it can be struck head-on using english-induced throw to bring it back in line.

Cheating the pocket--The term *cheating the pocket* means shooting the object ball to either side of center pocket while still

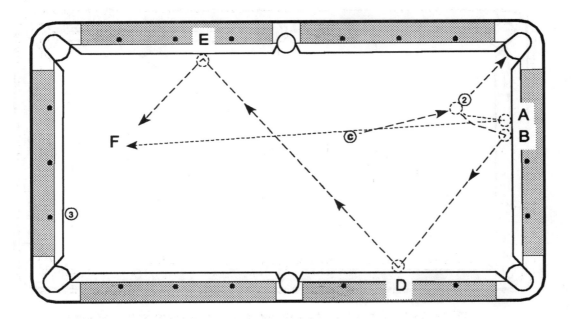

FIGURE 7-7. An example of using one or three cushions to get shape.

pocketing the ball. In doing so, the cut angle and consequent cue-ball deflection angle can be altered. The farther the object ball is from the pocket, the less effective cheating the pocket is. Cheating the pocket is generally restricted to shots in which the object ball is less than 2 or 3 feet from the pocket.

Figure 7-8 shows how cheating the pocket can be used to help get shape. The cue ball is on the center spot and the object ball (1-ball) is between the cue ball and side pocket. If cheating the pocket were not employed, the cue ball could only be left somewhere on or near the center string. However, cheating the pocket, while employing various types of english, will allow the cue ball to be positioned anywhere on the table. Assume position on the 2-ball is desired. The 1-ball can be shot slightly to the left of center pocket with bottom english. The cue ball will back up to the right side of the opposite side pocket. If the 1 ball were shot center pocket, there would be a possibility of backing the cue ball into the opposite side pocket. If shape on the 3-ball is desired, the 1-ball can

be shot the same as the previous shot but cheated to the right of center pocket. If shape on the 4-ball into pocket "A" is desired, the 1-ball can be shot as far as possible to the left side of the pocket with near maximum bottom english. The cue ball will back up toward pocket "B". Another way this shot can be executed is to cheat (about medium) to the left side of the pocket using top right english. The cue ball will go to the side cushion then rebound toward pocket "B". If shape on the 4-ball into pocket "B" is desired, the pocket can be cheated to the left (maximum) using center ball; or, the cue ball could be struck slightly above center with a firm stroke; the cue ball would go toward pocket "A". Shape on the 5-ball into pockets "D" or "E" can be gotten in the same manner by cheating the pocket to the right of center.

◐   ◓   ◑

EXAMPLES AND ANALYSIS

There is generally more than one way to get shape on a particular ball. The more

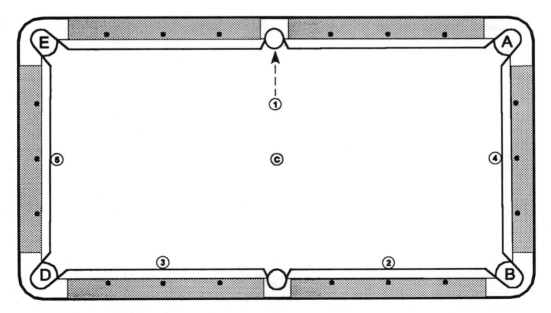

**FIGURE 7-8. The 1-ball can be shot while getting shape for any
of the other balls by cheating the pocket.**

skilled the player is, the more options that are available. For example, if a player can't back up the cue ball the length of the table then another option must be tried. A series of diagrammed shots (figure 7-9) are analyzed to demonstrate how shape can be gotten on the next ball. In these examples, only a few of the easiest options are explored. The terms "right" and "left" are referenced from the shooter's perspective.

1-BALL AS OBJECT BALL

Get shape on the 9-ball:
A slow to medium shot with top english will cause the cue ball to have normal roll when it strikes the 1-ball. It will go toward diamond "C" after impact and stop near the end cushion.

Get shape on the 8-ball:
Shoot the same as the previous shot but harder and with a little right english. The cue ball will strike the end cushion near diamond "C" then rebound straight back up the table.

Get shape on the 7-ball:
Shoot the same as the previous shot only harder.

Get shape on the 5-or 6-ball:
Use top with maximum right. The right side english will cause the cue ball to rebound toward side pocket "J". If the cut angle on the 1-ball were any larger, the shot would require center left english causing the cue ball to go to "B", "Z", then toward side pocket "J".

2-BALL AS OBJECT BALL

Note: In each of these shots, the speed of the cue ball after impact with the 2-ball will depend on how thin the 2 ball is cut.

Get shape on the 7-ball:
Soft shot, no english. Shoot for the center or right side of the pocket. If the 2-ball is cut too thin (left side of pocket) the cue ball will maintain its speed and may rebound too far from the end cushion.

Get shape on the 5-or 6-ball:
Use slow speed with a little left english

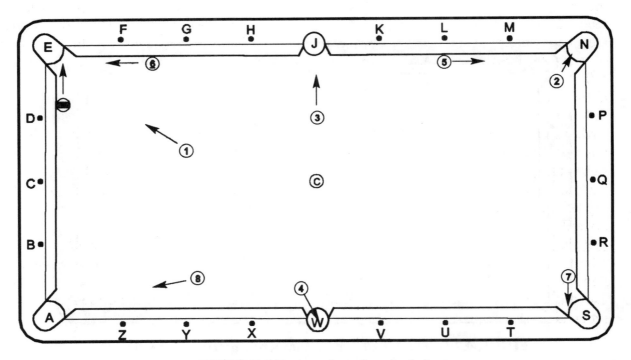

FIGURE 7-9. A series of typical shots.

and a thin cut. The cue ball will run straight into the end cushion after striking the 2-ball; the left english will cause it to rebound toward the 6-ball.

Get shape on the 1-ball:
Use a little right english to cause the cue ball to rebound off the end cushion toward the center of the table. Again, initial cue ball speed depends on how thin the 2-ball is cut.

3-BALL AS OBJECT BALL

Get shape on the 1-ball:
Use bottom english to draw the cue ball back. If the 3-ball is shot into the center of the pocket the cue ball may draw back into pocket "W". Shooting slightly to one side of center pocket (cheat the pocket) will alleviate this possibility.

Get shape on the 7-ball:
Use a medium speed stun stroke and shoot the 3-ball into the left side of the pocket. The cue ball will go toward diamond "P" or "Q". Shape could also be gotten using top right english. The cue ball would strike the side cushion near diamond "K" and rebound toward diamond "Q".

Get shape on the 4-ball:
A stun stroke can be used to stop the cue ball for a relatively easy shot at the 4-ball. If the 7-ball were to be shot after the 4-ball, it would be better to have the cue ball farther toward the left side of the table. In this case the 3-ball could be shot into the right side of the pocket using bottom to back the cue ball toward the 8-ball; or, use top left and go to the cushion then rebound toward the 8-ball.

Get shape on the 9-ball:
Cheat the pocket to the right and use bottom english to back up the cue ball; or, use top left and go to the cushion and rebound into position.

5-BALL AS OBJECT BALL

Get shape on the 1-ball:
If the shot is made without english, the cue ball will rebound toward diamond "T". Using a stun stroke, the cue ball will rebound toward diamond "U", but it may be going too fast to stop there. A combination of bottom and left will cause the cue ball to rebound toward diamond "V" for an easy shot at the 1-ball.

Get shape on the 7-ball:
With normal roll the cue ball will go toward diamond "T". If shot hard enough, the cue ball will rebound off the cushion toward the 2-ball. But, if the cue ball is struck that hard, it may not have time to attain normal roll before striking the 5-ball. To assure that it has normal roll when it gets to the 5-ball, a little top english must be used.

Get shape on the 4-ball:
Medium speed with bottom left english will cause the cue ball to rebound between diamond "V" and pocket "W" then rebound toward diamond "H". However, the best option is to use top right english causing the cue ball to strike the cushions at diamonds "R" and "T", then go toward "H".

8-BALL AS OBJECT BALL

Get shape on the 1-ball:
A stun stroke will cause the cue ball to go toward diamond "X" then rebound toward the middle of the table. The same shot could be used to get shape on the 3- or 4-ball.

Get shape on the 7-ball:
Shoot the same as the previous shot but with a little more speed and some left english. The left will cause the cue ball to rebound off the cushion toward the 2-ball rather than toward the 5-ball.

Get shape on the 9-ball:

Top english will cause the cue ball to strike the cushion near diamond "Y. A slow shot would yield a fair shot at the 9-ball. However, it may be better to shoot a little harder and go back and forth across the table to get back to where the 8-ball was.

CHAPTER 8
RAIL SHOTS

When the object ball is resting against a cushion and the intended pocket is at the end of that cushion, the shot is called a *rail shot*. Rail shots occur more often than random positioning might predict. The cushion causes a loss of up to 60 percent of a ball's rolling potential. The loss of energy at the rail increases the chance of the ball stopping at or near the cushion. Balls have a tendency to settle into the *rail track*. The rail track is a worn path 1.12 inch (1/2 ball diameter) from the cushion. The cushion is higher than the center of the ball. When a ball strikes the cushion it's forced back down into the cloth. This causes wearing and compacting of the nap thus forming the rail track. When the cloth is new the rail track is not obvious. As the cloth becomes worn the rail track turns a lighter color.

The rail shot has been cursed and otherwise maligned by just about every player. As shown in figure 8-1, only half the target area can be struck by the cue ball. The other half is sheltered by the cushion. However, if shot properly, the rail shot can be relatively easy. In fact, the permissible error of most rail shots is greater than similar shots away from the cushion.

So what is the proper way to shoot a rail shot? The common dictum holds that the cue ball should strike the object ball and cushion at the same time; the alignment of centers will be directly toward the pocket. Therefore, the object ball should go down the rail and into the pocket. This would be true were it not for the effects of collision-induced throw which causes the object ball to be thrown into the cushion and consequently rebound away from the cushion. Before exploring the proper way to shoot a rail shot, all the variables and their effects will be examined. The following are some of the variables that affect the rail shot: (1) which is struck first the cushion or the ball,

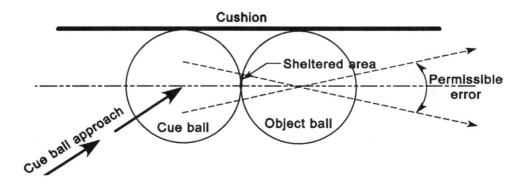

FIGURE 8-1. Half the target area can't be struck by the cue ball.

or both at the same time, (2) side english, (3) cue ball speed, and (4) distance to the pocket.

Before examining the rail shot in detail, it's necessary to define its component elements. Figure 8-2 shows some of these elements. Side english, used on a rail shot, may be described as either *cushion-side english* or *ball-side english*. Cushion-side english means that the cue ball is struck on the side nearest the cushion; ball-side english means the cue ball is struck on the side nearest the object ball. Cut angle is the same as any other shot and can be measured between the cushion and approach path of the cue ball.

In describing the path of the object ball, it is said to have *no error* if it is parallel to the cushion. Any error in the path of the object ball will either be *into* or *away* from the cushion. The error angle is measured between the direction that the object ball is propelled and the cushion. Regardless of which direction the error is, it always causes the ball to move away from the cushion.

The path of the cue ball can be described in relation to what it strikes first. It can: (1) strike the object ball and cushion at the <u>same time</u> as shown in figure 8-2, (2) strike the <u>cushion first</u>, then rebound into the object ball, or (3) strike the <u>ball first</u>, then carom into the cushion. In figure 8-2, if the cue ball was shot to the left of the path shown, it would strike the cushion first; if it were shot to the right of the path shown, it would strike the ball first.

Each of the three striking positions will be examined assuming no english, ball-side english, and cushion-side english.

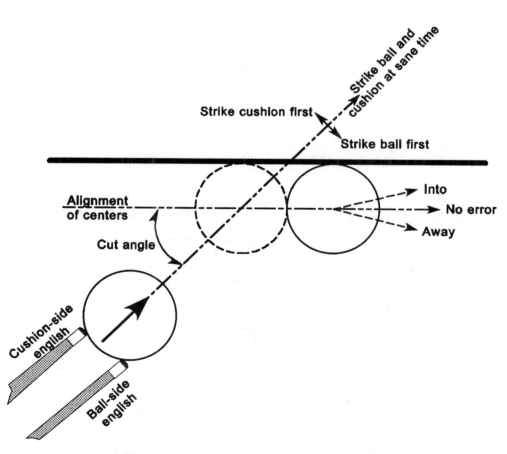

FIGURE 8-2. Terminology used in describing a rail shot.

STRIKING OBJECT BALL AND CUSHION AT SAME TIME

When the cue ball strikes the object ball and cushion at the same time the alignment of centers is directly parallel to the cushion, therefore there is no alignment error.

No english--(Figure 8-3a) It would seem that the best way to make a rail shot would be to strike the object ball and cushion at the same time. However, collision-induced throw causes an error <u>into</u> the cushion. The amount of the error depends on the cut angle. At small cut angles the error will be small. As the cut angle increases, so does the error.

Ball-side english--(Figure 8-3b) The error caused by english-induced throw is <u>into</u> the cushion. Both collision-induced throw and english-induced throw errors are <u>into</u> the cushion which compounds the net error. English-induced throw is greatest at small cut angles and becomes smaller as the cut angle

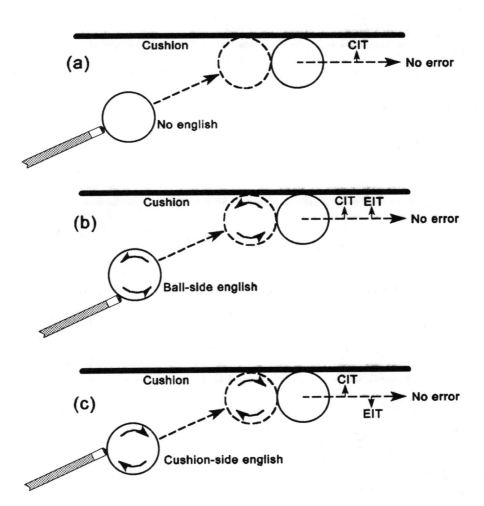

CIT - Error caused by collision-induced throw.

EIT - Error caused by english-induced throw.

FIGURE 8-3. Striking the object ball and cushion at the same time.

99

increases. This is opposite to the effects of collision-induced throw at various angles. Therefore, net error will be substantial regardless of cut angle.

Cushion-side english--(Figure 8-3c) The error caused by english-induced throw is <u>away</u> from the cushion, therefore it is acting in opposition to the error caused by collision-induced throw (into). At small cut angles the english-induced throw will predominate, and at large cut angles the collision-induced throw will predominate. At some combination of cut

angle and english, the errors will cancel each other and the path of the object ball will be parallel to cushion (no error).

STRIKING OBJECT BALL FIRST

When the object ball is struck first, the error caused by alignment of centers is always <u>into</u> the cushion.

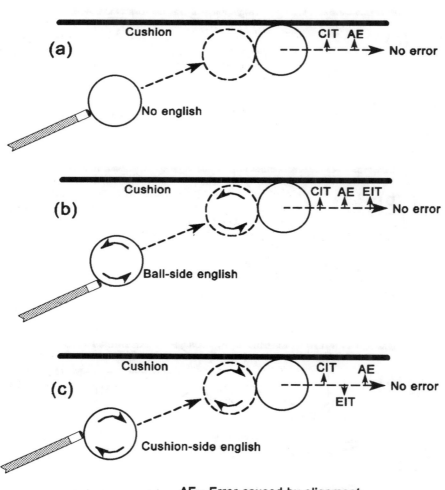

AE - Error caused by alignment.

CIT - Error caused by collision-induced throw.

EIT - Error caused by english-induced throw.

FIGURE 8-4. Striking the object ball first.

No english--(Figure 8-4a) The error caused by collision induced throw is <u>into</u> the cushion as is the error caused by alignment, therefore net error is always into the cushion.

Ball-side english--(Figure 8-4b) The error caused by alignment of centers, collision-induced throw, and english-induced throw are all <u>into</u> the cushion. Net error is compounded by each error causing it to be large regardless of cut angle.

Cushion-side english--(Figure 8-4c) The error caused by alignment of centers and collision-induced throw are both <u>into</u> the cushion. Error caused by english-induced throw is <u>away</u> from the cushion. At small cut angles the errors may cancel each other.

STRIKING CUSHION FIRST

When the cue ball strikes the cushion first, the object ball is struck as the cue ball is rebounding away from the cushion. The error caused by the alignment of centers is usually

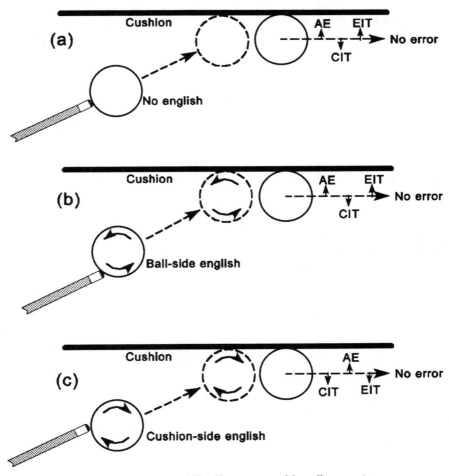

AE - Error caused by alignment.

CIT - Error caused by collision-induced throw.

EIT - Error caused by english-induced throw.

FIGURE 8-5. Striking the cushion first.

into the cushion.

No english--(Figure 8-5a) The cue ball strikes the object ball as it rebounds from the cushion. This is the equivalent of shooting at the object ball from the other direction which causes collision-induced throw to be <u>away</u> from the cushion and is opposite to the alignment error. The two errors may cancel each other at certain cut angles. Even though the cue ball is struck with no english, some side english is imparted by the cushion (cushion-induced english). The cushion-induced english is equivalent (in direction) to ball-side english and will cause an error <u>into</u> the cushion. The amount of cushion-induced english and resulting error depends on the cut angle. At very small and very large cut angles the cushion-induced english is small. Maximum cushion-induced english is imparted to the ball at cut angles between 30 and 45 degrees.

Ball-side english--(Figure 8-5b) The rebound angle of the cue ball is made smaller by ball-side english. Lessening the rebound angle, in effect, lessens the alignment error which is <u>into</u> the cushion. The error caused by collision-induced throw is <u>away</u> from the cushion and english-induced throw is <u>into</u> the cushion. If very little ball-side english is used, it will be retained after the cue ball strikes the cushion. However, if the cue ball initially has considerable ball-side english, some of it will be lost when it strikes the cushion.

Cushion-side english--(Figure 8-5c) The rebound angle of the cue ball is increased by the cushion-side english. Increasing the rebound angle, in effect, increases the alignment error which is <u>into</u> the cushion. The error caused by collision-induced throw and english-induced throw are both <u>away</u> from the

cushion. At moderate to large cut angles much of the cushion-side english is lost when the cue ball strikes the cushion. By the time it collides with the object ball the effect of english-induced throw is minimal. At small cut angles (less than about 15 degrees) very little english is lost on the cushion, in which case, the effect of collision-induced english is large.

INFLUENCE OF CUE BALL SPEED

Cue ball speed is not an influencing factor when the cushion and object ball are struck at the same time or when the object ball is struck first. When the cushion is struck first, cue ball speed must be considered.

The cushion compresses when it's struck by the cue ball. The higher the angle of incidence the more the cushion compresses, in which case, speed has a greater effect. The rebound starts at the point of maximum cushion compression. This point determines how the cue ball and object ball are aligned when they make contact. Figure 8-6a shows how cue ball speed affects the alignment direction. If the cue ball is moving slowly, it rebounds off the cushion then strikes the object ball. The error caused by collision-induced throw is <u>away</u> from the cushion and the error caused by alignment is <u>into</u> the cushion. If the cue ball is shot along the same path but faster, it will sink deeper into the cushion, and in effect, get closer to the object ball before it starts its rebound. In this case the error caused by collision-induced throw and alignment of centers are both <u>away</u> from the cushion.

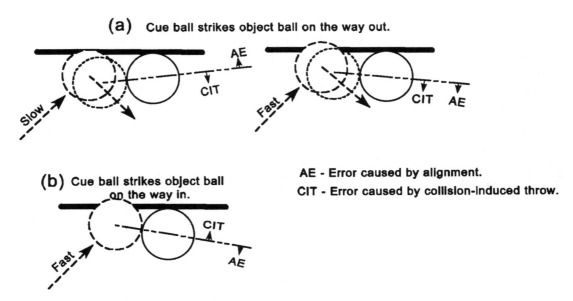

(a) Cue ball strikes object ball on the way out.

Slow

Fast

AE

CIT

CIT AE

(b) Cue ball strikes object ball on the way in.

Fast

CIT

AE

AE - Error caused by alignment.
CIT - Error caused by collision-induced throw.

FIGURE 8-6. Influence of cue-ball speed on a rail shot.

Figure 8-6b shows another manner in which speed influences the rail shot. If the cue ball is moving slowly, as in the previous example, the error caused by collision-induced throw is <u>away</u> from the cushion and alignment of centers is <u>into</u> the cushion. If the cue ball is moving fast and strikes the cushion very near the object ball, it will still be going into the cushion when it strikes the object ball. In this case the errors are still acting in opposition to each other but in opposite directions.

DISTANCE TO POCKET

One would tend to think that the distance between the object ball and pocket should not have any influence on how the shot should be executed. The logic being that the object ball must be propelled parallel to the cushion regardless of how far it is from the pocket. This is true, but the variable size of the target area causes permissible error to vary depending on distance to the pocket.

Figure 8-7 shows the error produced with a medium speed, 20-degree cut shot using various striking positions and english. When the cushion and ball are struck at the same time the aim is considered to be "0"; aiming to the cushion side or ball side is measured perpendicular to the "0" aim line at the point where the cue ball makes contact with the cushion and ball. The error, in degrees, either into or away from the cushion is shown using no english, ball-side, and cushion-side english. Only about 80 percent of maximum side english was used in order to avoid the possibility of miscuing.

In order to make functional use of the chart, the distance to the pocket must be converted to permissible error in degrees. Figure 8-8 shows this conversion assuming 5-inch pockets. As an example, if the object ball is 2 feet from the pocket it would have a permissible error of 4.8 degrees into the cushion and 4.8 degrees away from the cushion and still go into the pocket.

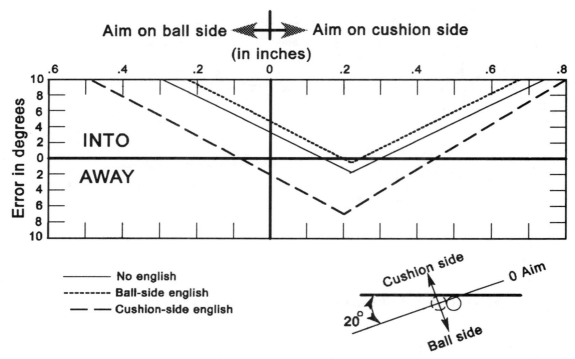

FIGURE 8-7. Chart showing the error (into or away from cushion) for a 20 degree cut, rail shot, when aim is toward the cushion or the ball.

In order to determine how to shoot a rail shot allowing the largest permissible error, both charts must be used. As an example, assume an object ball is 1.2 feet from the pocket and must be cut 20 degrees. Figure 8-8 indicates that at a distance of 1.2 feet the permissible error is about 8 degrees into or away from the cushion. From figure 8-7 it can be determined that with no english, cue ball aim could be from 0.20 inch on the ball side to 0.68 inch on the cushion side for a total target area of 0.88 inch; using ball-side english, aim could be from 0.15 inch on the ball side to 0.60 inch on the cushion side for a total target area of 0.75 inch; using cushion-side english, aim could be from 0.40 inch on the ball side to 0.75 inch on the cushion side for a total target area of 1.15 inches. The target area could be extended slightly by using somewhat more then 80 percent

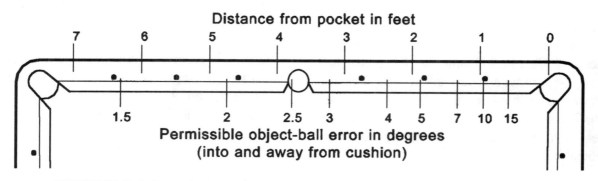

FIGURE 8-8. Permissible error in relation to distance from the pocket.

cushion-side english. Obviously, cushion-side english should be used to take advantage of the largest possible permissible error. The target <u>point</u> is the center of the target area or <u>0.18 inch</u> on the cushion side. Consider another 20-degree cut shot but this time assume the object ball is 3.2 feet from the pocket. From figure 8-8 it is determined that the object ball's permissible error is 3 degrees into or away from the cushion. From figure 8-7 it can be determined that with no english cue ball aim could be from 0.02 inch on the cushion side to 0.45 inch on the cushion side for a total target area of 0.43 inch; using ball-side english, aim could be from 0.04 inch on the cushion side to 0.40 inch on the cushion side for a total target area of 0.36 inch; using cushion-side english, there are two target areas; from 0.22 inch on the ball side to 0.02 inch on the cushion side and from 0.35 inch on the cushion side to 0.55 inch on the cushion side. Obviously, shooting between these target areas would cause a miss. However, if only 25 percent of maximum cushion-side english were used, there would be only one target area which would extend from about 0.05 inch on the ball side to about 0.48 inch on the cushion side for a total target area of 0.53 inch with a target point <u>0.21 inch</u> on the cushion side.

By increasing the distance between the object ball and pocket from 1.2 feet to 3.2 feet the optimum english went from more than 80 percent cushion side to 25 percent cushion-side english, and the target point went from 0.18 inch to 0.21 inch on the cushion side.

HOW TO SHOOT A RAIL SHOT

By now you know everything there is to know about a rail shot except *how* to shoot one.

In order to determine how all the variables interact, it was necessary to shoot thousands of experimentally controlled shots using no english, ball-side english, and cushion-side english at various cut angles while striking the cushion and object ball at the same time, cushion first, and ball first. Cue ball striking point was controlled to about 5-thousandths of an inch by running it through a specially designed alignment box. The cue ball and object ball were wiped clean before each shot to insure that there was no chalk or other contaminant on either ball which might influence throw. The cushion and rail track were brushed at about 5 shot intervals. The resulting data were used to produce a series of charts (like that shown in figure 8-7) for every 10 degrees of cut angle.

These charts are a bit bulky for practical application, therefore they were integrated into the one chart shown in figure 8-9. This chart indicates the optimum english and the target point for all cut angles at distances of 1, 2, 4, and 6 feet from the pocket. As indicated, **IN SHOOTING A RAIL SHOT, THE TARGET POINT IS ALWAYS ON THE CUSHION SIDE**. The target point varies somewhat depending on the distance to the pocket, an average was used for this chart. The target point shown is for a medium speed shot. If shot slower, the target point distance should be decreased up to 20 percent and increased up to 20 percent if shot faster.

As an example in using the chart, assume a 40-degree cut shot with the object ball 2 feet from the pocket, and shot at medium speed. To determine the type and amount of english, follow the 40-degree cut line from the left side of the chart to where it intercepts the 2 foot line; project this point down to the bottom of the chart. Reading from the bottom of the chart, the optimum english is about 35 percent of maximum cushion-side english. To determine the target point, extend the 40-degree cut line to the right where it intercepts

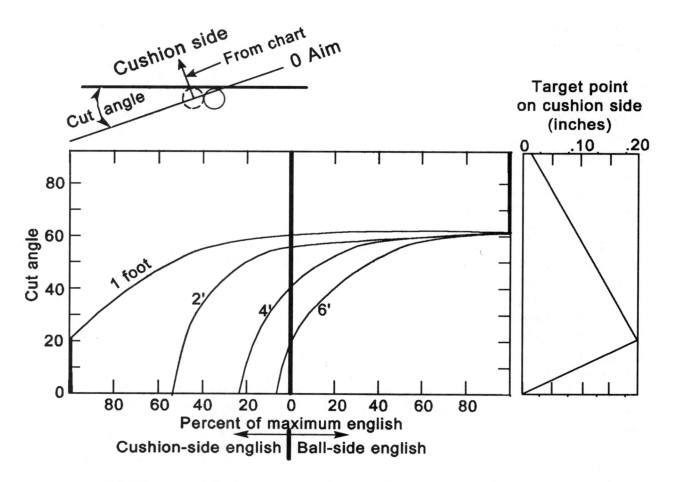

FIGURE 8-9. Optimum english and striking point for rail shots.

the line on the target point chart; project this point up to the top of the chart. The optimum target point is about 0.15 inch on the cushion side. Another example: Assume a 20-degree cut shot with the object ball 6 feet from the pocket and shot at medium speed. The chart indicates that no english should be used and the target point is about 0.20 inch on the cushion side.

For the casual pool player it may suffice to remember that most moderate cut-angle rail shots require striking the cushion first with some cushion-side english. The average barroom player should diagram a series of rail shots, guess the best english and target point, then determine from the chart how close the guess was. If you're a serious pool player, <u>you must memorize the rail shot chart</u>. A little

time spent memorizing the chart will avoid a lot of agony during your pool career.

⚫   ⚫   ⚫

CUE BALL REACTION

We now know the optimum english and target point which allow the greatest permissible error in shooting rail shots. However, pocketing the object ball may not be the only consideration. Quite frequently, one must deviate from this optimum in order to get shape on the next ball. Individuals must determine for themselves how much of a compromise (aiming point and english) they are able to make and still pocket the object ball.

The reaction of the cue ball depends on whether the object ball or cushion is struck first and the type and amount of english that is used.

Striking object ball first--Whether the object ball is struck first or the ball and cushion are struck at the same time, cue ball reaction is essentially the same. The cue ball caroms off the object ball and into the cushion at a 90 degree angle (perpendicular to path of object ball) regardless of cut angle. As shown in figure 8-10a, after striking the cushion the cue ball rebounds perpendicular to the cushion (direction "A"). If the cue ball is rolling at the time of impact, its path will curve after it rebounds from the cushion. The effective rebound angle will become smaller if the cue ball has forward rotation (top english or normal roll), or larger if it has reverse rotation (bottom english). If the cue ball has side english it will rebound at some angle other than 90 degrees as indicated by directions "B" or "C".

In controlling the cue-ball rebound angle, the stun stroke can be used as a reference. With a stun stroke the cue ball will rebound perpendicular to the cushion regardless of cut angle. If the effective rebound angle is to be made smaller, top english, ball-side english, or both can be used. If the rebound angle is to be made larger, bottom english, cushion-side english, or both, can be used. Using the stun stroke as a reference, one can better judge the type and amount of english required to produce the desired cue ball path.

Striking cushion first--If the cushion is struck first (as is optimum with all rail shots) the initial cue ball path after impact will be perpendicular to the cushion as shown in figure 8-10b. As in the previous example, the cue ball begins its path perpendicular to the cushion then curves if it has any forward or backward rotation. Side english doesn't have much affect on cue ball path because the cue ball has left the cushion before it contacts the object ball. That is why the effect of side english, on the cue ball's path, is somewhat unpredictable with rail shots. A slight error in aim can cause the reaction of the cue ball to be completely different depending on whether it strikes the ball or the cushion first.

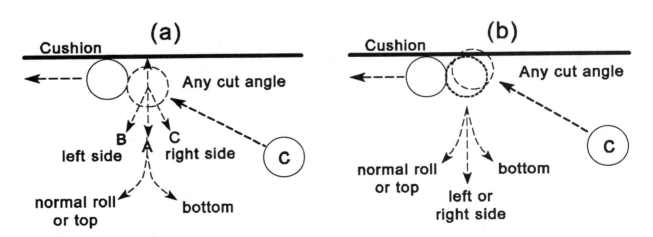

FIGURE 8-10. Cue-ball reaction on a rail shot using different types of english and striking point.

CHAPTER 9

COMBINATION SHOTS

A *combination shot*, as defined here, is a shot that has more than one ball-to-ball collision which are instrumental in pocketing the object ball. There are several variations of the combination shot, each will be examined.

SIMPLE COMBINATION SHOTS

A *simple combination shot* is one in which the cue ball strikes a ball which in turn knocks the object ball into the pocket. This is the most common of the combination shots and is generally referred to simply as a *combination shot* or a *two-ball combination shot*. An example of a simple combination shot is shown in figure 9-1a. The cue ball strikes the 1-ball which in turn knocks the 2-ball into the pocket. If more than one intermediate ball is involved, it's termed a three-ball combination, four-ball combination etc. in accordance with the number of balls involved (excluding the cue ball).

Permissible error--Inexperienced players generally don't attempt many combination shots because they don't recognize them. Average players recognize the potential combination shot. They attempt many but generally fail to pocket the object ball. Expert players recognize potential combination shots but generally avoid them because they know how difficult they are.

The problem with average players is that they think they can propel the intermediate ball more accurately than they really can. This results from conditioning. When they shoot a simple straight-in or cut shot, they aim for the center of the pocket. If the object ball goes in they assume they hit the center of the pocket. They may have missed the center of the pocket by a half inch or even an inch but the error doesn't register in their minds. In combination shots, errors of this magnitude are usually intolerable.

Consider the permissible error for a straight-in shot where the object ball is 1 foot from the pocket and the cue ball must travel 1 foot. The permissible error for the cue ball is 3.8 degrees. If another ball is added (as shown in figure 9-1a) making it a simple combination shot, the permissible error is 0.78 degree, thus making this shot about four times more difficult. By adding yet another ball (three-ball combination) as shown in figure 9-1b, the permissible error becomes 0.16 degree which is about twenty-four times more difficult than the original shot. If the travel distances are increased to 24 inches, the two-ball combination will have a permissible error of 0.098 degree; permissible error for the three-ball combination would be 0.0099 degree. These small permissible errors are difficult to conceptualize. Considered in another prospective; a permissible error of 0.098 degree is the equivalent of shooting the cue ball straight into a corner pocket 195 feet away. A permissible error of 0.0099 degree is

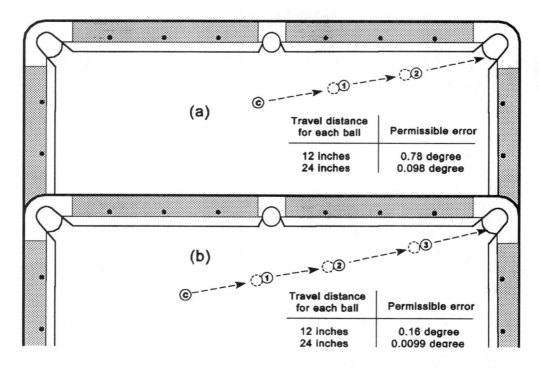

FIGURE 9-1. Permissible error for a two-ball and three-ball combination shot.

the equivalent of shooting the cue ball into a corner pocket 1,930 feet away (more than one-third of a mile).

If the two-ball combination shot, with each ball having to travel 12 inches, is set up so that each ball must be cut 20 degrees, the permissible error is 0.66 degree as opposed to 0.78 degree for the straight-in combination shot. Obviously, small cut angles do not substantially decrease the permissible error. However, their *difficulty* increases substantially because <u>judgment</u> is involved to a greater extent; if one cannot judge where to aim, the shot will be missed even if the cue ball strikes precisely where intended.

Do *not* use side english when shooting combination shots. Side english decreases cue ball accuracy. Combination shots require such great precision that any lessening of accuracy will most likely result in a missed shot. Side english also throws the first ball off-course (english-induced throw); gauging throw to the precise tolerance required in combination shots is extremely difficult. In fact, great care

must be taken to avoid inadvertently applying side english to the cue ball. Consider the two-ball combination shot shown in figure 9-1a. With a travel distance of 24 inches, the permissible error for the 1-ball is 0.96 degree. Assume aim is absolutely perfect. English-induced throw will have to be less than 0.48 degree to the left or right of this perfect aim. Striking the cue ball 0.6 inch to the side produces about 5 degrees of throw. By proportion it can be determined that inadvertently striking the cue ball more than 0.058 inch to the side will cause this shot to be missed. If this were a three-ball combination, inadvertently striking the cue ball more than 0.0059 inch (the thickness of two sheets of paper) to the side would cause the shot to be missed.

In summary; permissible error is much smaller for a combination shot than for a single ball shot. Accuracy required increases exponentially when additional balls are used in the combination or when the distance between balls is increased. Small cut angles

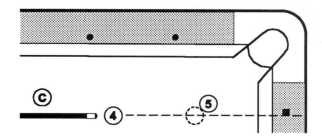

**FIGURE 9-2. Aiming technique
for a combination shot.**

do not appreciably affect permissible error, but they do increase the judgment factor which makes the shots more difficult. Even a small amount of inadvertent side english can cause a combination shot to be missed.

Aim and execution--Figure 9-2 shows a typical two-ball combination shot. The cue ball is shot into the 4-ball which in turn knocks the 5-ball into the pocket.

A common mistake is trying to visualize the entire shot while aiming and executing. There are so many angles, directions, and distances to be considered that making the required judgments while shooting is difficult. The proper technique is to first imagine that the 4-ball is the cue ball. Sight and align the 4-ball with the cue stick. Pick out some reference point on the rail (dirt, diamond, chalk, etc.) that is in line with the desired path of the 4-ball. When the 4-ball in figure 9-2 is aimed to pocket the 5-ball, its path is aligned with the right edge of the chalk. When executing the shot the 5-ball should be ignored; concentrate on shooting the 4-ball at the predetermined reference point (edge of chalk).

Care should be taken to shoot combination shots at a moderate speed. There's a tendency to shoot combination shots much too hard just to get them over with. And again, be sure a conscious effort is made to strike the cue ball in the center.

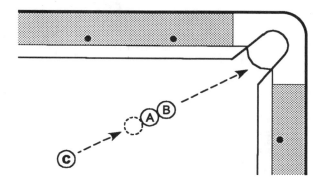

FIGURE 9-3. A frozen-ball combination.

FROZEN-BALL COMBINATION SHOTS

A *frozen-ball combination shot* is a shot in which two balls are frozen (in contact with each other). The first ball is struck by the cue ball and the second ball is pocketed. Figure 9-3 shows an example of a straight-in frozen-ball combination shot; the cue ball strikes ball "A" and ball "B" goes into the pocket.

Throw--In the example shown in figure 9-

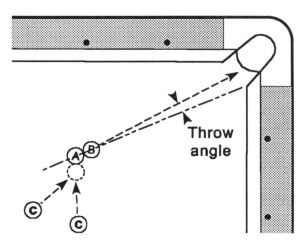

**FIGURE 9-4. Ball "B" will be thrown
relative to the direction
ball "A" is propelled.**

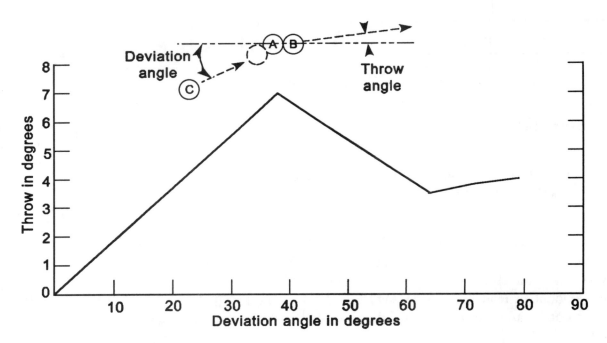

**FIGURE 9-5. The amount of collision-induced throw
depends on deviation angle.**

3 there is no throw. Ball "B" will go in the direction in which it is aligned with ball "A". If ball "A" is propelled in some direction other than its alignment direction, the path of ball "B" will be affected by collision-induced throw. As shown in figure 9-4, regardless of which direction the cue ball comes from, ball "B" will be thrown relative to the direction that ball "A" is propelled.

Collision-induced throw, relative to simple cut shots, has previously been examined. Collision-induced throw, relative to frozen balls, is similar but greater in magnitude. Figure 9-5 shows the magnitude of collision-induced throw when the first ball is struck head-on at various deviation angles. The difference in the magnitude of throw is due to the difference in friction; when balls are frozen, friction is greater. This is because static friction is greater than kinetic friction.

The path of the second ball is also affected by collision-induced english. When the cue ball strikes the first ball head-on, there is no collision-induced english; when it's struck at

an angle it picks up some side english (collision-induced english) which in turn causes throw (english-induced throw) of the second ball. The magnitude of english-induced throw can be anywhere from zero to about 1 degree.

English-induced throw is subtracted from, but not added to, collision-induced throw. Figure 9-6 shows two examples of a frozen-ball combination cut in two directions. In each case ball "A" is cut 45 degrees and its path is 30 degrees from its alignment with ball "B". At 30 degrees, collision-induced throw is about 5.5 degrees (figure 9-5). At a cut angle of 45 degrees the english-induced throw is about 0.5 degree. In figure 9-6a the throw forces are acting in opposition to each other, therefore net throw is 5 degrees (5.5 - 0.5 = 5.0). In the shot shown in figure 9-6b, english-induced throw is acting in the same direction as collision-induced throw and therefore is negated, and net throw is still 5.5 degrees.

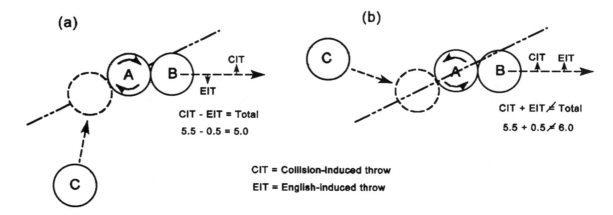

(a)

CIT - EIT = Total
5.5 - 0.5 = 5.0

(b)

CIT + EIT ≠ Total
5.5 + 0.5 ≠ 6.0

CIT = Collision-Induced throw
EIT = English-Induced throw

FIGURE 9-6. When throw forces are in opposite direction they can be subtracted, when they are in the same direction they are not additive.

Accuracy required-- The accuracy required for this type of combination shot is less than that of a comparable straight-in shot. For example, the shot shown in figure 9-3 has a permissible error of about 20 degrees. If ball "A" were not there the permissible error would be only 3.3 degrees.

FROZEN-BALL CAROM SHOTS

A *frozen-ball carom shot* is similar to a frozen-ball combination shot except that the first ball struck is the object ball. Figure 9-7 shows a typical frozen-ball carom shot. Ball "A" can be struck anywhere between the alignment line and a line through the center of ball "A" perpendicular to the alignment line, and its path will be perpendicular to the alignment line. The principle is the same as with the stun stroke; ball "A" has no roll or spin at the time of collision with ball "B", therefore its path will be perpendicular to the path of ball "B".

Accuracy required--Frozen-ball carom shots generally do not require great accuracy. The permissible error for the cut shot shown in figure 9-7 is 12 degrees. If ball "B" were

not there, the permissible error would be 0.75 degree.

Effect of english--Side english on the cue ball does not significantly affect the frozen-ball carom shot. Top or bottom english will transfer to the first ball and therefore will affect its course. The first ball struck is pinned between the cue ball and the second ball which allows the torsional force of the cue ball more time to act on the object ball. The longer a force is applied, the more energy that is transmitted.

Top english on the cue ball causes the equivalent of bottom english on the first ball

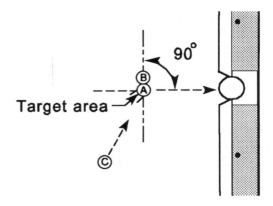

FIGURE 9-7. Target area for a frozen-ball carom shot.

113

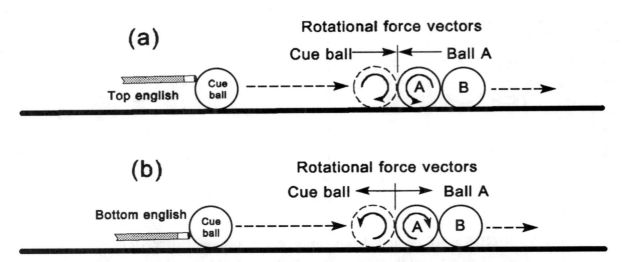

FIGURE 9-8. Effects of top and bottom english on a frozen-ball carom shot.

struck. As shown in figure 9-8a the rotational force of the cue ball is toward ball "A" and the rotational force of ball "A" is toward the cue ball. These forces, being in opposite directions, substantially cancel each other so there is no net effect on the path of ball "A".

As shown in figure 9-8b, bottom english on the cue ball causes the equivalent of top english on ball "A". This means that the rotational forces are acting in opposite directions. The cue ball wants to back up and ball "A" wants to go forward. Since ball "B" is gone as a result of the collision, the rotation of ball "A" is converted to linear movement. If all three balls are in a line, as shown in figure 9-8b, the cue ball will back up and ball "A" will follow ball "B" (but only for a short distance). If ball "A" is struck at a slight angle from the alignment line (as shown in figure 9-9), the english will cause its path to curve. The curve is caused by two forces working in different directions; the carom force is perpendicular to the alignment line and the english force is in the direction the cue ball was originally traveling. As shown in figure 9-9, the path of ball "A" starts out in the carom direction then curves as the rotational force is converted to linear movement.

The amount of bottom english that can be transferred (and resulting curve) depends on how full the first ball is struck, and the cue ball's direction relative to the alignment of the frozen balls. The nearer to head-on that the first ball is struck, the more english that is transferred; and the smaller the angle between the cue ball path and the alignment of the frozen balls, the more english that is transferred. However, the straighter the three

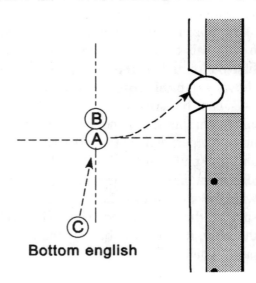

FIGURE 9-9. Bottom english on the cue ball causes the object ball to curve.

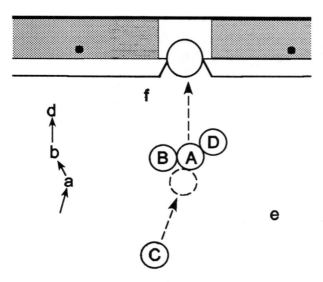

**FIGURE 9-10. If ball "A" strikes
ball "D" first it will go
into the pocket.**

balls are aligned, the less distance the object
ball will travel.

Third ball complication--Another frozen
ball can be added to the first two to
complicate the shot. Figure 9-10 shows such
an example; balls "A" and "B" are set up

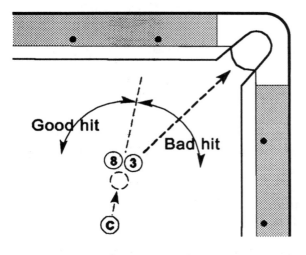

**FIGURE 9-11. Cue ball exit direction
can be used to distinguish
a good hit from a bad hit.**

perfect for a frozen-ball carom shot but ball
"D" blocks the path of ball "A" to the pocket.
Ball "A" can be shot into ball "D" which
leaves the vicinity; ball "A" then caroms into
ball "B" and goes into the pocket. This shot is
hard to visualize because the movement of
ball "A", as it caroms into ball "D", then "B",
is small. It's easier to visualize if you imagine
that you're looking at it with a microscope so
that the little movements are magnified. Ball
"A" actually goes in three different directions
as shown by "a", then "b", then "d".

The principle demonstrated by this shot
can frequently be used to identify bad hits. A
bad hit is when the cue ball strikes the wrong
ball first which constitutes a foul. When the
involved balls are far apart a bad hit is fairly
obvious; the closer together they are, the
more difficult it is to detect a bad hit by
simple observation.

Referring to figure 9-10, the final direction
of ball "A" is determined by its alignment
with the second ball that it strikes. If the cue
ball were shot from position "e" such that ball
"A" would strike ball "B" first, ball "A"
would end up going in direction "f"
(perpendicular to the alignment of balls "A"
and "D"). Therefore, by observing the exit
direction of ball "A" one can determine which
ball was struck first, "B" or "D". Figure 9-11
shows a typical situation in which a bad hit is
possible while still pocketing the object ball.
Assume the 3-ball is struck first (good hit).
The cue ball will then carom into the 8-ball
and go perpendicular to their alignment. If it
goes anywhere to the right of that direction
it's a bad hit.

OBJECT-BALL CAROM SHOTS

An *object-ball carom shot* is defined as a
shot in which the cue ball strikes an object
ball which in turn caroms off another ball
before going into a pocket. Figure 9-12

115

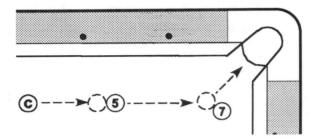

**FIGURE 9-12. An object ball
carom shot.**

shows an example of this type of combination shot. This shot is similar to the frozen-ball carom shot except that the object ball (5-ball) travels some distance before striking another ball (7-ball).

Variables--This type of shot has two variables not present in the frozen-ball carom shot. First, the exact contact point and subsequent alignment between the involved balls will vary depending on the approach path of the 5-ball. And second, the 5-ball will be rolling when it strikes the 9-ball which affects its path after the carom. Figure 9-13 shows how its path is affected by roll. Ball "A" will have anywhere from no roll to normal roll (dependent on travel time) when it strikes ball "B". The consequent path of ball "A" will be the same as the cue-ball deflection path described in Chapter 5.

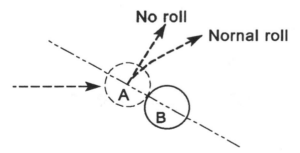

**FIGURE 9-13. The carom direction
of ball "A" depends on
its state of roll.**

Accuracy required--This shot generally requires somewhat more accuracy than a comparable straight-in shot without a carom. The permissible error for the shot shown in figure 9-12 is 1.1 degrees. The same shot without the carom would have a permissible error of 2.4 degrees. In addition to greater aim accuracy, greater judgment is also required. These shots should be examined closely before being attempted. Imagine the exact point at which the object ball must contact the other ball. When aiming, concentrate on that contact point.

Versatility of shot--If this shot requires more accuracy than the straight-in shot, then why use it? It's most often used when the straight-in path of the object ball is blocked by an intervening ball. It can also be used to nudge the contacted ball (7-ball in figure 9-12) into a more advantageous position or away from the pocket if it's your opponent's ball. It also allows more cue ball position options. For example, in the shot shown in figure 9-12, if the 5-ball were shot straight-in it would have to be cut at an angle. Using the object-ball carom shot allows striking the 5-ball head-on. Having both options allows the cue ball to be positioned anywhere on the table for the next shot.

●   ●   ●

CUE-BALL CAROM SHOTS

A *cue-ball carom shot* is a shot in which the cue ball caroms off another ball before striking the object ball. Figure 9-14 shows a typical cue-ball carom shot. The first ball struck by the cue ball (ball "A") serves only to change the cue ball's direction so that it can strike the object ball (ball "B").

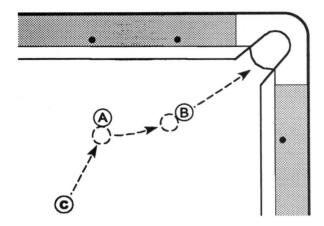

FIGURE 9-14. A cue-ball carom shot.

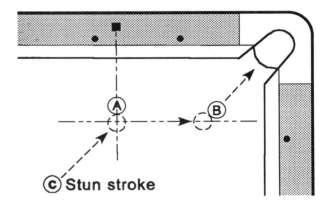

FIGURE 9-15. When a stun stroke is used the cue ball's path does not curve.

Limiting the variables--It's difficult to accurately determine where to strike ball "A" if the cue ball has rotation at the time of impact. Some of the variables that must be considered are: (1) cue ball speed, (2) distance between the cue ball and ball "A", (3) arc of the cue-ball curve after impact with ball "A", and (4) distance between ball "A" and the object ball. This shot is much easier if some of these variables are avoided by using a stun stroke. As shown in figure 9-15, with a stun stroke the cue ball will carom off ball "A" at 90 degrees from the alignment of centers and will not curve after impact. This makes it much easier to determine the proper contact point on ball "A".

Accuracy required--The permissible error for the shot shown in figure 9-15 is 0.24 degree. If ball "B" were shot directly into the pocket the required accuracy would be 1.9 degrees.

As with any carom shot, the judgment required makes the shot more difficult than the permissible error suggests. As previously described, the shot should be examined very closely before being executed. Determine the proper contact point on ball "A", then aim the cue ball such that it makes contact at that point.

In some cases it is better to determine the proper contact point on ball "A", then observe the direction ball "A" would take when struck at that point (center of chalk in figure 9-15). When executing the shot concentrate on shooting ball "A" in the predetermined direction.

CHAPTER 10

BANK SHOTS

A *bank shot* is a shot in which the striking of a cushion is instrumental in pocketing the object ball. If the object ball makes coincidental contact with a cushion adjacent to the pocket, it is not considered to be a bank shot. A *kick shot* is a form of bank shot in which the cue ball strikes one or more cushions before striking the object ball.

To successfully execute a bank shot, the proper point on the cushion at which the ball must strike must be determined. There are several techniques or systems that can be used to determine this point. Most of these systems actually determine the *geometric banking point*. The geometric banking point is the point at which the angle of incidence equals the angle of rebound. The geometric banking point must be corrected for ball speed, spin, rotation, etc. in order to determine the actual banking point. Before considering corrections, the various banking systems will be examined. They include the following:

1. Diamond system
2. Equal angle system
3. Equal distance system
4. Crisscross system
5. Image table system
6. Parallel system
7. Rail track system
8. Rote system

DIAMOND SYSTEM

Few pocket billiard players are familiar with the diamond system. Many uninformed players think the diamond system is some sort of mystical pool panacea. Actually, the system was devised for the game of three-cushion billiards (no pockets) where points are scored only after three cushions and two balls are struck. Therefore, the system has somewhat limited application to pocket billiards. The analysis presented here will allow you to determine if it can be applied to your game. In any case, you will be able to decide if it is your pool panacea.

The diamond system requires that the initial ball speed be medium or slightly faster. As with any banking system, speed is nearly as critical as aim. The system also requires that the cue ball be struck with a little running english. In this analysis, shooting at or through a diamond means aiming at its actual location in the rail, not at the cushion or rail track adjacent to the diamond.

The diamond system actually consists of two subsystems; the *5-SYSTEM* in which the side rail is struck first, and the *PLUS SYSTEM* in which the end rail is struck first. Each of these subsystems will be examined individually.

5-System--The rails are numbered in the order in which they are struck (first, second, and third). The second rail is generally ignored in the diamond system. Emphasis is on the first and third rail because they are the critical rails in three-cushion billiards.

The diamonds on the first and third rail are numbered as shown in figure 10-1. These numbers are called *rail diamond numbers* and are used to determine where to aim on the first rail, and where the ball will strike the third rail. Figure 10-2 shows a second set of numbers that are called *cue-ball position numbers*. The diamond nearest the second rail is assigned cue ball position number 1.5. The value of each succeeding diamond is increased by 0.5 so that the diamond in the corner has the value of 5. The numbers continue around the end rail where the value of each diamond is increased by 1.

To determine where the cue ball will strike the third rail, subtract the first rail number from the cue-ball position number. For example, in figure 10-2 cue ball "A" is in position 5. If the cue ball is shot at diamond number 3 on the first rail it will strike diamond number 2 on the third rail (5 - 3 = 2). Cue ball "B" is at position 4. Assume you want to strike the third rail at diamond number 3. By subtracting 3 from 4 it is determined that the aiming point is diamond position 1 on the first rail. Do not be confused by the cue-ball position numbers shown in figure 10-2. Once the cue-ball position number is determined, further analysis is made in terms of rail diamond numbers. The three-cushion player must know where the cue ball will go after it strikes the third rail. Its path, off the third rail, is called a *track*. The tracks are numbered in relation to the diamond numbers of the third rail. Figure 10-3 shows the third rail tracks 1 through 3. These tracks are slightly different for each cue ball position and must all be committed to memory if the system is to be of maximum usefulness.

How to use the system: Consider the situation shown in figure 10-4. The object ball (8-ball) is near the corner pocket; intervening balls force a three-cushion shot. We know that track 2 starts near the second diamond on the third rail and goes into the corner where the object ball is. Therefore, the cue-ball position number minus the first rail number must equal 2. The aiming point on the first rail must be determined by regression. If the aim is at rail diamond number 3, the cue-ball position number is 4.4. This aim will be incorrect because 4.4 minus 3 equals 1.4. If the aim is at rail diamond number 2, the cue ball number will be 4.6 which would yield 2.6, which is too high. Sighting at diamond number 2.5 results in a cue-ball number of 4.5 (4.5 - 2.5 = 2) which is perfect. If the cue ball is shot through rail diamond number 2.5 on the first rail it will take track 2 into the object ball.

Plus system--The *plus* system is also referred to as the *2-plus* system or the *plus 2* system. This system is used when the end rail must be struck first.

Figure 10-5 shows how the diamonds are numbered in this system. The corner diamond (over the pocket) has the value of 1, and the value of each succeeding diamond is increased by 2. With this system the cue ball is shot through one of the diamonds on the end rail. It strikes the third rail an equal number of diamonds away from its origin. In figure 10-5 the cue ball is at position "A"; if it is shot at diamond position number 2 on the first rail, it will be aligned with position number 4 on the originating rail. To determine where the ball will strike the third rail, add 2 to 4 and the answer is diamond position number 6. If the cue ball is at position "B", which is diamond position 2 when shot at diamond position 5 on the first rail, it will strike the third rail at 2 plus 5 or diamond number 7.

It is difficult to maintain a proficiency with the diamond system without constant practice. The practice requirements are probably warranted for the three cushion player but are questionable for the ordinary pool player. Now that you know all about the diamond system, you can judge its value for yourself.

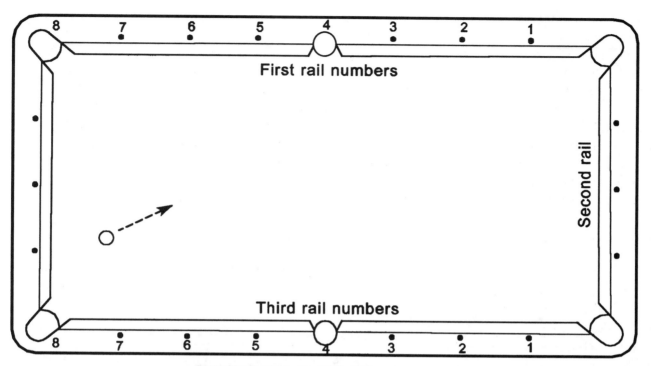

FIGURE 10-1. Rail diamond numbers.

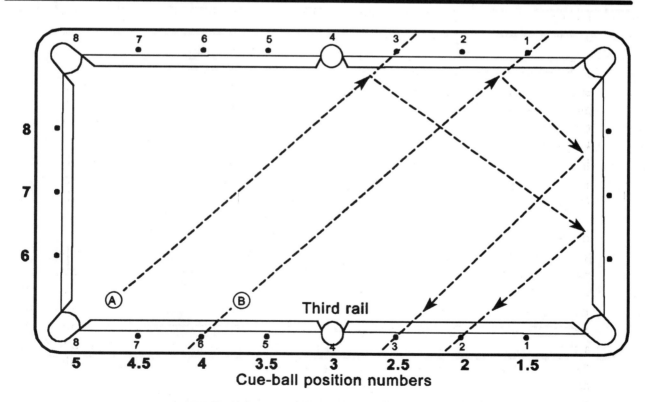

FIGURE 10-2. Cue-ball position numbers.

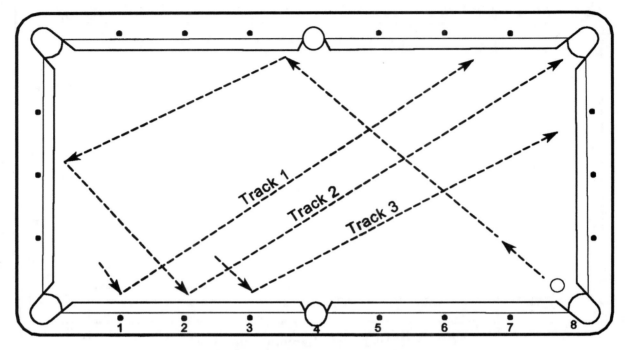

FIGURE 10-3. Track numbers.

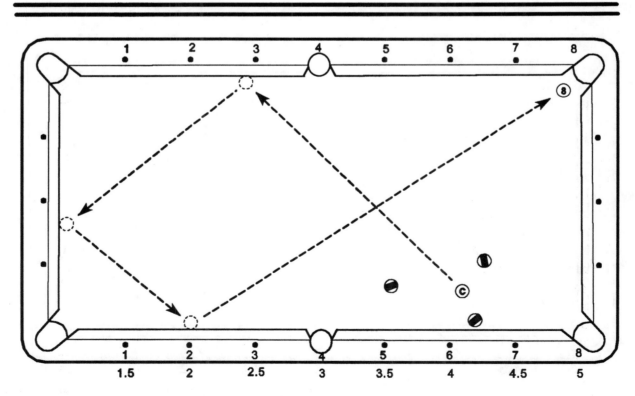

FIGURE 10-4. Example of using the diamond system.

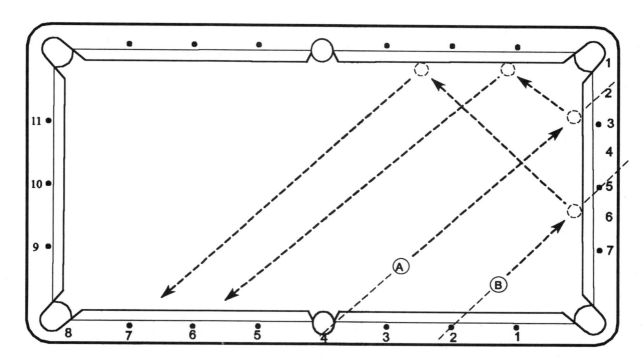

FIGURE 10-5. The "plus" system in which the end rail is struck first.

EQUAL ANGLE SYSTEM

The *equal angle system* is the simplest and probably the most often used banking system. It requires imagining two lines that represent the path of the ball into and away from the cushion. The apex of these lines is moved until the angle of incidence equals the angle of rebound. When these angles are equal, the apex of the lines represents the geometric banking point.

Figure 10-6 shows an example of this system. An imaginary line is drawn from the ball to an arbitrary point (first guess) on the rail track of the banking cushion (point "A"); another line is imagined running from point "A" to the pocket. It can be observed that the angle of incidence is larger than the angle of rebound, therefore point "A" is incorrect. The banking point is moved toward the pocket to point "B" where the angle of incidence equals the angle of rebound. This is the geometric banking point.

This system works best when the angle of incidence is large and the ball is a good distance from the banking cushion. The smaller

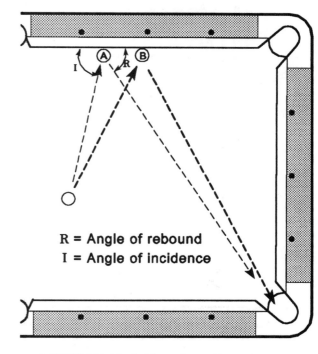

R = Angle of rebound
I = Angle of incidence

FIGURE 10-6. Equal angle system.

the angle of incidence and/or the shorter the distance to the banking cushion, the more difficult it is to accurately visualize the lines and angles.

● ● ●

EQUAL DISTANCE SYSTEM

With the *equal distance system*, distances rather than angles are used to determine the geometric banking point. Figure 10-7 shows an example of this system. First make your best guess as to where the geometric banking point is (point "A"). Imagine a line from point "A" through the ball to the near cushion (point "B"). The cue stick can be held with the tip at "A" to help visualize line "AB". Imagine a perpendicular line from point "A" to the near cushion (point "C"). Compare distance "BC" to distance "CD". If they are equal, point "A" is the geometric banking point. If they are unequal, point "A" must be moved in the direction of the largest distance and the test repeated. For example in figure 10-7, if distance "BC" is greater than distance "CD", point "A" would have to be moved to

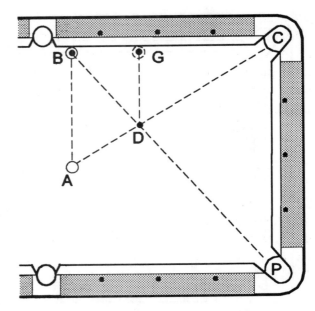

FIGURE 10-8. Crisscross system.

the left.

● ● ●

CRISSCROSS SYSTEM

The *crisscross system* is probably the most promulgated of all the banking systems. Figure 10-8 shows an example of this system. The following steps are required to determine the geometric banking point:

1. Draw a line from the ball (point "A") to point "B" on the rail track perpendicular to the cushion.
2. Draw a line from point "B" to the intended pocket (pocket "P").
3. Draw a line from point "A" to the opposite pocket (pocket "C").
4. Find point "D" where lines "AC" and "BP" cross.
5. Draw a line from point "D" to point "G" perpendicular to the cushion. Point "G" is the geometric banking point.

It's difficult to visualize all of these lines at the same time. Therefore, it is recommended

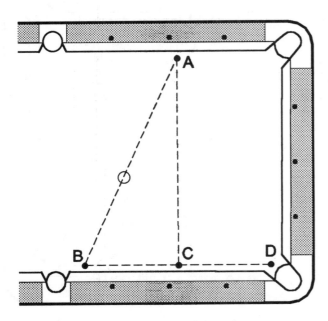

FIGURE 10-7. Equal distance system.

that the cue stick be used to represent line "BP" so that only lines "AC" and "DG" need be imagined. This system becomes less and less accurate the closer the ball is to the banking cushion. It can't be used at all when the ball is on the cushion.

IMAGE TABLE SYSTEM

With the *image table system* another table is imagined adjacent to the real table, and the ball is aimed for the pocket on the imaginary table. An example of this system is shown in figure 10-9. The ball is at point "A", the intended

pocket is labeled "P", and the image pocket is "P'". Aim the ball as though it were being shot directly into image pocket "P'". The geometric banking point is where the aim line crosses the rail track (point "G").

Sounds simple but most people have trouble imagining the pocket of the image table, in space, without visual references. If this is a problem try this: Stand near the image pocket "P'"; holding the cue stick vertically, place the butt on the floor directly below "P'"; sight through the stick back to the ball; point "G" is where the line of sight crosses the rail track of the real table. Remember where point "G" is, then go back and shoot the shot.

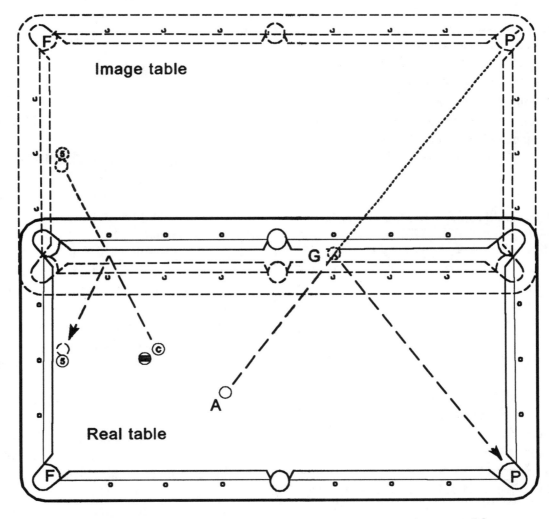

FIGURE 10-9. Aim at the ball or the pocket on the image table.

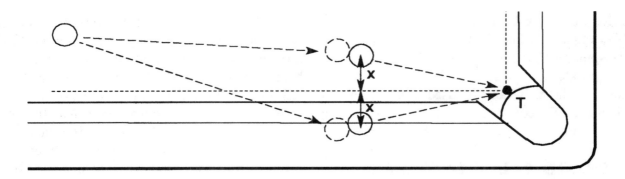

FIGURE 10-10. The image system can be used for short kick shots.

If you have your own table (or are otherwise allowed), mark the floor at each image pocket. This will take the guesswork out of estimating where the image pocket is when using the vertical stick technique. The distance from the real table to the image pocket is the distance between the rail tracks, not between the cushions. For example, when marking the floor for the side pocket of a 44-inch table, mark the floor 41.8 inches (44 - 2.2 = 41.8) from the cushion of the real table.

The image table system is superior to the previous systems because it primarily indicates the direction the ball must be shot; from this direction the geometric banking point is determined. When the ball is on the cushion, the banking point is predetermined by virtue of its position; therefore, banking <u>direction</u> is the primary unknown. Most of the other systems are the opposite. They indicate the geometric banking point from which the proper direction can be determined.

This system can also be used for kick shots. The 5-ball in figure 10-9 can't be shot directly into the pocket because of the intervening ball. To execute the kick shot, imagine that the 5-ball is in the exact same position on the image table, then shoot for the image 5-ball.

The image table system can also be applied to short kick shots as shown in figure 10-10. This shot is very useful when an intervening ball prevents a direct shot into the pocket or when good position cannot otherwise be gotten. To implement, observe the distance between the center of the object ball and rail track; imagine that the center of the image ball is the same distance on the other side of the rail track; aim as to shoot the image ball into the pocket. In figure 10-10 the object ball is distance "x" from the rail track, and the edge of the image ball is distance "x" on the other side of the rail track; shoot for the image ball.

●   ●   ●

PARALLEL SYSTEM

The *parallel system* is similar to the image table system in that it primarily indicates the direction that the ball must be shot rather than the banking point. This makes it applicable when the object ball is at or very near the banking cushion. The parallel system can be used for single rail or two-rail bank shots.

Single rail--The parallel system is very simple which makes it easy to implement. Figure 10-11 shows an example of this system. The objective is to bank ball "A" into the corner pocket "P". Find the midpoint (point "M") directly between ball "A" and pocket "P"; imagine a line from point "M" to the opposite pocket "N"; imagine another line parallel to line "MN" from "A" to the banking cushion. The point where this line crosses the rail track (point "G") is the geometric banking

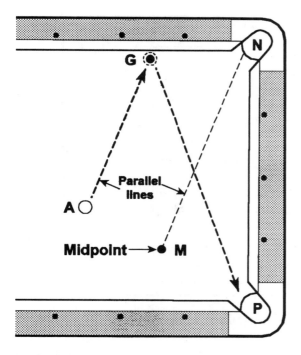

FIGURE 10-11. The parallel system.

point. The line "AG" may be easier to visualize if the cue stick is held over the midpoint "M" with the tip pointing at pocket "N".

Estimating the line "AG" is difficult when the ball is a long way from the pocket even when the cue stick is used as an aid. In these cases a variation of this system can be employed. This variation is shown in figure 10-12. Find the midpoint "M"; use the cue stick, as shown, to define line "MN"; observe where the butt of the stick crosses the rail track of the near cushion. This point will be called the "complimentary banking point." The geometric banking point is this exact point on the rail track of the opposite cushion. In figure 10-12, the complimentary banking point is on the rail track at a diamond. The geometric banking point is at the same position on the rail track of the opposite side rail.

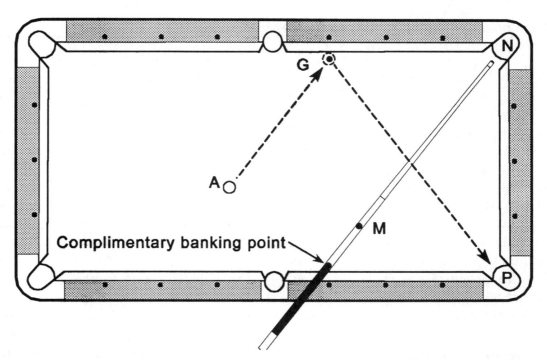

FIGURE 10-12. The parallel system using the complimentary banking point.

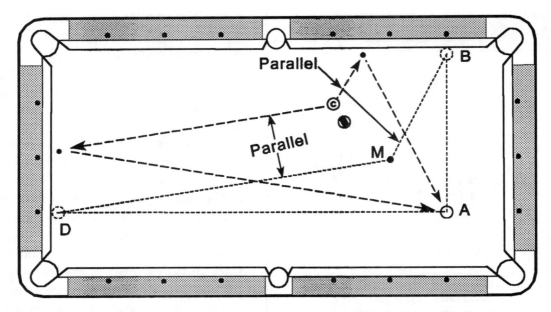

FIGURE 10-13. The parallel system used for kick shots.

The parallel system is also effective in determining the geometric banking point for kick shots. Figure 10-13 shows an example of a kick shot at ball "A". Imagine a point on the rail track of the banking cushion perpendicular to ball "A" (point "B"); find the midpoint "M" between the cue ball and the ball "A"; imagine a line from point "M" to point "B"; shoot into the cushion parallel to line "MB". The same system can be used in kicking to the end rail at ball "A". Using the same midpoint "M", imagine point "D" on the rail track of the end rail perpendicular to ball "A"; shoot into the end rail parallel to line "MD".

Two rails--The parallel system can also be used for two-rail bank shots. As shown in figure 10-14, the two-rail bank shot is similar to the one-rail shot except that a different pocket is used for parallel alignment. First, find the midpoint "M" between ball "A" and the intended pocket "P"; draw a line through the midpoint to the corner pocket where the two banking rails meet (pocket "E"); shoot into the rail parallel to line "ME". Note that the path of ball "A" is an equal distance (distance "s")

from the midpoint line both going to the first cushion and coming off the second cushion. This makes the system easy to use when shooting a kick shot.

Figure 10-15 shows how the two-rail parallel system can be used to kick into another

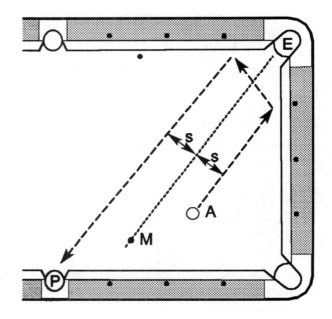

FIGURE 10-14. The parallel system used for a two-rail bank shot.

128

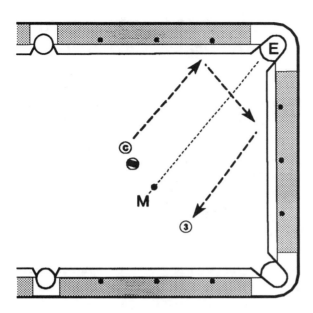

FIGURE 10-15. The parallel system used for a two-rail kick shot.

RAIL TRACK SYSTEM

The *rail track system* is one of the simplest and easiest to use of all the banking systems. An example of this system is shown in figure 10-16, to implement:

1. Find point "A" which is perpendicular to the ball and on the rail track opposite the banking cushion.
2. Determine the midpoint "M" between the ball and point "A". 3. Draw a line from the opposite pocket (pocket "E") through the midpoint to the rail track (point "B").
4. Draw a line from point "B" through the ball to the opposite rail track (point "G"). Point "G" is the geometric banking point and line "BG" represents the banking direction.

ball. Find the midpoint "M" between the cue ball and the ball to be kicked (3-ball). Draw line "ME" from the midpoint to the corner pocket where the banking rails meet; shoot into the rail parallel to line "ME". Note: The midpoint line can be drawn to any of the four corner pockets allowing several options for the two-rail kick shot.

Although the two-rail parallel system is geometrically correct, in reality, the ball comes off the second rail moving away from the midpoint line. This error is caused by several variables which will be discussed in detail later. For kick shots, a correction for the error can sometimes be made by using english. The slower the shot and/or the smaller the angle of incidence, the less english that is required. When this system is used to shoot an object ball two rails, obviously english can't be used to correct for the variables; in these cases the error must be anticipated and the banking point moved closer to the pocket at the end of the midpoint line.

As with some of the other systems, it's easier to visualize if the cue stick is used to represent one of the lines. Hold the stick over point "M" with the tip pointed toward pocket "E". Point "B" is where the stick crosses the rail track. Sight from point "B" over the ball to

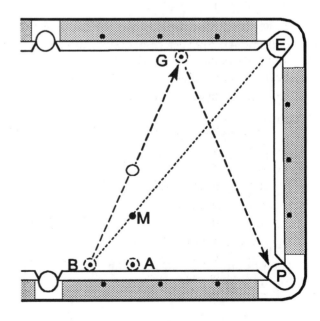

FIGURE 10-16. Rail track system.

find point "G" on the rail track or to some other reference point on the cushion, rail, or beyond. Another technique can be used in the case of a kick shot; hold the butt of the stick over point "B" as the ball is being addressed. Aim will automatically be at point "G".

This system principally indicates direction and is therefore applicable even when the ball is at or near the banking cushion.

ROTE SYSTEM

All the previously discussed banking systems help to determine the geometric banking point and/or the direction the ball must be shot. After executing a particular bank shot many times it is no longer necessary to divide angles, imagine lines, points, etc. For example, in practicing a particular bank shot; one of the systems can be used to determine the banking point. After shooting the same shot several times it will not be necessary go through the same analysis each time; it will be remembered from the previous analysis. This is essentially what the *rote system* is; many bank shots are shot often enough so that their banking points are committed to memory.

Most professional pool players use the rote system. Any player that plays long enough and often enough will build up a memory bank of bank shots. This means less and less analysis will be required. This system is learned by constant practice. The only way it can be maintained is by repeatedly refreshing the memory with more practice.

The greatest advantage of this system is that it automatically corrects for all the variables that will be discussed shortly. The worst thing about this system is that it can't be passed on to another player. The greatest players in the world can pass on their knowledge but not their memories.

VARIABLES AFFECTING ANGLE OF REBOUND

Most books on pool state that "*the angle of rebound is equal to the angle of incidence.*" If this were true the geometric banking point would be the proper banking point and we could go on to the next chapter. Unfortunately, the rebound angle is usually *not* equal to the angle of incidence.

There are three variables that affect angle of rebound: (1) cushion distortion, causing rebound angle to be larger, (2) roll, causing the effective rebound angle to be smaller, and (3) english, which affects the rebound angle in several ways. Each of these variables will be examined in detail.

Cushion distortion--When a ball with no spin or rotation runs into a cushion the angle of rebound is larger than the angle of incidence. This is due to the mechanical distortion of the cushion as the ball compresses the rubber. Figure 10-17 diagrammatically depicts the lines of force within the cushion. Note that there is a greater force trying to push the ball back in the direction from which it came than in the

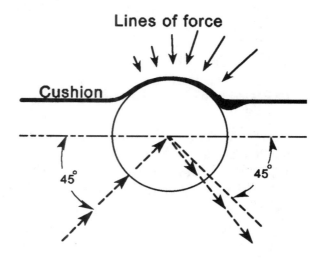

FIGURE 10-17. Cushion distortion causes the rebound angle to be larger than the angle of incidence.

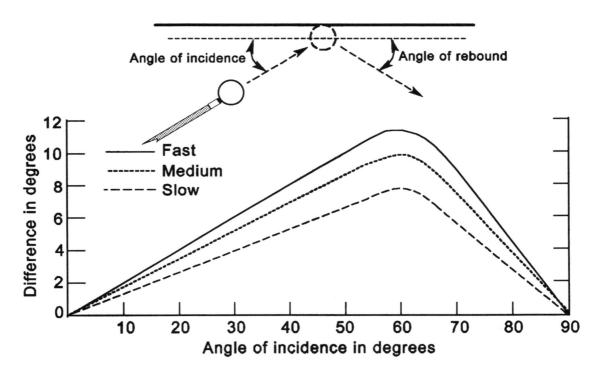

**FIGURE 10-18. Difference between angles of incidence and rebound
due to cushion distortion.**

direction of the rebound path. The resultant of these forces causes the rebound angle to be larger than the angle of incidence.

The difference between incidence and rebound varies with the speed of the ball and the angle of incidence. As the speed is increased the ball sinks deeper into the cushion. This causes a greater imbalance of forces which results in a larger disparity of angles. Figure 10-18 shows the difference between incidence and rebound at different speeds and angles (assuming the ball has no spin or rotation). As indicated, the difference becomes larger as the angle of incidence increases to about 60 degrees, then it begins to decrease.

Figure 10-19 shows an example of using cushion distortion to one's advantage. Ball "A" cannot be shot directly at the geometric banking point because the 1-ball is blocking its path. However, if ball "A" is struck very hard, the rebound angle will be larger than the angle of incidence allowing it to strike the cushion to

the left of the geometric banking point. In so doing, the 1-ball can be avoided while successfully banking ball "A" into the opposite side pocket. In banking ball "B", the angle of incidence cannot be made smaller because the 2-ball is in the way. Therefore, ball "B" must be struck as slowly as possible in order to keep the rebound angle as small as possible.

Roll--When a ball strikes a cushion it is generally rolling in the direction of its original path. Upon striking the cushion it loses some of its roll due to friction between ball and cushion. If the ball has enough rotation, some will remain after it rebounds from the cushion. This rotation causes the ball to curve as shown in figure 10-20. The arrows represent the force caused by roll. The force is greatest as the ball leaves the cushion and diminishes as it is converted to direction change (curve).

The amount of curve depends on the amount of rotation the ball has as it leaves the

131

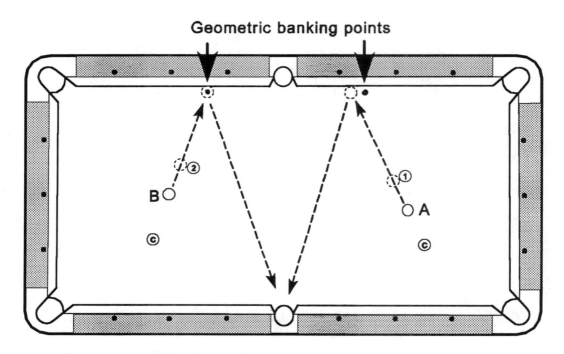

FIGURE 10-19. Cushion distortion can be used to help make ball A.

cushion. The shape of the curve depends on its speed. The amount of roll that a ball has when it strikes the cushion depends on its travel distance and how hard it is struck. The principles of normal roll apply; the harder a ball is struck the greater the distance required to obtain normal roll. If two balls an equal distance from the cushion are banked at medium and fast speeds, the one that is struck hardest will curve less because it has less time to accumulate roll before striking the cushion.

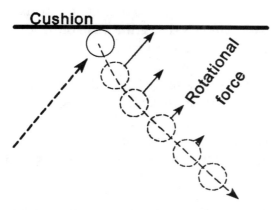

FIGURE 10-20. Curve caused by roll.

When a ball is shot slow or very slow, most of the roll is lost on the cushion and therefore the resulting curve is insignificant.

The speed at which a ball comes off the cushion determines the arc of the curve. A ball that is moving slowly will curve nearer the cushion and will have a smaller arc than a fast moving ball. Since the rebound path is curved, it is difficult to quantify and describe in terms of rebound angle deviation. In this analysis the rebound angle will be considered the same as the effective rebound angle (figure 10-21) measured after the ball has moved 3 feet from the cushion.

Figure 10-22 shows the difference between the angles of incidence and rebound caused by normal roll at medium speed. Most experienced players generally shoot bank shots at medium to fast speed. This doesn't allow the ball to accumulate much roll before striking the cushion. Figure 10-23 (figure 5-2 repeated here for convenience) shows the distance required for a ball to attain normal roll at various speeds. If the ball doesn't have normal roll, only a portion of the difference shown in figure

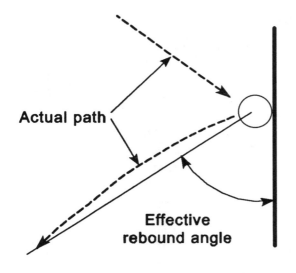

FIGURE 10-21. Effective rebound angle.

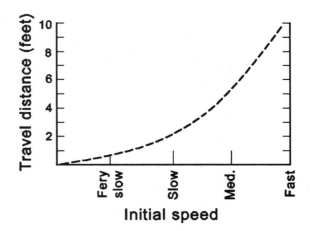

FIGURE 10-23. Distance required for a ball to attain normal roll.

10-22 will apply. For example, assume an object ball is 2 feet from the cushion and requires a 60-degree angle of incidence. If it is shot at medium speed it will have about 35 percent of normal roll (figure 10-23) when it strikes the cushion. With normal roll the deviation of rebound angle would be 5 degrees (figure 10-22); with only 35 percent of normal roll the deviation will be only 1.8 degrees (0.35 x 5 = 1.8). If it is shot at a fast speed the deviation will be less than 1 degree. Shooting bank shots at a very fast or very slow speed reduces the complications caused by roll.

English--English, relative to bank shots, is of four different types: (1) cue-ball english, (2) collision-induced english, (3) cushion-induced english, and (4) transferred english. Each of these types of english were discussed in Chapter 6. How each affects bank shots will be examined here.

Cue-ball english: Cue-ball english is the

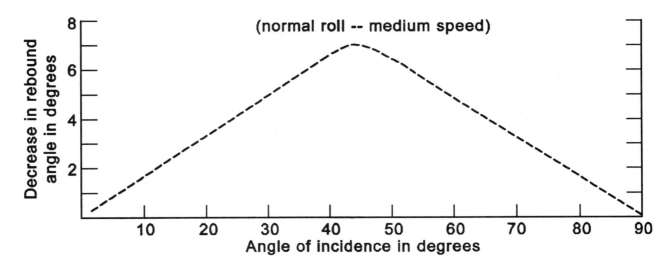

FIGURE 10-22. Decrease in rebound angle caused by normal roll.

english imparted to the cue ball by striking it off-center with the cue stick. Top and bottom english have no significant application in bank shots, side english does. The major practical application of side english is with kick shots. An example of using side english to make a kick shot is shown in figure 10-24. The object ball (1-ball) is near the pocket but can't be shot directly in because of an intervening ball. Another intervening ball is blocking the cue ball's path to the geometric banking point (point "A"). To avoid striking the intervening ball, the angle of incidence must be increased and the rebound angle decreased. The cue ball must be shot to point "b" using right side english to reduce the rebound angle. Another intervening ball is blocking the geometric banking point (point "D") for a kick shot at the 2-ball. However, the shot can be made by shooting at point "e" using left english, or shot at point "f" using right english.

When the cue ball is shot perpendicular into the cushion, 100 percent side english produces

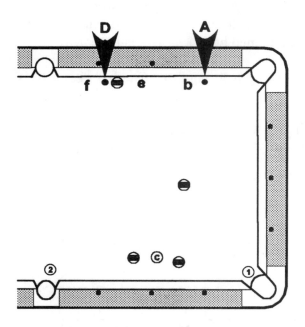

FIGURE 10-24. When the geometric banking point can't be struck, english can be used to help make a kick shot.

about 30 percent change in rebound angle. The smaller the angle of incidence, the less effect side english has on rebound angle. The amount of side required to cause the desired change of rebound angle is easier to learn by rote than by analytical explanation.

Note: The deviation of rebound angle, caused by side english, varies depending on the surface characteristic of the ball and cushion; and therefore may vary somewhat from table to table.

A word of caution; never use side english on a kick shot unless it is absolutely necessary. Many players are good at regular bank shots but have difficulty with kick shots. This is usually because they are inadvertently applying side english or otherwise misusing side english. When shooting a kick shot, always double check the striking point on the cue ball before executing the shot. More kick shots are missed by striking the cue ball incorrectly than by aim error or miscalculating the banking point.

Collision-induced english: When a ball is struck at an angle by another ball, it picks up some side english from the collision. This english is called *collision-induced english*. When the cue ball strikes an object ball head-on, no english is imparted to the object ball. As the cut angle increases (up to about 30 degrees) the amount of english increases. At cut angles over 30 degrees, friction between the two balls begins to decline and so does collision-induced english. The amount of collision-induced english is small in comparison to the side english that can be imparted to the cue ball by a cue stick. Therefore, collision-induced english can generally be ignored except in calculating the rebound angle of a bank shot.

Figure 10-25 shows how collision-induced english affects the rebound path of an object ball. When the cue ball is shot from position "A" it collides head-on into the object ball imparting no collision-induced english and the object ball rebounds along path "a". If the cue

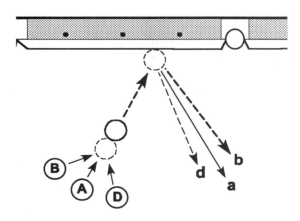

FIGURE 10-25. Collision-induced english affects rebound angle.

ball is shot from position "B" it will impart the equivalent of right side (running) english to the object ball causing it to rebound along path "b". If the cue ball is shot from position "D" it will impart the equivalent of left side (reverse) english causing the object ball to rebound along path "d".

The maximum deviation of the rebound angle, caused by collision-induced english at various cut angles, is shown in figure 10-26a. This assumes that the angle of incidence is 90 degrees (perpendicular to cushion). As indicated, the maximum deviation of rebound angle is about 5 degrees at a cut angle of 30 degrees. (Maximum deviation will vary somewhat depending on ball-to-ball friction).

If the angle of incidence is less than 90 degrees, the deviation of rebound angle will be less than that shown in figure 10-26a. Deviation varies slightly depending on whether the english is running or reverse; however, the difference is small and can be ignored. Figure 10-26b shows how much (average of running and reverse) the deviation of rebound angle is reduced at angles of incidence between 30 and 90 degrees. For example, if the angle of incidence is 60 degrees, the deviation of rebound angle is about 75 percent of the maximum shown in figure 10-26a. Consider a bank shot where the object ball has to be cut

25 degrees and the angle of incidence is 60 degrees. A cut angle of 25 degrees causes the rebound angle to deviate 4 degrees at an incidence angle of 90 degrees (figure 10-26a); at 60 degrees the deviation is only 75 percent of that or 3 degrees (0.75 x 4 = 3).

Collision-induced english starts out as spin on a vertical axis; as soon as the ball starts moving, friction between ball and cloth causes the axis to tilt to the side. Effective side english diminishes as the axis tilts. For this reason, most of the english is lost in the first few inches of travel. Figure 10-26c shows how much collision-induced english remains on the object ball as it moves away from the point of collision (at medium speed). English diminishes rapidly at first; as travel distance increases, english dissipates at a slower rate. After about 6 inches only 50 percent of the initial english remains on the ball.

Figure 10-27 shows three examples of computing the deviation of rebound angle caused by collision-induced english. In example (a) the cut angle is 60 degrees. Figure 10-26a indicates a maximum deviation of 2.5 degrees; at an angle of incidence of 60 degrees, deviation is about 75 percent of maximum or 1.9 degrees (0.75 x 2.5 = 1.9). The object ball is 4.0 inches from the cushion, therefore about 55 percent of the english will remain on the ball at the time of impact with the cushion; this reduces deviation to about 1 degree (0.55 x 1.9 = 1.0). The english is equivalent to running english which causes the rebound angle to be reduced by 1 degree. In example (b), the maximum deviation at a cut angle of 40 degrees is about 4.0 degrees. This is reduced to 3.2 degrees due to angle of incidence and further reduced to 1.6 degrees due to distance from cushion. The english is equivalent to reverse english which increases the rebound angle. In example (c), the maximum deviation for a 50-degree cut angle is 3.3 degrees; this is reduced to 1.9 degrees due to angle of incidence. In this example there is no

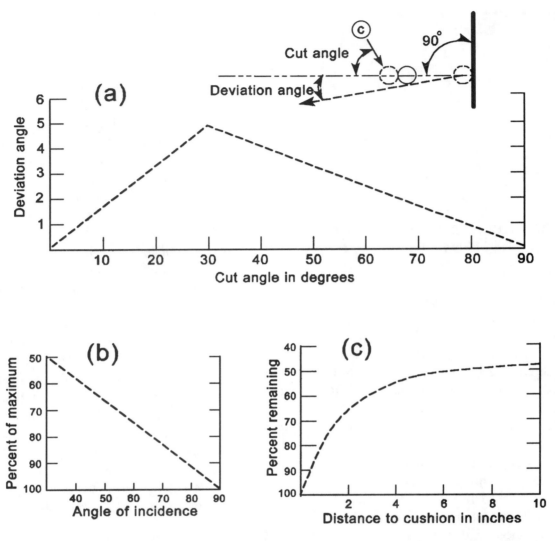

FIGURE 10-26. The effect of cushion-induced english depends on cut angle, angle of incidence, and distance to cushion.

correction for distance from cushion because the object ball is touching the cushion.

It is obvious that calculating rebound angle deviation due to collision-induced english is complicated; one must consider cut angle, angle of incidence, and distance to cushion. It would be nice if the effects of collision-induced english could be alleviated. Well, HALLELUJAH!! It *can* be alleviated. If the proper amount of side english is applied to the cue ball there will be no collision-induced english. The two balls will make contact like meshing gears, therefore no torque forces and no english. If the object ball is cut to the left, right side english must be applied to the cue ball. Conversely, if it is cut to the right, left english must be used. The percentage of maximum side english that must be applied to the cue ball is equal to twice the cut angle (in degrees). For example, if the object ball must be cut 20 degrees to the right, about 40 percent of maximum left english must be applied. Negating collision-induced english can be practiced by placing a striped ball on the foot

136

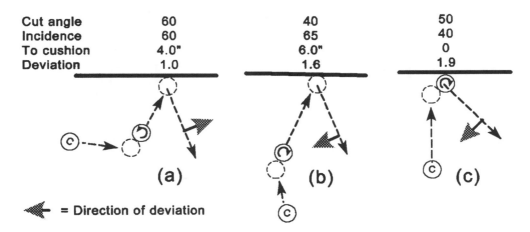

Cut angle	60	40	50
Incidence	60	65	40
To cushion	4.0"	6.0"	0
Deviation	1.0	1.6	1.9

(a)   (b)   (c)

= Direction of deviation

FIGURE 10-27. Calculating the effects of collision-induced english.

spot with its stripe parallel to the side rails. Shoot it toward the center of the head rail at various cut angles. If it rolls on its stripe the proper english was applied and collision-induced english was successfully negated.

Whenever possible, cue ball english should be used to avoid the effect of collision-induced english when shooting bank shots. There will be situations when it can't be used due to cue ball positioning considerations. Therefore, a few hypothetical bank shots should be analyzed occasionally so that the effects of cut angle, angle of incidence, and distance to cushion are brought to focus.

Cushion-induced english: When a ball strikes a cushion at an angle the cushion imparts english to the ball. This english is called *cushion-induced english* and is equivalent to side english. Cushion-induced english can generally be ignored because the ball comes off the cushion and *hopefully* goes into a pocket. However, cushion-induced english must be considered if the ball is to strike a second cushion.

In figure 10-28, the cue ball is near corner pocket "M". It is shot (center-ball) at the rail track adjacent to the first diamond on the opposite rail. If the angle of rebound would

equal the angle of incidence the ball would strike the cushion at positions 1, 2, 3, and go into side pocket "N". In reality this does *not* happen, its actual path is similar to that shown in figure 10-29. After striking position 1, it rebounds to position 4 which is short of the second diamond due to the effect of cushion

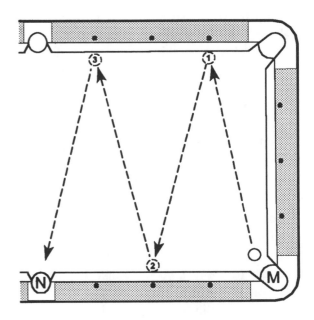

FIGURE 10-28. Theoretical path of a ball assuming rebound equals incidence.

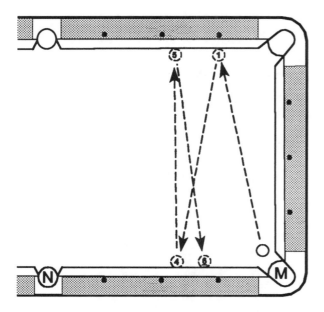

**FIGURE 10-29. Actual rebound path
of a ball that is struck hard.**

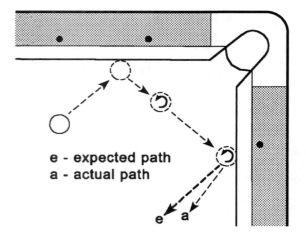

e - expected path
a - actual path

**FIGURE 10-30. The rebound angle
off the second cushion is affected
by cushion-induced english.**

distortion. The cushion-induced english picked up at position 1 causes it to rebound to position 5, then to position 6.

Figure 10-30 shows what happens when a ball strikes two adjacent cushions. The ball picks up some cushion-induced english at the first cushion which, in this case, is equivalent to right side english. This english takes affect when the ball strikes the second cushion causing the rebound angle to be smaller than it would otherwise be. Note that the effect of cushion-induced english, acting on the second cushion, is opposite to that of cushion distortion. At various combinations of incidence and speed the effect of either may be dominant, or they may cancel each other.

In the case of a two-cushion kick shot, the use of running english helps to negate the cushion distortion effect on the first cushion and cushion-induced english helps negate

cushion distortion on the second cushion. If all these forces are equal the two-cushion parallel system will work perfect without additional corrections.

Transferred english: When an object ball is struck by a cue ball that has english, a small portion of that english is transferred to the object ball. The english transferred to the object ball is opposite to that of the cue ball. For example, if the cue ball has right side english the object ball will pick up left side english. The amount of transferred english is small and can generally be ignored except for bank shots with high angles of incidence.

Maximum rebound angle deviation resulting from transferred english is about 4 or 5 degrees. This varies somewhat depending on ball surface and consequent ball-to-ball friction. The maximum transferred english decreases rapidly as cut angle increases. At cut angles over 30 degrees, the transferred english is insignificant and can be ignored.

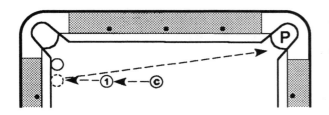

FIGURE 10-31. Using transferred english to make a bank shot.

Rebound angle deviation caused by transferred english can be used to make some bank shots that could not otherwise be made. Figure 10-31 shows such an example. The 1-ball can't be banked into corner pocket "P" because an intervening ball is blocking its normal rebound path. The shot can be made by applying maximum left english to the cue ball and striking the 1-ball head-on. The left english will throw (english-induced throw) the 1-ball a little to the right and will transfer right english to the 1-ball. The right english will lessen the rebound angle causing the ball to go into corner pocket "P". Some players prefer to use english-induced throw and transfer of english on all bank shots with low cut angles. Being able to strike the object ball head-on, or nearly so, offers an easier target; and varying the amount of side english can be easier than varying the cut angle. When playing exclusively with familiar equipment this technique works fairly well. However, if one plays with a variety of equipment the technique may fail due to several variables. Variable ball-to-ball friction, depending on the balls being used, varies the collision-induced throw and transferred english. Variable ball-to-cushion friction will cause the rebound angle to vary. These and other variables must be taken into consideration when deciding whether or not to use side english as an aid in banking a shot.

DETERMINING NET REBOUND ERROR

Before a correction can be applied to the angle of incidence the net error of the rebound angle must be determined. Deviation of rebound angle caused by english on the cue ball in kick shots, and transferred english on the object ball are not considered errors because they are generally purposely applied. Net error is the sum of the errors caused by cushion distortion, roll, and collision-induced english. As shown in figure 10-32, if the error causes the rebound angle to be <u>larger</u> than the angle of incidence, it has a <u>positive</u> (+) value; if it causes the rebound angle to be <u>smaller</u>, it has a <u>negative</u> (-) value. Cushion distortion always

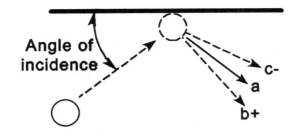

a Assumed if rebound equals incidence

b Error is positive making rebound larger

c Error is negative making rebound smaller

FIGURE 10-32. Net rebound error can be positive or negative.

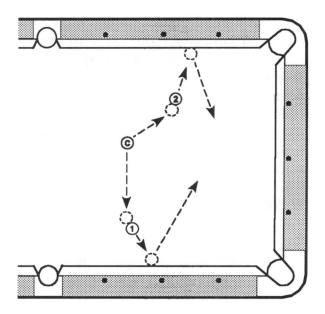

FIGURE 10-33. Typical bank shots (analyzed in Table 10-1).

causes the rebound angle to be larger, therefore it always has a positive value; conversely, error caused by roll is always negative. Since these errors are opposite in value they tend to decrease net error. The error caused by collision-induced english can be either positive or negative depending on cut direction relative to the angle of incidence.

Figure 10-33 shows two bank shots. Table

10-1 shows how net error is calculated.

CORRECTING ANGLE OF INCIDENCE

After determining the net error of the rebound angle, a correction must be applied to the angle of incidence. The sign of the correction must be opposite to the sign of the net error. As shown in figure 10-34, if the angle of incidence must be made larger (to correct for a negative net error) it is given a positive value; if it must be made smaller (to correct for a positive net error) it is given a negative value.

It would seem that if the net rebound error is (x) degrees, then the angle of incidence could simply be corrected by (x) degrees in the opposite direction. Unfortunately, it is not that simple. When the angle of incidence is changed the ball strikes the cushion at a different point which must be taken into consideration. If the ball is at the banking cushion the banking point will not change even when the incidence angle is changed. Therefore, the angle of incidence must be corrected the total amount (100 percent) of the net rebound error. As the distance between ball and banking cushion increases, a smaller percentage of the net error

		1-ball	2-ball
Data	Shot speed	medium	medium
	Cut angle	30	45
	Incidence angle	60	70
	Distance to cushion	9"	11"
Errors	Cushion distortion	+10	+8
	Roll	-.5	-.3
	Collision-induced english	+1.9	-1.6
	Net error	+11.4	+6.1

TABLE 10-1. Error analysis of the bank shots shown in Figure 10-33.

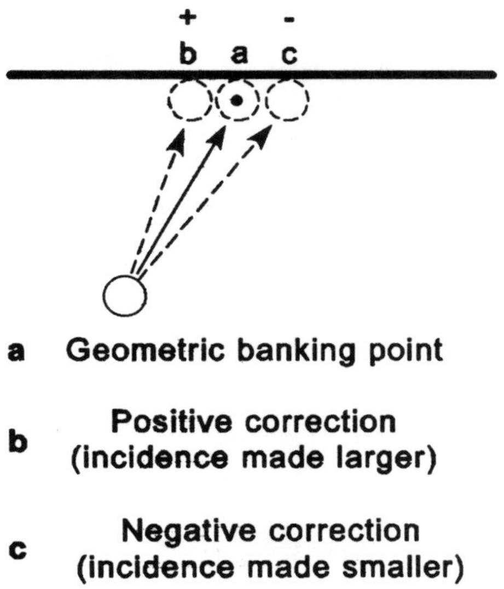

+   -
b a c

a   Geometric banking point

b   Positive correction
        (incidence made larger)

c   Negative correction
        (incidence made smaller)

FIGURE 10-34. Net error correction.

is required. As shown in figure 10-35, when the ball is at the opposite cushion only 50 percent of the net rebound error is applied to the angle of incidence. When the object ball is between these two extremes an interpolated percentage of the net error must be applied. This

correction system is not mathematically perfect but is reasonably close without being unreasonably complicated.

Figure 10-35 shows two typical bank shots. Assume that it has been determined that the net rebound error for ball "A" is +8.5 degrees. The interpolated percentage of net error, to be applied to the angle of incidence, is about 85 percent or 7.2 degrees (0.85 x 8.5 = 7.2). Since the net error has a positive value the correction must have a negative value. The angle of incidence to the geometric banking point is 65 degrees; 65 degrees minus the correction results in a corrected angle of incidence of 57.8 degrees (65 - 7.2 = 57.8). Assume the net rebound error for ball "B" is +1.2 degrees. The interpolated correction that must be applied to the angle of incidence is 70 percent. Therefore the correction is -0.84 degree (0.70 x 1.2 = 0.84). The angle of incidence to the geometric banking point is 85 degrees. Therefore the corrected angle of incidence is 84 degrees (85 - 0.84 = 84.2).

Once the correction is known it can be

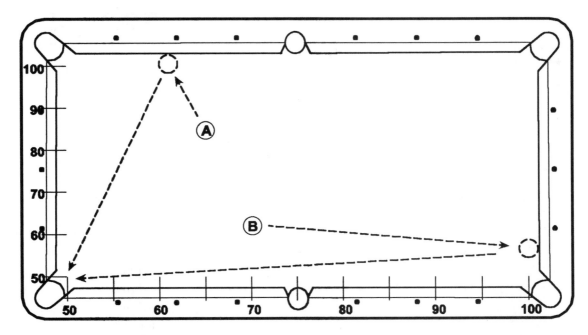

FIGURE 10-35. The proper percentage of net error that must be applied to the angle of incidence depends on how far the ball is from the banking cushion.

applied directly to the angle of incidence. The cue stick can be used to facilitate the application of the correction; figure 10-36 demonstrates the technique. After the geometric banking point and correction to angle of incidence have been determined, proceed as follows:

1. Place the tip of the stick on the table as close as possible to the ball to be banked.
2. Aim the stick directly at the geometric banking point.
3. Move the butt end of the stick 1 inch for

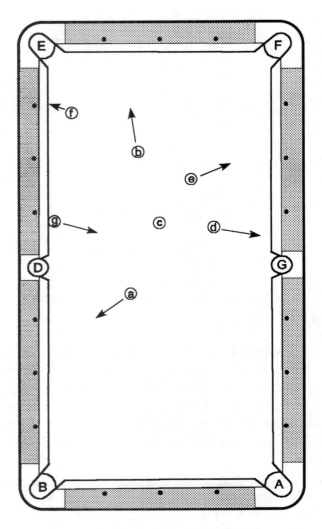

FIGURE 10-37. Typical bank shots (analyzed in Table 10-2).

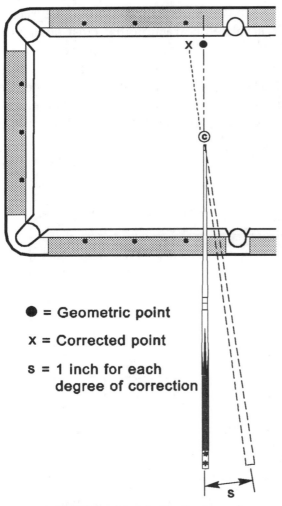

● = Geometric point

x = Corrected point

s = 1 inch for each degree of correction

FIGURE 10-36. Technique for applying a correction to the angle of incidence.

every degree of correction required.
4. Observe where the corrected stick alignment crosses the rail track. That is the corrected banking point and direction.

Figure 10-37 shows six typical bank shots. Table 10-2 shows the data for, and the analysis of, each shot at medium and slow speeds. Note that all the shots made at the slower speed require less correction; this is because cushion distortion is smaller at the slower speed.

Ball and pocket	Angle of incidence	Cut angle	Object ball to cushion	Speed	Cushion distortion	Roll	Collision english	Net error	Applicable percentage	Incidence correction
a-A	57	43	18"	slow	+6.0	0	-1.3	+4.7	83	+3.9
				med.	+9.7	-1.4	-1.3	+7.0	83	+5.8
b-B	80	6	19"	slow	+2.0	0	-0.4	+1.6	89	+1.4
				med.	+3.5	-0.4	-0.4	+2.7	89	+2.4
d-D	80	12	11"	slow	+2.0	0	+1.0	+3.0	87	+2.6
				med.	+3.5	-0.3	+1.0	+4.2	87	+3.6
e-E	65	42	16"	slow	+5.0	0	-1.4	+3.6	82	+3.0
				med.	+9.0	-1.0	-1.4	+6.6	82	+5.4
f-F	75	42	4"	slow	+3.0	0	-1.9	+1.1	95	+1.0
				med.	+5.5	0	-1.9	+3.6	95	+3.4
g-G	78	15	0	slow	+2.5	0	+2.2	+4.7	100	+4.7
				med.	+4.5	0	+2.2	+6.7	100	+6.7

TABLE 10-2. Analysis of the bank shots shown in Figure 10-37.

CUSHION REBOUND EFFICIENCY

Cushion rebound efficiency, or simply *cushion efficiency,* refers to the ability of the cushion to preserve the linear motion of a ball after it rebounds from the cushion. It is determined by comparing the distance the ball travels after striking the cushion to the distance it would have traveled had it not struck the cushion and is expressed as a percent. For example, if a ball is going sufficiently fast to travel 10 feet past the cushion but rebounds only 4 feet, the cushion has a rebound efficiency of 40 percent.

As the angle of incidence decreases, cushion efficiency increases. Figure 10-38 shows the rebound efficiency for an unpolished ball on an average table. The efficiency decreases from 100 percent at zero angle of incidence to about 40 percent at 90 degrees. The main reason the cushion is so inefficient at high incident angles is because the ball loses the energy contained in its forward roll (rotation). Roll accounts for 28.6 percent of a ball's total energy (assuming normal roll). Additional energy losses are caused by friction between ball and cushion, and between ball and cloth.

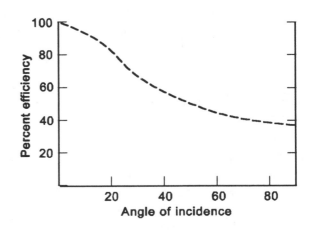

FIGURE 10-38. Rebound efficiency expressed as a percent.

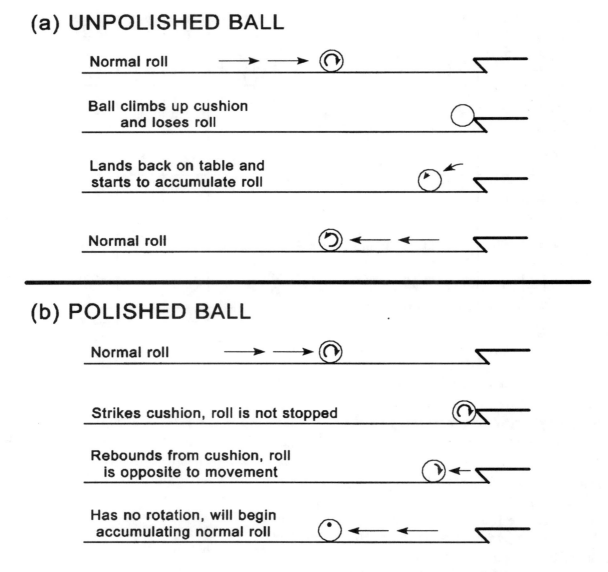

(a) UNPOLISHED BALL

Normal roll

Ball climbs up cushion
and loses roll

Lands back on table and
starts to accumulate roll

Normal roll

(b) POLISHED BALL

Normal roll

Strikes cushion, roll is not stopped

Rebounds from cushion, roll
is opposite to movement

Has no rotation, will begin
accumulating normal roll

FIGURE 10-39. Rebound efficiency is less for a polished ball because its rotation is opposite to its direction after rebounding from the cushion.

A well-used unpolished ball will react differently than a smooth polished ball when it strikes a cushion, this is due to friction differences. Figure 10-39a shows what happens when an unpolished ball with normal roll runs into a cushion. The rotation causes the ball to climb up on the cushion (jump). High friction between ball and cushion causes the rotation to be stopped and the ball bounces back with little or no rotation. As it moves away from the cushion it accumulates roll until at some point it will attain normal roll. Figure 10-39b shows what happens when a polished ball with normal roll runs into a cushion. The ball does not climb up the cushion; it rebounds from the cushion while still rotating toward the cushion. This causes it to slow down. At some point the rotation stops and it begins to rotate in the direction in which it is moving. Because rotation is initially opposite to its movement, it rebounds a shorter distance. Consequently, the cushion is viewed as being less efficient. With a slow shot (one table length and rebound one table length) a polished ball will rebound about 1.5 to 2 feet less than an unpolished ball.

Friction between ball and cushion also varies due to the surface condition of the cushion. Chalk or other gritty substances increase friction causing the ball to jump and cushion efficiency to increase. Conversely, if the cushion has talcum powder or other slippery substances on it, rebound efficiency will be less.

SUMMARY OF BANK SHOTS

By this time you're probably wondering how anyone could ever make a bank shot because of all the variables and complications involved. It doesn't seem likely that anyone could remember all the charts and graphs necessary to analyze a bank shot when one is encountered while playing. Fact is, most can't. Therefore one must condition the mind to make an accurate estimate of the proper banking point and angle of incidence. Conditioning the mind can be done by analyzing many bank shots on paper. The more bank shots that are analyzed on paper, the more accurate one's estimates will become. To conduct a paper analysis proceed as follows:

1. Sketch a table with a few object balls and cue ball in random positions.
2. Decide on a speed for the shot.
3. Estimate the position of the geometric banking point and corrected banking point and/or angle of incidence.
4. Determine the geometric banking point using one or more of the banking systems.
5. First estimate then calculate effects of:
   (a) cushion distortion
   (b) roll
   (c) collision-induced english
   (d) net error
   (e) correction to angle of incidence

6. Compare the corrected banking point and angle of incidence to your original estimate.

Repeat the paper exercise using different ball positions until your estimates are the same as your calculations. Analyze the same bank shots executed at different speeds to familiarize yourself with the effect of speed. Those people that don't play very often must rely on analysis to make bank shots. The more one plays, the more the rote system can be used which relies on memory rather than analysis.

Balls do not bank the same on all tables. Some of the table variables that affect bank shots are:

1. Rubber in the cushions - the type and age of the rubber affects its rebounding characteristics.
2. Cloth on cushion - the wear and stretch of the cloth affects ball - cushion friction which alters the effects of roll and english.
3. Table inertia - the heavier the table the more efficient the cushions.
4. Loose rails - poorly attached rails lose the inertia effect causing the cushions to be less efficient (dead).
5. Misaligned rails - occasionally, opposite rails are not parallel to each other; two-piece side rails may not be assembled straight.
6. Height of cushion - the higher the cushion the less efficient it is, and height also effects cushion-induced english.

Before playing any serious pool on a strange table, be sure to check the rails. Shoot a series of bank shots at different angles to determine if the cushions have any strange quirks.

CHAPTER 11

MISCELLANEOUS SHOTS

There are several other shots that have not been discussed which warrant individual attention. They are: *POWER BREAK SHOTS, LAG SHOTS, SPOT SHOTS, JUMP SHOTS,* and *CURVE* and *MASSÉ SHOTS.* Each will be examined here.

POWER BREAK SHOTS

The *power break shot* is a shot in which the cue ball is propelled as hard as possible into the racked balls. The three principal games in which the power break is used are EIGHT-BALL, NINE-BALL, and ROTATION. The greater the player's skill level, the more important the power break shot becomes. Assume you and your opponent run an average of 1.5 balls per inning (turn at table). If you fail to make a ball on the break you're behind 1.5 balls at the start; if you average 5 balls per inning, you're effectively 5 balls behind.

The three main objectives of the power break shot are: (1) pocket as many balls as possible, (2) scatter the balls, and (3) position the cue ball for the next shot.

Variables--Several variables make the power break somewhat unpredictable. They include resiliency of the balls, ball surface irregularities, cushion efficiency, and ball configuration in the rack.

The resiliency of the balls determines how fast and how far they bounce off each other. Resiliency varies somewhat depending on the type of plastic used in fabricating the balls. As balls become older they develop microscopic stress fractures which tend to reduce resiliency.

Ball surface impurities or irregularities tend to make the break shot unpredictable. The reaction of the balls when they collide depends largely on the friction between their surfaces. The next time you play, examine a few balls very closely. Check for manufacturer defects, nicks and scratches from being knocked off the table; and smudges from finger prints, chalk, powder, or other contaminants. The way these surface irregularities come together when the balls are racked determines (to a large extent) how they will react to the break shot.

Cushion efficiency determines how much of the ball's speed is retained after striking a cushion. The greater the ball speed, the greater the travel distance; the farther each ball travels, the greater the chance of it going into a pocket.

When the balls are racked they should all be in contact with each other. If they're loose, the shock wave will not propagate uniformly through the entire pack. This means that the balls will tend to rebound back into each other resulting in a loss of kinetic energy.

Aim point-- Ideally, all of the energy contained in the cue ball should be transferred to the racked balls on impact. If the cue ball moves after impacting the pack, it did not transfer all of its energy. The only way to keep the cue ball from moving after impact is for it to strike another ball head-on. The only ball that can be struck head-on is the first ball in the pack, therefore the cue ball must be aimed for the center of the first ball.

Cue ball placement-- The only legal requirement is that the cue ball be positioned behind the head string. Beyond that, logic must dictate where the cue ball is placed. Three things that must be taken into consideration in deciding on a cue ball placement are: (1) cue ball approach direction, (2) aim accuracy, and (3) bridge type. In each specific type of game there are other unique considerations.

From what direction should the pack be broken up? Even the experts disagree; when experts on a subject disagree there is generally some validity for each opinion. If there is an argument for each position then perhaps it doesn't make much difference. And, so it is with the power break shot. The cue ball approach direction does not significantly affect the scattering of the balls. (In the game of NINE-BALL the placement of the cue ball may increase the odds of pocketing the front ball and/or a corner ball). Statistically speaking, there is a slightly smaller chance of scratching (cue ball going into a pocket) when the cue ball approaches from the center of the table.

The closer the cue ball is to the racked balls the more accurately the first ball in the pack can be struck. This would dictate that the cue ball be placed the shortest distance from the pack or just behind the head string in the center of the table. If the cue ball is positioned at the side rail it will have to travel about 6 inches

farther. By increasing the distance 6 inches, any error in striking point will be increased by about 15 percent. An error of 0.1 inch at the pack would be increased by 0.015 inch. This aim error magnification is small but is something to consider.

In selecting a cue ball placement, the type of bridge to be used must be taken into consideration. There are three different bridge options; the normal bridge with bridge hand on the table surface, the side-rail bridge, and the end-rail bridge. The normal table bridge is the least stable. Any body movement while applying power is likely to affect the bridge hand. Or worse, maximum power won't be applied for fear of moving the bridge hand. The normal hand bridge must be used if the cue ball is to be placed adjacent to the head string more than about 6 inches from the side rail. The superior stability of the side or end rail bridge may be desirable because of the body movement associated with the power break shot. The end-rail bridge is probably easier to use and is more stable because the fingers can be wrapped around the edge of the cushion providing added stability. By gripping around the edge of the cushion the upper body can be pulled forward during the stroke which adds to the power. Even extreme body movement will not affect the stability of this bridge.

When an end-rail bridge is used, the cue ball must be placed some distance back from the head string so that it can be reached; this causes a slight loss of accuracy. However, the loss of accuracy is small and is more than gained back by the increased stability of the bridge. The cue ball should be placed **as far as possible** from the bridge while still allowing it to be struck accurately. This permits a longer stroke which allows more time for the stick to accelerate before striking the cue ball.

Cue ball reaction--Hopefully, a ball will be pocketed on the break, therefore cue ball position for the next shot must be considered.

Since it is not known where the balls are going to stop it's difficult to plan, in advance, the best cue ball position. Leaving the cue ball in the center of the table provides the greatest statistical probability of getting shape on another ball. Therefore, a little bottom english should be used so that the cue ball backs up to the center of the table after striking the pack. Breaking from the center of the table makes it easier to position the cue ball in the middle of the table. If the pack is broken from the side, the first ball would have to be struck off-center in order to bring the cue ball back to the center of the table. Having the cue ball in the center of the table has another advantage -- it is as far as it can be from all the pockets, therefore it would have to be struck fairly hard by another ball in order for it to be pocketed accidentally.

Consider some of the alternate breaking techniques that have been promulgated. Some advise using extreme top english so that the cue ball drives forward after striking the pack. Supposedly, the cue ball has a second chance at driving another ball into a pocket. There are several flaws in this reasoning. Putting extreme top english on the cue ball means that some of the energy contained in the stick was used to rotate the cue ball. This means that less energy was delegated to linear movement (less velocity). With top english the cue ball strikes the pack then stops. Most of the rotational energy is lost to friction as it spins on the cloth while trying to accelerate forward. This loss of energy decreases the change of pocketing a ball. And, there are more problems; after stopping, the cue ball never really gains enough speed to be of much help in knocking another ball into a pocket. It actually enters a zone where there are many balls moving collectively at a high velocity. It is quite likely that the cue ball will get in the way of a fast moving object ball, thereby reducing its speed and likelihood of going into a pocket. The cue ball is ricocheted about which increases its chance of going into a pocket.

Another popular break shot causes the cue ball to bounce straight up into the air after colliding with the pack. The reasoning is that while the cue ball is in the air it won't be struck by another ball and thus won't be knocked into a pocket. This is true, but this reduced risk is being paid for by a large energy loss. Assume the cue ball jumps one foot into the air; insurance is being bought for 0.5 second (the time the ball is in air); the energy loss is the equivalent of a ball rolling a distance of 75 feet (providing no cushions were struck). Statistically speaking, it is a poor trade-off. It would be better to take the extra rolling distance rather than the short term insurance.

Cue stick--Your normal playing stick should never be used for the power break. A good stick won't be damaged but the leather tip will flatten and harden prematurely.

Many players believe that using a heavier stick will produce a more powerful break. This may be true for some players but others may break better with a lighter stick. The optimum stick weight depends on the individual's physical stature and reflexes. As stick weight is increased its speed is reduced, and at some point the reduction in speed will cause total stick energy to decline. Generally speaking, the maximum stick velocity generated by a small quick person will diminish rapidly with increased stick weight. The stick velocity of a large muscular person will diminish less rapidly and therefore stick weight can be increased considerably before resulting in diminishing returns.

Cue stick energy is much more sensitive to stick speed than to stick weight. This is because energy increases linearly with weight but exponentially with speed. For example, if stick _weight_ is increased by 10 percent, total energy will increase by 10 percent; if stick _speed_ is increased by 10 percent, total energy will increase by about 20 percent. Another factor that must be considered is the efficiency

149

in which the energy of the stick is converted to cue ball velocity. Assume a freight train moving at 10 mph strikes a cue ball. The cue ball will be propelled away at about 10 mph. If the cue ball is struck by a baseball bat moving 20 mph the ball will be propelled away at nearly 20 mph. The train has thousands of times more energy (because of its massive weight) but it can't be transferred to the cue ball by a simple collision. Each individual should experiment with sticks of different weight, then use a stick weight that works best. The break-shot practice technique described in Chapter 13 can be used to gauge relative power.

The leather cue tip acts as a shock absorber in that it compresses and absorbs energy when it makes contact with the cue ball. It is not resilient, therefore it does not give this energy back as the cue ball leaves contact with the tip. This shock absorbing affect lessens the transfer of energy from the stick to the cue ball. For this reason, the tip of your break stick should be as <u>hard</u> and as <u>thin</u> as possible.

Stance and stroke--With the normal shooting stance, the chin should be fairly close to the stick. This allows for maximum aim accuracy and adequate power for most shots. The emphasis with the break shot is on **power**, therefore the body should be <u>more upright</u> allowing greater freedom of arm movement and extreme follow-through. The stick should be griped tighter and several inches closer to the butt end.

The cue stick should accelerate throughout the break stroke. At a distance of 6 inches the stick may be traveling 10 mph; at a distance of 10 inches it may be traveling 15 mph. Therefore, the bridge distance should be as <u>long</u> as possible to allow time for the stick to accelerate before striking the cue ball. Even a small increase in bridge distance will increase power considerably. The limiting factor is being able to strike the cue ball where desired.

The longer the bridge distance, the less accurately the cue ball can be struck. In practicing the break shot, the bridge distance should be increased in small increments until the cue ball is mis-struck about 10 percent of the time. In actual play, shorten this maximum bridge distance slightly to insure an accurate solid hit on the cue ball. Most players miscue less frequently when they have their <u>visual focus on the cue ball</u> during the stroke rather than on the pack.

The upper body should move forward during the execution of the power stroke. The distance moved doesn't have to be far as long as it is quick and coordinated with arm movement. Assume arm stroke speed is 15 mph; if the upper body is moved forward at a speed of 3 mph (walking speed) the speed of the stick will be increased by 20 percent. This 20 percent increase in stick speed means a 44 percent increase in stick energy. This translates into pocketing many additional balls on the break

Summary--Having the capability of a good power break gives the shooter a decided advantage. Always shoot for the center of the first ball in the pack. Cue ball placement is not critical but shooting from the middle of the table has some advantages. The power-break practice described in Chapter 13 can be used to determine your personal optimum cue stick weight and bridge distance. The various types of bridges should be experimented with to determine which produces greatest power and accuracy.

⚫   ⚫   ⚫

SPOT SHOTS

In some game situations the rules call for spotting (placing) the object ball on the foot spot and shooting at it from anywhere behind the head string; this is called a *spot shot*.

In determining the best cue ball placement, several options must be considered. Placing the cue ball in the center of the table adjacent to the head string offers the shortest possible shot, but the high cut angle requires great accuracy and judgment. Placing the cue ball adjacent to the head string at the side cushion presents the smallest cut angle, but this position makes striking the cue ball somewhat awkward. Most players place the cue ball adjacent to the head string about one or two ball diameters from the side rail. Shooting from this position requires a balance of judgment and ability. Players that play regularly maintain fairly good judgment and therefore are able to make the spot shot from this position. However, judgment capability diminishes quickly if a person doesn't play regularly. For those people, there is a better way to shoot a spot shot -- one that doesn't require judgment.

Place the cue ball such that the spot shot can be made using a half-ball hit. The aiming point will be the edge of the object ball, therefore no judgment need be used while aiming. Figure 11-1 shows how to determine the proper cue ball position for the half-ball hit. Sight from the center of the corner pocket to the center of the foot spot. Place the cue ball on this line-of sight immediately behind the head string.

This same cue ball position can be used in another respect. Assume that both corner pockets, at the foot of the table, are blocked by other balls. The spotted ball can be banked into the corner pocket at the head of the table by striking it head-on with a hard stroke. If a medium-speed stroke is used, the cue ball must be placed one diamond distance from the side cushion.

Another technique that has been widely touted is to place the cue ball 1.5 diamonds from the side cushion and immediately behind the head string; then aim directly at the center diamond on the foot rail. This system is not very good because of its sensitivity to the

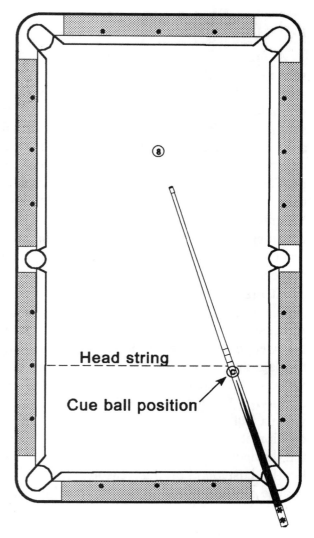

FIGURE 11-1. Cue ball position for a half-ball spot shot.

placement of the object ball. The spot mark itself may be off just a little or the ball may be placed just slightly off the spot. An object ball placement error of 1/16 or 1/8 inch to either side of the spot will cause an object ball error of 2.1 and 4.3 degrees respectively. With the half-ball hit technique, the error is negligible even if the object ball is placed 1/4 inch to either side of the spot.

LAG SHOTS

A *lag shot* can loosely be defined as any shot in which the cue ball is struck slowly and purposefully. As used here, the term lag shot refers to a specific shot in which the cue ball is shot from behind the head string to the foot rail and it rebounds toward the head rail. The objective is to stop the cue ball as near as possible to the head rail. The lag shot is usually used to determine which player shoots first. Winning the lag shot offers a decided advantage because, statistically speaking, the winner will have an additional inning 50 percent of the time.

At first glance the lag shot appears to be a simple cue ball speed control test requiring physical ability only. However, a little knowledge can improve the chance of winning the lag shot. With the lag shot, there is one variable that usually is not considered -- *cushion efficiency*. As previously discussed, when a ball with normal roll runs directly into a cushion it rebounds only about 40 percent of the distance that it would have gone had it not hit the cushion. For this reason it is best to choose a target point *beyond* the head rail and

err on the strong side rather than to leave it short. For example, assume a person has an error of plus or minus 12 inches. As shown in figure 11-2a, if the cushion is the target point the error will be <u>12 inches</u> too short, or <u>4.8 inches</u> (40 percent of 12 inches) too long for an average error of 8.4 inches. If the target is 6 inches beyond the cushion (figure 11-2b) the errors will be <u>6 inches</u> too short, or <u>7.2 inches</u> (40 percent of 18 inches) too long for an average error of 6.6 inches. The average error is 1.8 inches (21%) less when the target is 6 inches beyond the cushion. The optimum target position depends on the ability of the shooter. The target should be shifted about 45 percent of the person's average distance error. That is, if a person using the cushion as the target has an average error of 10 inches, then the target point should be shifted 4.5 inches beyond the cushion. When the target shift technique is done properly, the cue ball should come up short only about 30 percent of the time. If the cue ball comes up short more than 30 percent of the time, the target point should be moved farther beyond the cushion and vice versa.

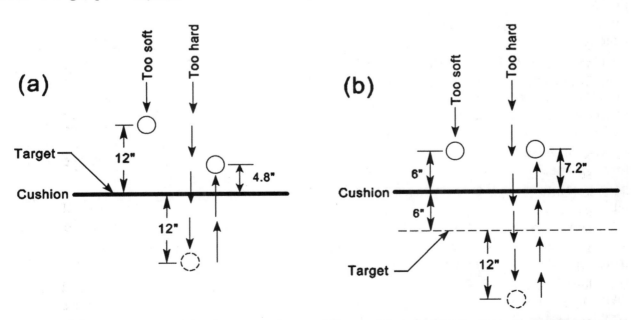

FIGURE 11-2. Positioning the target beyond the cushion results in less average error.

JUMP SHOTS

The *jump shot* is defined as a shot in which the cue ball is deliberately made to leave the table surface upon being struck with the cue stick. The jump shot can be used to jump over an intervening ball (or portion thereof) that may be obstructing the cue ball's path to the object ball. There are legal jump shots and illegal jump shots. The cue ball must be bounced off the table surface for it to be a legal jump shot. If the cue ball is scooped off the table by being struck below center, it's an illegal shot.

Note: The cue ball can be made to jump much higher and with greater accuracy if a special *jump stick* is used. These jump sticks are shorter (down to about 18 inches), thicker (up to about .75 inch), and have a much harder tip (sometimes made of plastic). It is currently being debated as to whether to allow these sticks to be used.

Execution--To execute a legal jump shot the butt of the stick must be raised above horizontal allowing a downward stroke at the cue ball. The height and distance that the ball jumps is determined by how high the butt end is held and how hard it is stroked. The easiest way to envision the action of the cue ball is to imagine that it is being thrown down at the table from the direction of the cue stick.

As an experiment, place a coin about 2 inches in front of the cue ball; shoot directly at the coin using a fast speed. Most average players won't hit the coin with the cue ball because they habitually shoot every shot with the cue butt elevated. (If care is taken to keep the stick level, the coin can be struck because the cue ball won't bounce). The coin can be moved progressively forward to determine where the cue ball lands at various speeds and butt elevation. The highest point of the jump is about halfway between where it lands and its original position. The height of the jump can be determined by progressively stacking more coins until the cue ball hits the stack.

Aim adjustment--The cue ball may bounce several times after it comes back down to the table. It may even be in the air when it strikes the object ball. This doesn't matter much on a straight-in shot but it will change the cut angle of a cut shot. Figure 11-3 shows how this occurs. If the cue ball is above the table when it strikes the object ball, the effective diameter of both balls is smaller. The top view shows how the centers are aligned when the cue ball is on the table (real ball diameter), and when the cue ball is in the air (effective ball diameter). As shown, the cut angle is greater when the cue

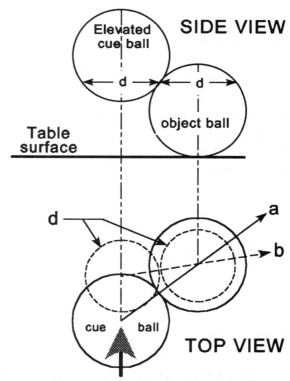

a = Normal path of object ball
b = Elevated path of object ball
d = Effective diameter

FIGURE 11-3. When the cue ball is elevated the cut angle is much greater than when it is on the table.

ball is in the air. The larger the cut angle, the larger the error. For example, if the cue ball is 0.5 inch above the table when it makes contact with the object ball, the cut error will be 0.85 degree for a 30-degree cut shot and 1.5 degrees for a 45-degree cut shot. Therefore, if there is a chance that the cue ball will be in the air when it strikes the object ball, the object ball should be cut slightly less than normal.

Getting position--If the cue ball is in the air when it strikes an object ball, it may carom even higher into the air. This can be used advantageously in getting position when the desired cue ball path, after contact with the object ball, is blocked by an intervening ball. To experience this type of shot, place an object ball in the center of the table one diamond from the end rail; place the cue ball directly between the object ball and side rail. Shoot the object ball into the corner pocket using the jump shot technique; observe the height and direction of the cue ball as it caroms off the object ball. When the cue ball jumps off the table it is usually the result of this type of shot done unintentionally.

Object ball jump--The object ball can also be made to jump, this is called an *object-ball jump shot*. The object ball can be made to jump over the edge of, or even completely over, an intervening ball. The object ball is made to jump by being struck by a cue ball that is above the table surface. The object ball reacts as though it were struck downward with a cue stick and therefore bounces off the table surface as it caroms away. To experiment with the object-ball jump shot, place a coin about 2 inches in front of the object ball; shoot at it using the cue-ball jump shot technique. The object ball should jump over the coin. The height and distance of the object-ball jump can be determined by moving the coin and stacking coins as was done with the cue-ball jump shot.

Figure 11-4 shows **an upper division object-ball jump shot**. Place an object ball (8-ball) on the head spot. Position the cue ball about 3 inches from the head rail so that the shot is aligned straight into the opposite corner pocket. Place an intervening ball on the center string directly between the object ball and the intended pocket. Elevate the butt of the stick about 10 to 12 inches above horizontal and shoot at the 8-ball using a hard stroke. With a little practice you should be able to make the 8-ball jump over the intervening ball and go into the pocket about 20 percent of the time.

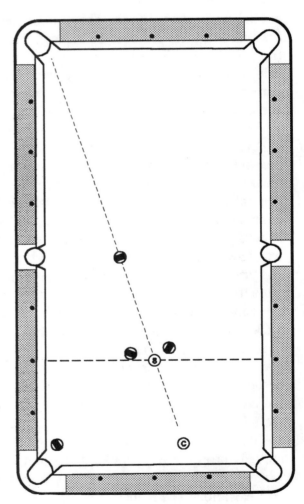

FIGURE 11-4. The 8-ball is made to jump over the intervening ball.

CURVE AND MASSÉ SHOTS

If the butt of the stick is elevated above horizontal when side english is applied, the cue ball's path will curve. This accounts for the popular belief that the cue ball curves when side english is used. It usually does but only because the stick is not held horizontal. The amount of curve and where it occurs depends on the proportional mix of side english, butt elevation, and cue ball speed. When practicing cue ball curve shots, change only one variable at a time. That is; repeat the same shot using a constant amount of side english and butt elevation while varying only the speed; shoot another series of shots keeping two different variables constant and changing the other.

If the cue ball curves more than about 90 degrees it is called a *massé shot*. The massé shot is executed by holding the stick nearly vertical and striking the cue ball sharply. When the massé shot is first being learned, it should be practiced with an expendable stick and on a table that needs recovering. The downward stroke must be forceful. Not only is there a chance of damaging the equipment, but there is a tendency toward timidity when using good equipment. Once learned, the massé shot offers no danger to stick or table. Few players have mastered the massé shot sufficiently to make it a viable part of their game. It was devised for pure billiards where it has greater application potential.

●　　　●　　　●

CHAPTER 12
STRATEGY

Strategy, as defined here, is planning and maneuvering to best advantage. The quality of one's strategy determines the difficulty of the individual shots. Good strategy makes any given sequence of shots easier. To reduce the difficulty of individual shots, one need only increase the quality of strategy. Appropriate strategy is somewhat dependent on the player's skill level. The strategy of a novice is limited to selecting an object ball and pocket with the objective being to pocket *a* ball. As the player's ability increases, strategy becomes progressively more important and the objective broadens to include ball sequence selection, and everything else that is required to ultimately win the game. Most top professional players are about equal in ability. When they play each other the winner is generally determined by superior strategy. Good strategy doesn't elicit raves from the spectators but it does win games. Players that employ superior strategy win consistently and seemingly without effort because they are not forced to make spectacular shots.

The finer points of strategy vary depending on the type of game being played. Strategy, as discussed here, is referenced to the games of EIGHT-BALL or NINE-BALL. In the game of EIGHT-BALL there are two groups of balls, the *solids* (numbered 1 through 7) and *stripes* (numbered 9 through 15). The first player to pocket a ball is assigned all of the balls in that group, and the other player gets the remaining group. When players pocket all of the balls in their group (in any order) they get to shoot at the 8-ball. The player that legally pockets the 8-ball wins the game. In the game of NINE-BALL only balls numbered 1 through 9 are used. The balls must be pocketed in numerical order, and the player that pockets the 9-ball wins the game. The 9-ball, or any other ball, can legally be pocketed out of sequence providing it is a part of a combination in which the lowest ball on the table is struck first. Not striking the lowest ball first constitutes a foul. Rules vary, but generally, when a foul is committed the opponent gets *ball-in-hand*. Ball-in-hand means that the player can place the cue ball anywhere on the table for the next shot. These two games represent the basic differences in strategy requirements. In EIGHT-BALL the player has to select the object ball and sequence of succeeding shots. In NINE-BALL the object ball and the sequence of all succeeding balls are predetermined by virtue of the game rules.

SHOT SELECTION

In games like EIGHT-BALL, shot selection is the most critical aspect of strategy. The easiest ball should always be considered first. The next consideration is whether shape can be gotten for the succeeding shots. Usually, the issue of getting shape is not black or white but rather varying shades of gray. A difficult shot may be selected where there is greater probability of getting good shape; or, an easy shot may be selected even though the probability of getting shape is small. Another influencing factor in shot selection is the number of shots being planned in advance.

Three-ball sequence--It is often asked, how far ahead should a player look and plan shots? It varies depending on the player's competence. A neophyte must be concerned only with the ball that's being shot; the average barroom player plans a two-ball sequence; and, except for problem balls, the expert plans a three-ball sequence. I know -- some players claim to look fifteen balls in advance; they may have a general idea of how they wish to play each ball but they don't have a specific plan. Planning more than three shots in advance is more akin to a fantasy than to a plan. Suffice to say; if you plan three shots in advance you can successfully compete with anyone, that is, providing you have the other necessary skills.

Figure 12-1 shows a typical three-shot sequence. The average player would shoot the 1-ball and stop the cue ball for best shape (straight-in) on the 2-ball. However, with the 2-ball being straight-in, it will be difficult to get shape on the 7-ball. A good player would be concerned about the 7-ball before shooting the 1-ball. The pocket could be cheated when shooting the 1-ball so that the cue ball is left at position "a". From position "a" the 2-ball could easily be made; the cue ball would strike the cushion at "b" then rebound to "d" for an easy shot at the 7-ball. Obviously, positioning the cue ball while shooting the 1-ball is essential in running all three of these balls. The difference in positioning is only a few inches, but often a few inches can determine the outcome of the entire game.

After shooting the first ball in the three-ball sequence, another ball must be added to the sequence. In adding another ball, the

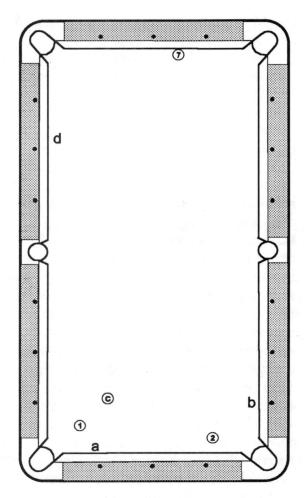

FIGURE 12-1. Typical three ball sequence.

original plan may have to be scrapped and an entirely new plan devised. Many players resist changing their original planned sequence. They unconsciously feel that any change may indicate a flaw in the original plan. Changes are logically justified because a new variable (another ball) has been introduced. Think of any change as refining and perfecting.

Pocket selection--Balls are generally always shot into the nearest pocket. Because we repeatedly select the nearest pocket, our thinking becomes so conditioned that we might not even consider other pockets. In the initial examination of the table, mental note should be made of the best pocket for each ball *and* all possible alternate pockets. Occasionally, alternate pockets must be used because of getting improper shape or to facilitate getting shape.

Consider the situation shown in figure 12-2; the 1-, 2-, and 5-ball must be made. The 1-ball is the easiest shot and should be shot first. It would be easy to get shape on the 2-ball for the second shot, but that would make it difficult to get shape on the 5-ball. Another plan would be to shoot the 1-ball such that the cue ball strikes the cushion at "a" and rebounds toward "b" for a shot at the 5-ball into the same pocket. However, from position "b" it would be difficult to get shape on the 2-ball. If a slight position error were made while shooting the 1-ball, the situation would be even worse. The problem here is wanting to shoot the 5-ball into corner pocket "P". If the mind-set of putting the 5-ball into pocket "P" is changed, the three-ball sequence becomes easy. The 1-ball can be shot so that the cue ball moves just slightly forward. From there the 5-ball could be shot into the opposite

corner pocket; using bottom english the cue ball could be stopped for an easy shot at the 2-ball.

The best way to avoid a difficult situation is to mentally shoot each shot in the planned sequence prior to shooting the first ball. If getting shape on any of the balls is questionable, the first thing that should be considered is changing the sequence; if that doesn't help then alternate pockets should be considered -- then alternate balls.

Estimating probabilities--In order to determine which balls to shoot, which pockets to shoot for, and the proper sequence of shots, the mind must estimate the probabilities for all the various combinations. Your mind must take into consideration your own particular skills. Players of different skill levels or players that have different skills would and should select different shots and shape. Mentally processing the visual input is so complicated that it would require a good-size computer to duplicate. Usually, we are not even aware of the processes that our mind must go through to select the shot or sequence of shots. Aware of it or not, the mind must systematically process the visual data. The more accurately it processes these data, the better we play pool. The mind can be trained to process data more accurately by consciously calculating the odds of success.

If there is only one object ball on the table, and it is positioned such that it could be made 50 percent of the time, there would be a 50 percent chance of running the table. If there was a second object ball on the table and shape could be gotten on it such that it too could be made 50 percent of the time, there would be a 25 percent chance (0.50 x 0.50 = 0.25) of running the table. Any additional object balls would accordingly reduce the chance of running the table. The selection of shot sequence should be such that it affords the greatest chance of running the table and

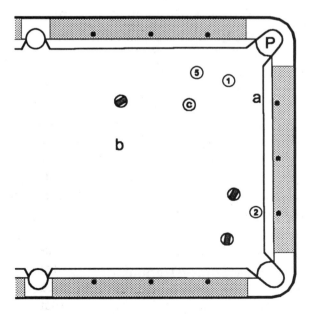

FIGURE 12-2. Solving a typical three ball sequence.

winning the game. Consider the example shown in figure 12-3. There are only three balls so only the sequence need be calculated. The following sequence analysis is subjective but has a valid procedural basis.

1-ball first: Assume that the player could cut the 1-ball into the corner pocket (pocket "P") one out of ten shots (10 percent chance). Even if the player could get 80 percent shape on each of the other balls (good enough that each could be made 80 percent of the time), the probability of running all three balls would be about 6.4 percent (0.10 x 0.80 x 0.80 = 0.064).

3-ball first: Assume the player could pocket the 3-ball about 70 percent of the time. The cue ball would rebound off the cushion and stop somewhere near position "a". From "a" the shooter could make the 1-ball 80 percent of the time while getting an 80 or 90 percent shot at the 2-ball. With these percentages the shooter would have a 48 percent chance (0.70 x 0.80 x 0.85 = 0.48) of running all three balls.

2-ball first: The 2-ball is an easy shot so the shooter could probably make it 95 percent of the time. The cue ball would go to the cushion and rebound back toward the 3-ball. On average, it would end up near position "b" leaving about a 90 percent shot at the 3-ball. While shooting the 3-ball, it would be fairly easy to get a 95 percent shot at the 1-ball. In this scenario, the probability of running the table is 81 percent (0.95 x 0.90 x 0.95 = 0.81).

Even though this analysis is subjective, it is obvious that the 2-ball should be shot first, 3-ball second, and 1-ball third. A better player would have higher percentages but the relative percentages, which are more significant, would remain about the same.

Whether it is done consciously or otherwise the mind must go through a similar

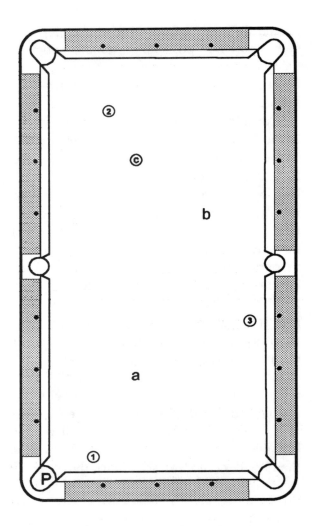

FIGURE 12-3. An exercise in estimating the probability of making a three ball sequence.

process each time a three shot sequence is evaluated. In order to condition the mind to consider all alternatives, this type of analysis should be done repeatedly, on paper, with randomly positioned balls. The more this procedure is practiced, the easier and more accurate the process becomes.

Defense considerations--If one of your easiest object balls is blocking one or several of your opponents balls, consideration should be given to leaving it there for defensive purposes. In figure 12-4 the 1- and 2-ball are

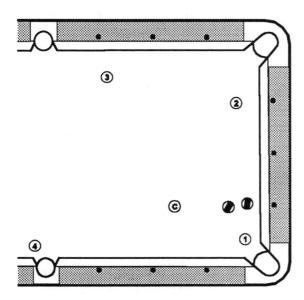

FIGURE 12-4. The 2-ball should be shot first due to defensive considerations.

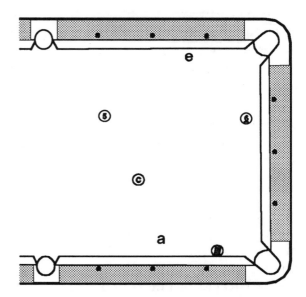

FIGURE 12-5. After pocketing the 5-ball the cue ball should be left at position "e" rather than at position "a".

of equal difficulty, but the 1-ball is blocking two of the opponent's balls. Therefore, the 2-ball should be shot first. In the process of shooting the 2-ball, shape should be gotten on the 3- then the 4-ball. If a miss occurs during any of these shots the opponent will be left with a very difficult situation.

Frequently, shape on the second or third ball in a sequence is selected on the basis of defensive posture. That is, a shape position is selected that will yield a lower percentage shot for yourself but your opponent won't have a shot in case you miss. Figure 12-5 shows such a situation; while shooting the 5-ball the cue ball will go to the cushion then rebound to position "a" for a high percentage shot at the 6-ball. However, if the 5-ball is missed the opponent will have a high percentage shot at the striped ball. A better strategy would be to think defense as well as offense; the 5-ball should be shot with a stun stroke causing the cue ball to go to position "e"; the 6-ball would be a few percentage points more difficult, but in case of a missed

5-ball, your opponent would be left with a difficult shot.

The judgment as to the proper proportion of defense and offense depends on the individual. Each individual must pay particular attention to the results of judgments made during competitive play. If, after missing shots, your opponent is given too many easy shots, consideration must be given to increasing the proportion of defense into your strategy. The effectiveness of your offense-defense proportion must be reassessed occasionally. If your skills are rapidly increasing, the reassessment must be made more frequently.

Key ball--A *key ball* is a ball that can be pocketed while accomplishing a second objective. Usually, the key ball is a ball that can be used to get shape on the game-winning ball. A key ball can also be used to facilitate the breaking up of clusters or for performing some other vital function.

161

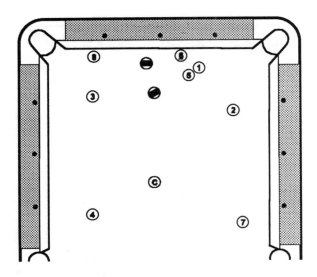

FIGURE 12-6. The 2- and 3-ball are both key balls.

Figure 12-6 shows an example of two types of key balls. Assume the game is EIGHT-BALL and the shooter has solids. The 2-and 3-ball are both easy shots. Either could be shot first but they are both key balls. The 2-ball can be shot into the corner pocket while using the cue ball to break up the 1-5-6 cluster. The 3-ball can be used for getting shape on the 8-ball and therefore should be reserved for that purpose. The shooter is well advised to shoot either the 4- or 7-ball first even though they are slightly more difficult.

PROBLEM BALLS

Problem balls as defined here, are balls that are difficult or impossible to make without first being moved. Many players tend to leave the problem balls until last. For the beginner, this is a good policy; the problem balls will probably be moved accidentally by the time the other balls are pocketed. The better the player, the sooner the problem balls must be attended to. In the following analysis

the player is assumed to have average or greater skill.

Problem balls should be identified in the initial examination of the table. An attempt should be made to get shape on, or move, the problem balls as soon as possible. Early in the game there may be other balls that can be used as alternate shots in case the problem balls can't be moved or made. For example, in figure 12-7 the 5-ball is a problem ball. It can only be made into the far corner pocket, and the position zone is a small area near "a". An attempt should be made at getting to the position zone at every opportunity. If the attempt fails there are still other balls to shoot at. For example, the 3-ball can be shot into the side pocket using bottom english to back the cue ball to position "a". Assume the cue ball didn't back up far enough; the 1-ball can still be shot into corner pocket "P", and in doing so the cue ball can be made to go to the cushion near "e" and rebound back to "a". Again, if the cue ball fails to roll far enough,

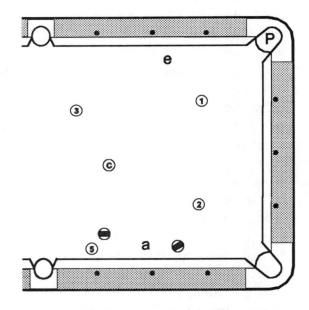

FIGURE 12-7. The 5-ball is a problem ball, it should be dealt with at the earliest opportunity.

the 2-ball can be used as an alternate shot. In shooting the 2-ball, another attempt can be made to get to position "a", or at least, the cue ball could be left in the vicinity of the 2-ball for a lower percentage, but possible, shot.

As a rule, **THE EASIEST BALL SHOULD BE SHOT WHILE TRYING TO GET SHAPE ON THE HARDEST BALL**. However, this is not always possible or even prudent. In some cases an easy ball can be shot while getting shape on another easy ball which in turn will facilitate getting shape on the hardest ball. In any case, a plan as to how to get shape on the hardest ball should be formulated *before* shooting any shot.

⚫   ⚫   ⚫

SHAPE CONCESSIONS

Some players try too hard to get perfect shape and in so doing frequently end up with no shape and no shot. Figure 12-8 shows a situation of this type. The 1-ball can be shot into the side pocket causing the cue ball to go three rails to position "e" for perfect shape on the 8-ball into the corner pocket. Anyone could execute the shot as diagrammed -- some of the time. The expert could do it most of the time but the average player could not consistently predict the cue ball path that accurately. The cue ball would probably run into an intervening ball, stop short, or roll too far resulting in random position on the 8-ball. A safer shot, for most players, is to shoot the 1-ball very gently stopping the cue ball somewhere between "a" and "b". This would result in a lower percentage shot at the 8-ball, but all things considered, a better chance of making the two-ball sequence.

There are some tradeoffs in selecting ball sequence and shape. One must frequently decide between a high percentage shot or high percentage shape. As with most other

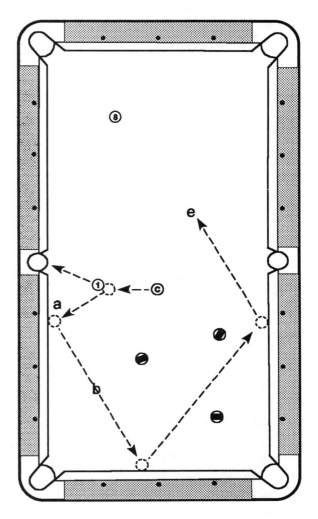

FIGURE 12-8. The cue ball could be stopped at "a", "b", or "e" for a good shot at the 8-ball.

strategy considerations, the decision depends largely on ability; the more experienced players usually are better able to predict the cue ball's path and therefore go for the better shape. Regardless of skill level, most players make more errors trying to get better shape than is actually required. All players must evaluate their own shape strategy; each time they fail to make a sequence of balls they must reevaluate.

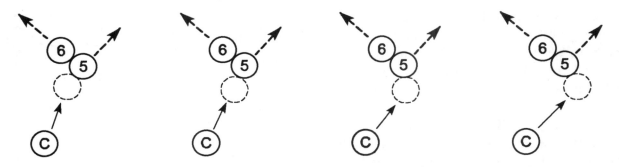

FIGURE 12-9. The 5- and 6-ball will go in the same direction regardless of where the 5-ball is struck.

CLUSTERS

It is relatively easy to run several balls when they are scattered around the table. It's much more difficult to sustain a run when the balls are clustered. A *cluster,* as defined here, is two or more balls touching or in proximity to each other.

In the initial examination of the table, pay particular attention to the clusters, and examine them carefully. Occasionally one or more of the balls can be made with a combination or carom shot. If none of them can be made, the balls in the cluster must be moved or broken up (rearranged).

A novice shouldn't be too concerned about clusters as long as there are other balls to shoot at. The clusters will probably be accidentally bumped and rearranged during the normal course of the game. As a player's skill level increases, longer runs are expected which requires breaking up the clusters progressively earlier in the game. Expert players try to break up clusters, or at least formulate a plan to do so, at the first opportunity. There are several good reasons for this strategy. First, each time a ball is removed from the table, fewer opportunities remain to break up the cluster with a cue-ball carom off another ball. Second, while attempting to break up clusters, cue-ball

position accuracy is diminished. The fewer balls that remain on the table, the less chance there is (statistically) of getting shape on one of them. And third, if a miss occurs as a result of attempting a break-out shot, it is better to happen early in the game when there are more balls on the table to act as interference for your opponent's shots.

Most players tend to slam into clusters with the intent of giving the balls a good long roll. This is usually an error -- one should know, in advance, exactly what direction each ball will go and where it will stop. Since the balls are close to each other, predicting what direction they will go is relatively easy. For example, consider the two-ball cluster shown in figure 12-9. The 5- and 6-ball will move away in a specific direction regardless of where the cue ball strikes the 5-ball. The second ball (6-ball) always moves away along the line passing through the center of the two balls (alignment direction). The first ball struck (5-ball) goes perpendicular to the second ball.

In a three-ball cluster, one need only move two balls in order to effectively break up the cluster. Figure 12-10 shows the break up of a three-ball cluster. Note that the same rules for predicting exit direction apply here.

With most simple cut shots, the direction the balls carom off each other is generally

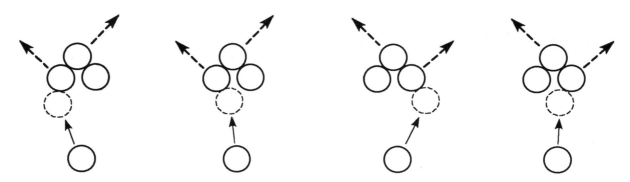

FIGURE 12-10. In a three ball cluster, one need only move two balls to effectively break up the cluster.

determined by visualizing the alignment of their centers as they make contact with each other. With clusters, it is generally easier to determine the path of each ball relative to *contact point.* Figure 12-11 shows how a three-ball cluster is analyzed using contact points. It is fairly easy to determine the contact point between balls "A" and "B"; ball

"B" will go in direction "e", directly opposite this contact point. The path of ball "A" will be perpendicular to the path of ball "B", therefore the contact point with ball "D" can be predicted; the path of ball "D" will be directly away from this point as indicated by direction "f". The final path of ball "A" will be perpendicular to the path of ball "D" as shown by direction "g".

The distance each ball travels is a function of how fast the cue ball is moving at impact, and the alignment of the clustered balls. Figure 12-12 shows a two-ball cluster (3- and 4-ball) that must be broken up before either ball can be made. The player shoots the 1-ball (key ball) into the corner pocket. The cue ball

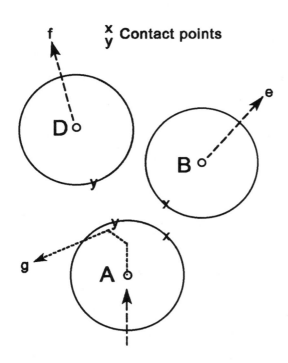

FIGURE 12-11. Contact points can be used to help predict the path of each ball.

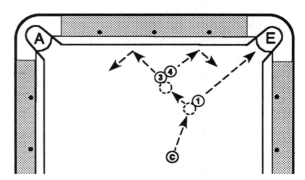

FIGURE 12-12. The speed at which the key ball is shot determines where the clustered balls will end up.

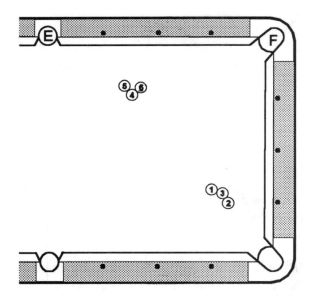

FIGURE 12-13. Two typical clusters.

caroms off the 1-ball into the 3-ball. If the shooter intends to shoot the 3-ball next, the shot must be executed gently so that the 3-ball stops shortly after contacting the first cushion. If the shooter intends to shoot the 4-ball next, it must be shot harder because the 4-ball won't move nearly as far as the 3-ball due to the angles involved. The proper sequence is a gentle shot at the 1-ball, then the 3-ball into pocket "A", then the 4-ball into pocket "E".

Examine the 1-, 2-, and 3-ball cluster shown in figure 12-13. The 2-ball can be made by striking the 1-ball. Since there is a makable ball, there is no need to break up the cluster while shooting another ball. The biggest concern here is to be sure that the 1- and 3-ball are moved to an advantageous position for the succeeding shots.

Examine the 4-, 5-, and 6-ball cluster in figure 12-13. Probably none of these balls can be pocketed, therefore this cluster must be broken up while shooting another ball. Even when none of the balls can be made, there is still a best way to break up a cluster. In this example the 4-ball can be struck such that the

5-ball will end up near pocket "E" and the 6-ball near pocket "F".

NUDGING BALLS

As a rule one should **NEVER MOVE BALLS UNNECESSARILY**. There are good reasons for this rule. First, if the cue ball is involved in more than one carom, it is difficult to predict where it will end up. And second, if balls are not moved, their positions are known with certainty thus allowing strategy to be planned further in advance. When balls are moved it frequently requires revamping the entire game plan.

Even so, there are still situations where a little nudge can win the game. Your own ball can be nudged into a better position or your opponent's ball can be nudged out of position. Nudging can be done with the object ball before it goes into a pocket or with the cue ball before or after it strikes the object ball.

Figure 12-14 shows three examples of nudging one's own ball into a better position. It would be difficult to get good shape on the 2-ball in its present position. The 1-ball should be shot so that it nips the 2-ball before going into the side pocket. The 2-ball will move into the open area toward corner pocket "A". The 4-ball is also in a bad position behind an intervening ball. The 3-ball should be caromed off the edge of the 4-ball as it goes into corner pocket "B"; the 4-ball will go to the cushion and rebound into the open area near the pocket. The 6-ball can't be made in any pocket because it's up against the opponent's ball. The 5-ball should be shot into corner pocket "D". The cue ball will carom off the 5-ball into the 6-ball nudging it into the open.

Figure 12-15 shows three examples of nudging your opponent's ball while pocketing your own ball. The 2- and 3-ball are difficult

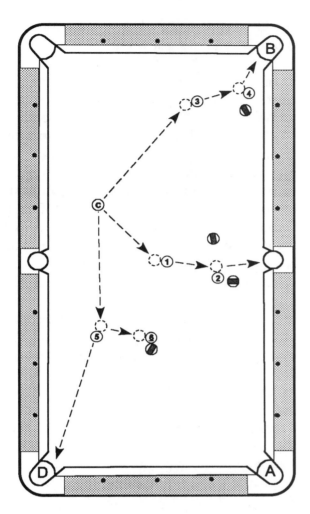

**FIGURE 12-14. Examples of nudging
one's own ball into
a better position.**

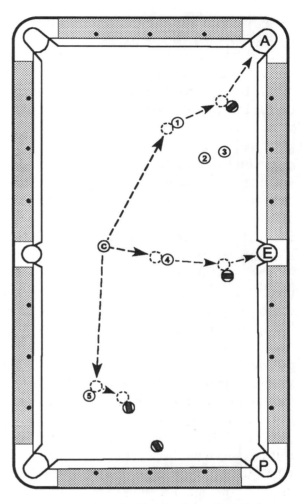

**FIGURE 12-15. Examples of nudging
your opponent's ball into
a more difficult position.**

to make because the opponent's ball is blocking their easiest pocket (pocket "A"). The 1-ball should be caromed off the opponent's ball before going into the corner pocket. The 4-ball could be shot directly into the side pocket "E", but this would leave your opponent with an easy side pocket shot. It is best to nip the opponent's ball with the 4-ball, sending it to the rail and away from the pocket. The 5-ball can easily be made with a gentle center-ball shot, but the cue ball will probably bump the opponent's ball toward corner pocket "P". Some bottom english

should be used so that the opponent's ball is struck very thin sending it to the cushion where it will be more difficult to make.

SAFETIES

In most games of pool, most shots are offensive; the shooter's prime objective is to pocket an object ball. However, there are situations in which pocketing a ball is not even a consideration. The only objective may be to leave a difficult shot for your opponent. These shots are called *safeties*.

Safeties are a vital part of all pool games but are especially important in the game of NINE-BALL. In NINE-BALL the lowest ball on the table must be struck first. Not striking it first constitutes a foul and the opponent gets ball-in-hand. Having ball-in-hand is a distinct advantage, therefore shooting a safety and thereby causing your opponent to foul, can be a potent strategy maneuver. Since safeties are so critical in NINE-BALL, the following discussion of safeties refers to NINE-BALL.

The two most common types of safeties involve hiding the object ball or hiding the cue ball. Figure 12-16a shows an example of hiding the object ball. The 1-ball is cut thin so that it strikes the cushion and rebounds to a position behind three other balls. The incoming player has to shoot a difficult kick shot just to hit the 1-ball, and failing to do so

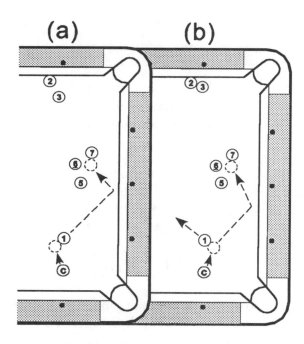

FIGURE 12-16. A safety situation in which either the object ball or the cue ball can be put into a difficult position.

would constitute a foul. The same situation could be shot as shown in figure 12-16b. Here, the 1-ball is struck on the right side causing the cue ball to end up behind the clustered balls.

Whether it is better to hide the object ball or the cue ball depends on the particular circumstances and the shooter's competence. Most players can predict the _direction_ of the object ball more accurately than the direction of the cue ball after the collision. This is because the success of every shot depends on the direction of the object ball. On the other hand, most players can control the rolling _distance_ of the cue ball better than the rolling distance of the object ball. This is because, in the normal course of play, the rolling distance of the cue ball must always be controlled. The object ball stops in the pocket regardless of how fast it is going. When deciding whether to hide the object ball or the cue ball, one must decide whether the shot is more direction sensitive or speed sensitive, then shoot accordingly. All things being equal, it is usually better to hide the cue ball. You may do such a good job of hiding the object ball that you can't get a good shot at it even with ball-in-hand. Such is the case with the 1-ball in figure 12-16a. Keep in mind that if the safety is good, and your opponent fouls, you get to move the cue ball, not the object ball.

Figure 12-17 shows another situation that demonstrates the value of a safety at a crucial time. When confronted with the ball arrangement as shown, most players would shoot the 1-ball into the corner pocket and proceed with the run. However, the shooter can elect to shoot a safety by positioning the 1-ball near the 9-ball while nestling the cue ball behind the 6-, 7-, 8-ball cluster. If the next player is unable to hit the 1-ball first and fouls, the game could be won by shooting an easy 1-9 combination.

The judicious use of safeties can obviously be an effective weapon in pool strategy. Your

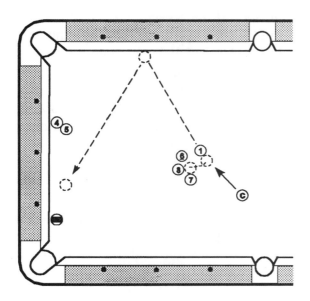

**FIGURE 12-17. A safety may
help assure a win.**

opponent will probably also come to this realization and use safeties against you. Therefore, you must learn how to react to a safety.

When your opponent has executed a good safety, your main concern is to execute a good hit thereby avoiding a foul. If a good hit can be made fairly easily then consideration should be given to pocketing the object ball or at least leaving a difficult shot for your opponent. If a good hit is difficult or impossible, the next best option should be considered. Several of these options are listed:

1. Roll another ball between the object ball and the easiest pocket. Taking away the easiest pocket may not stop your opponent's run, but it will make it more difficult.
2. Create a difficult cluster that may stop your opponent's run. In figure 12-16a the 2- and 3-ball are in the open where each can be made. In figure 12-16b the 2-ball has

been moved next to the 3-ball creating a difficult cluster.
3. Disturb any easy 9-ball combinations.

If left with the safety shown in figure 12-17, first consider a cue ball kick shot at the 1-ball to either of the side cushions. Even if a foul is committed by striking the 9-ball first -- at least the easy combination is taken away. If the cue ball position is such that a successful kick shot is very unlikely or impossible, the next best option is to consider a deliberate foul that will remove the easy combination. Possibly the 6- or 7-ball can be banked into either the 1- or 9-ball. Another possibility is to move another ball between the 1- and 9-ball, or if there is room, between the 9-ball and the pocket. The best of these options will depend primarily on the exact location of the cue ball.

9-BALL COMBINATIONS

In the game of NINE-BALL, combination shots on the 9-ball are a major part of the basic game, therefore they must be given special consideration in planning strategy.

The question often arises, is it better to go for the combination shot on the 9-ball, or go for the run. It depends on the individual's particular skills, the position of the other balls, and the number of balls remaining. Players that usually run only a few balls should decide in favor of trying the 9-ball combination. The more balls remaining before the 9-ball, the more the situation favors a combination shot. If there are clusters such as the 4- and 5-ball in figure 12-17, a combination shot may be more viable. If a run requires going back and forth from one end of the table to the other, there is a greater chance of getting out of shape and missing a shot; thus, the combination may be more viable. Even a very low probability

169

combination shot at the 9-ball should be attempted if one can be assured of leaving the cue ball safe.

Once a decision to go for the 9-ball combination has been made, a plan of execution must be formulated. Quite frequently there is a choice of using a simple combination shot into the 9-ball, as shown in figure 12-18a, or using a cue-ball carom shot as shown in figure 12-18b. Several factors must be considered in deciding which to use:

1. Most players can judge the path of the object ball more accurately than the path of the cue ball after impact.
2. When using the cue-ball carom combination, the cue ball's path will be curved if it has any roll. Always use a stun stroke to avoid cue ball curve.
3. Consider what will happen if the shot is

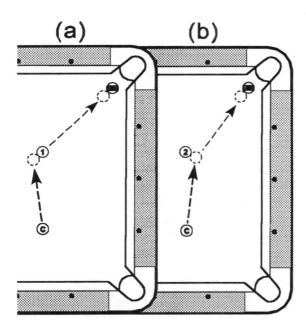

FIGURE 12-18. In some situations either the object ball or the cue ball can be used in a 9-ball combination shot.

missed. If the object-ball carom shot is used (figure 12-18a) and missed, the object ball and 9-ball will probably be left near each other allowing a possible combination shot for the next player. If the cue-ball carom shot is used (figure 12-18b) and missed, the object ball will end up on the opposite rail out of harm's way.

In the event that your opponent fouls, giving you ball-in-hand, the first thing to consider is a possible combination shot at the 9-ball. The proper procedure for setting up the 1-9 combination is shown in figure 12-19a.

1. Imagine the path the object ball (1-ball) must take in order to pocket the 9-ball.
2. Pick out a spot on the rail (point "s") which represents the proper 1-ball direction.
3. Set the cue ball on the table such that the cue ball, object ball, and point "s" are all aligned.
4. When executing the shot, concentrate on shooting the 1-ball at point "s". Trying to judge where the 1-ball should strike the 9-ball while aiming the cue ball overtaxes the mind.

Assume that the 2-ball in figure 12-19b is the object ball; shooting a simple combination shot (2-9) would require a thin cut, therefore a cue ball carom shot should be used. To implement:

1. Determine where the cue ball must be when it strikes the 9-ball and the path it must take off the 2-ball.
2. Imagine a line through the center of the object ball perpendicular to the desired path of the cue ball; the point where this line emerges from the object ball is the proper contact point.

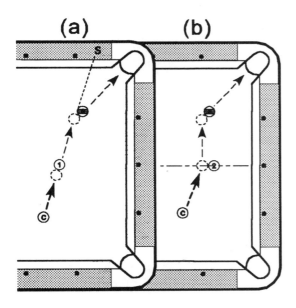

FIGURE 12-19. Setting up a 9-ball combination when you have ball-in-hand.

3. Place the cue ball near the object ball so that the contact point can be struck easily.
4. Execute the shot with a stun stroke while concentrating on the contact point. For some people it is easier to note what direction the object ball will go when the proper contact point is struck. Then when aiming, concentrate on shooting the object ball in that direction.

STRATEGY OVERVIEW

It is difficult to be specific in suggesting proper strategy because of the many situations requiring different strategies. As in the game of chess, a general strategy can be suggested, but the number of pieces and positions are so numerous that one specific strategy cannot be promulgated. Playing chess is a good way to learn strategy; the rules are different and the pieces are different, but the thinking processes are similar. Learning and playing chess helps condition

the mind to be cognizant of all available options and accurately appraise the logical progression of events with each option.

As previously stated, appropriate strategy is dictated, to a large extent, by the individual's ability. For example, in the game of NINE-BALL, a beginner need not be concerned about the position of the 4-ball while shooting the 1-ball. As ability improves the player must look and plan further in advance. Be careful not to let your knowledge of strategy lag behind your ability; once you're able to run the table, your strategy must _allow_ you to run the table. It is one thing to know strategy and quite another thing to employ it. Experiment with various strategy options during practice play. Even beginners should try to learn the finer points of strategy so that when their ability allows, they will be properly prepared. Being aware of the various strategy options will encourage beginners to stretch their abilities.

The strategy of professional players should be observed and studied at every opportunity. When observing the experts, consider these aspects:

1. Try to anticipate shot selection, sequence of balls, and position technique. When the expert does something unexpected try to determine why.
2. Do they use more or less english than you do?
3. Do they use the cushions more than you do in getting shape?
4. Do they rearrange problem balls and clusters the same way you do?
5. Do they employ more or less defensive strategy than you do?
6. How do they shoot safeties -- do they hide the cue ball or the object ball?

When playing a friendly practice game, discuss strategy with your opponent while the game is in progress. Discuss all the strategy

171

options that you can both collectively think of. This will help you recognize more options when playing a serious game.

Each time a ball is missed or a game is lost, try to isolate and identify the cause. The problem may be the lack of ability but quite often it can be traced to an error in strategy. The strategy error usually occurs one, two, or more shots before the miss occurs. The sooner strategy errors are identified, the sooner they can be corrected.

It doesn't take several strategy mistakes to lose a game. One must always strive to avoid that first mistake. In this regard, a pool game is similar to a long mathematical problem; one small mistake early in the game (problem) will significantly affect the final outcome (answer).

Learning and applying new strategy techniques during a competitive game is difficult. Try to utilize a variety of strategy techniques while practicing. Usually, strategy mistakes are made because the player is not aware of the options available at all times. Players that are not aware of the strategy options cannot possibly even recognize strategy errors. If errors are not recognized they can't be corrected and thus the learning process is stymied. Quite frequently, strategy options are not recognized because of a particular mind-set, the brain stops thinking about strategy when the first option is recognized.

The easiest way to learn to apply appropriate strategy is to practice on paper. Analyzing hypothetical situations on paper allows more time to be spent on strategy. The extra time generally revels more viable options and the best option is more often identified. Practicing on paper will be discussed in more detail in Chapter 13.

CHAPTER 13
PRACTICE

INTRODUCTION

A person can know all there is to know about pool, or any other sport, and still not be able to play worth a hoot. Knowledge must be blended with ability before excellence can be achieved. The knowledge part must be stored in the brain's memory then recalled when the situation calls for it. For example, a person can experiment by shooting a specific bank shot at a certain speed. Once the shot is made, the proper banking point is committed to memory. If the shot must be repeated, the mind's memory will indicate the exact banking point. As long as it is fresh in the mind, the shot can be repeated time and time again. Unfortunately, memory has a tendency to fade with time. If the same shot is tried a month or year later it may have to be learned all over again. To prevent the memory from fading, the shot must be repeated occasionally to refresh and reinforce memory. Therefore, practice is required to acquire and maintain a memory bank of information (shots).

With regard to the previous example, even after the proper banking point is determined, the shooter must have the *ability* to make the ball strike that point to successfully execute the shot. The ability to execute the shot depends, in large part, on memory also, but in this case it's muscle memory. In order to perform a physical task, many individual muscles must be trained to function in unison. Once the muscles are trained to perform a task, they can repeat the task with little or no conscious thought. Every muscle in the body must be trained before it can function efficiently. Muscles had to be trained before we could walk, talk, or scribble our first word. Muscle memory also fades with time and therefore must also be refreshed and reinforced by practicing. Professional basketball players practice shooting baskets; professional golfers practice on the driving range and on practice putting greens; they're probably not learning anything new but their muscle memory is being refreshed and refined. It is most important to practice just prior to playing which allows less time for the muscle memory to fade.

Coordination and timing are also important aspects of shot execution. Consider a situation that requires a stun stroke. The cue ball must be struck below center causing it to start out with backspin; the backspin must wear off completely by the time the cue ball strikes the object ball. The dissipation of backspin depends on travel time. That is, if the cue ball is struck too slow or too fast, travel time will be too long or too short causing the ball to have forward or backward rotation at the moment of impact. The success of this shot is a function of time, therefore timing is critical. And again, proper timing is achieved only with practice.

There has always been the question of which is better, practicing with drills (repeat positioning of the balls) or practicing by playing. The basketball player drills by shooting free throws; the baseball player has batting drills and fielding drills. Any game that requires numerous and divergent skills must be practiced with a large percentage of drills. Pocket billiards, with its great diversity of shots and required skills, should logically be practiced with a large percentage of drills.

The initial training of mind and muscles requires a different type of practice than does the refreshing and reinforcing. Beginners should spend about **80 percent** of their time doing practice drills and **20 percent** of their time on practice play. As the basic skills are acquired the percentages should change; by the time they become professionals, they should spend **80 percent** of their practice time playing and **20 percent** on drills. Regardless of skill level, a person that doesn't play often, or has long layoffs, should concentrate on drills. A playing slump should be treated with large doses of drills.

All successful competitors thrive on the challenge. Each time you practice you should be challenged to do better. Bowlers have their game averages, golfers have their handicaps, and ball players have their batting averages. These numbers serve as a gauge as to how well a particular task is performed. Very often, the numbers themselves represent the competition which stimulates the challenge.

Devise a scoring system for each type of pool practice. Record and chart the results of each practice session. Improving your record will serve as a challenge to your competitive nature and will stimulate improvement. Setting numerical goals helps to encourage practice. When setting goals, be sure they are time dependent. For example, your goal may be to become 100 percent better at rail shots, in two months. This type of goal encourages a high frequency of practice in the next two months to insure the improvement. In contrast, if your goal is to improve X percent each time you practice, it doesn't contain a built-in incentive to practice often.

In the ensuing discussion, reference will be made to marking ball positions. Simple paper hole cutouts (from a hole punch) can be used for this purpose. They can be set to one side of the ball much like golf ball markers are used. If a more permanent marker is desired, the hole punches can be made from glued paper, either the type that must be wetted or the label type with removable backing. Or, going one step further, self-adhesive colored dots can be used. They can be purchased by the roll from any stationary store. These dots come in various sizes and colors, and one roll should last a lifetime. In some cases, ball positions can be marked with another ball or piece of chalk.

When practicing, always **STRIVE TO BALANCE YOUR ERRORS**. For example, you should miss just as many shots by cutting the object ball too thin as by cutting it too thick. If you find that you're cutting most shots too thin, you must make a conscious effort to cut all shots a little thicker. By balancing your errors, you will miss the fewest number of shots.

PRACTICE DRILLS

A *practice drill* is a process of training or teaching by the continued repetition of an exercise or shot. In order to make practice drills most effective, particularly for beginners, the basic fundamentals should be isolated and practiced individually. As the skill level increases more and more of the fundamental skills can be blended together.

The more diverse the drills are, the more often the learned skills can be applied during competitive play. When shots that you have practiced in drills occur during competitive play, their execution should be nearly automatic because of the prior training of mind and muscles. It is almost like being allowed to practice the shot before actually shooting it. If the shot is not identical to the one in the practice drill, small adjustments can be made by interpolation or extrapolation. For example, if bank shots are practiced from one and two diamonds out from the cushion, the exact banking point for each of these shots is known. If, in competitive play, you encounter a similar bank shot 1.5 diamonds out from the cushion, by interpolation, the proper banking point is determined to be between the two known banking points. In other words, your drill shots can be used as a reference by which all similar shots are judged.

When a critical shot is missed during an important game, it should be remembered. Missing a shot generally represents a deficiency of some sort, therefore a drill should be devised incorporating that particular shot or deficiency. For example, if a thin cut shot is missed, a drill should be devised incorporating thin cut shots from various places on the table and at various distances. Practice the drill until the thin cut shot is perfected. If no progress or improvement is made in the area of deficiency, your problem may be rooted deeper. For example, if there is no improvement in the thin cut shot, the problem may be inaccurate aim or a defective stroke; in which case, another drill for improving aim and stroke must be devised.

The following are some examples of practice drills designed to teach various aspects of the game. They can be modified somewhat to make them more difficult for the advanced player or easier for the beginner. The estimated scores that a barroom player would get assumes a 44-inch table with large pockets.

Speed control-- Speed is the most important of the prime commands given to the cue ball in executing each and every shot. Without speed control there is no shape, no runs, and no wins. Speed control is progressive; beginners usually have only two speeds, fast and slow. As they develop speed control they will be capable of dividing these two speeds into more, and smaller increments.

Even the most expert pool players must constantly work on and refine their speed control. Because speed control is so important, the following speed control drills should be practiced often. In doing so, communication between the mind and muscles, which is paramount in speed control, is refined and perfected.

To set up a speed drill, place the cue ball behind the head string as shown in figure 13-1a. Shoot the cue ball as softly as possible toward the foot rail. Mark the place where the cue ball stops. Replace the cue ball behind the head string and shoot it again but just a little harder so that it barely rolls past the last marker. Continue doing this until the ball strikes the foot rail. The more times it can be shot before striking the foot rail, the better the speed control. If the ball fails to roll farther than the last marker, one point is deducted. A good barroom player should score about 8 or 10 points before striking the foot rail. It is good policy to record your best effort as well as your average. A person who tries for excessive increments will have a high best effort but a low average. Compare your speed control with that of your friends.

The second phase of this drill is to do the same thing for the second length of the table as shown in figure 13-1b. Shoot to the foot rail and rebound as little as possible. Mark the ball position and shoot again trying to rebound just a little past the previous marker. Deduct one point if the ball fails to roll farther than the last marker. Again, record your average and best effort on the second table length. The drill can continue for a third table length (figure 13-1c) and more. A good barroom player will average about 5 or 6

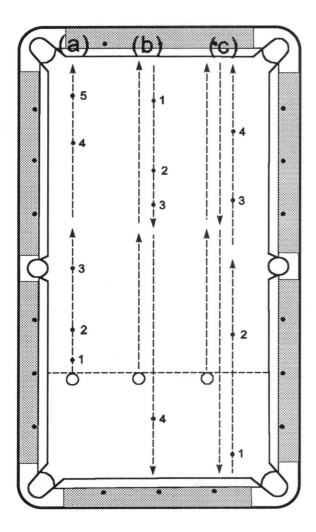

FIGURE 13-1. Ball-speed drills.

ball behind the head string in front of one of the diamonds as demonstrated by position "A". Aim and shoot the cue ball directly at the corresponding diamond on the foot rail. The objective is to make the cue ball rebound directly back along its original path. Care must be taken to avoid inadvertent side english which will cause the rebound path to deviate. This exercise can be made more difficult by starting with the cue ball touching the head rail.

A more difficult aim and shooting drill is also shown in figure 13-2. Place the cue ball

points on the second table length and about 7 or 8 points on the third table length.

These speed drills can be repeated using an object ball instead of the cue ball. Place the object ball just behind the head string, and shoot into it with the cue ball from about 6 inches away.

Aim accuracy--Aim accuracy is the ability to make the cue ball go in the direction you intended for it to go. All the knowledge in the world won't do any good if your aim accuracy is lacking. A rudimentary accuracy drill is shown in figure 13-2. Place the cue

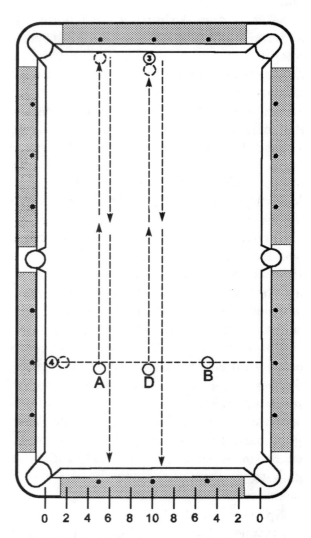

FIGURE 13-2. Accuracy drills. Try to strike the ball on the cushion and bounce straight back.

directly on the head string one diamond from the side rail as indicated by position "B". Place a target ball (4-ball) on the rail at the opposite end of the head string. Shoot for the center of the target ball so that the cue ball rebounds directly back along its original path. Any cue ball error will be magnified because of the round surface of the target. This drill can be made more difficult by placing the cue ball on the rail thus requiring a rail bridge. To further increase difficulty, set up the same shot using the length of the table as shown by cue ball position "D" with the target ball (3-ball) on the foot rail. Some bottom english must be used in order to make the cue ball rebound all the way back to the head rail. This is because the target ball does not stop the forward roll of the cue ball like the cushion would; therefore, roll is acting in opposition to its rebound direction. Scoring can be done by temporarily marking the head rail as shown. If the ball rebounds back to the center diamond it is scored as a 10. If it strikes the side rail it's a zero. A good barroom player should average about 6 points per shot.

As discussed in Chapter 9, combination shots require great accuracy. It follows that they can be used in a drill to help improve accuracy. Set up a series of combination shots with the cue ball in the center of the table as shown in figure 13-3. Make distances "a", "b", and "d" different for each shot (the shot is the most difficult when all three are equal). Try to position the balls so that the combination is straight-in. The straighter they are, the less judgment that is required. A good barroom player should average about 5 successes in each series of 6 shots on a 44-inch table. Since combination shots are so distance sensitive, average success rate will vary depending on table size.

Another simple accuracy drill is shown in figure 13-4. Place an object ball on the center spot and the cue ball about 6 inches from the

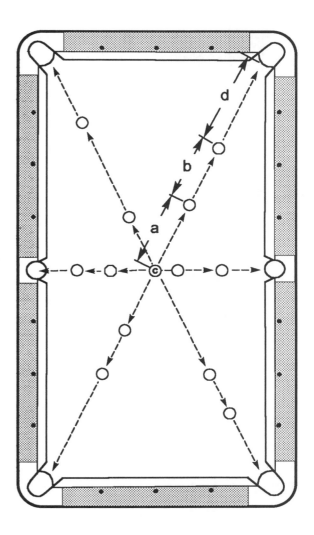

FIGURE 13-3. Combination shots used for accuracy drills.

corner pocket (pocket K). The object ball is shot directly into the opposite corner pocket (pocket P). This shot is not extremely difficult (permissible error is shown in figure 13-4 for different size tables) but it does require good shooting technique. A good barroom shooter should make this shot about 7 out of 10 attempts. This drill can also be used to help diagnose the cause of shooting slumps. If the shot is consistently missed on the same side, it is generally the result of improper eye positioning relative to the stick. The eye position, distance the chin is above the stick,

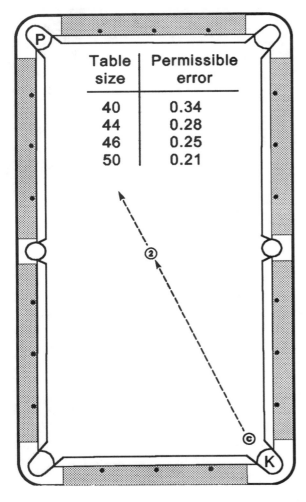

Table size	Permissible error
40	0.34
44	0.28
46	0.25
50	0.21

FIGURE 13-4. An accuracy drill.

Your success rate should not drop more than about 50 percent with your eyes closed.

English--Top and bottom english are the easiest to learn and use because they don't throw (english-induced throw) the object ball off-course. Figure 13-5 shows a practice drill using bottom english. Place the object ball (2-ball) on the center spot, place the cue ball one-half ball diameter to the side of the foot spot. Shoot the object ball with enough bottom english to cause the cue ball to stop; mark the cue ball position. Keep repeating the shot with progressively more bottom so that the cue ball backs up just past the previous

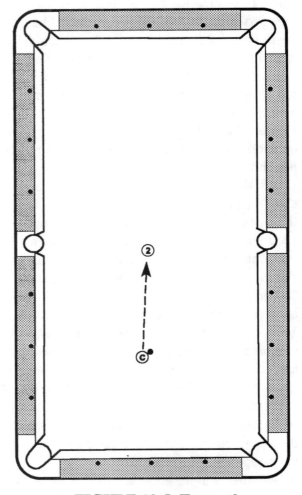

FIGURE 13-5. Top and bottom-english drills.

etc. can be adjusted until your normal accuracy returns. Regardless of skill level, this drill should be shot about 10 times at the beginning of every practice session. This will help avert a shooting slump by allowing accuracy problems to be recognized when they begin creeping into your game.

The same drill can also be used to help alleviate the bad habit of last-second aim corrections. Set up the shot as described and assume your normal shooting stance; when aim is thought to be perfect, close your eyes, take a few more preliminary strokes, then execute the shot. With the eyes closed, there is less tendency to change aim alignment.

marker. If the cue ball fails to back up farther than the previous marker, deduct one point from your score. Continue until you don't think you can improve your score. Record your average and best effort. A good barroom player should average between 6 and 8 points.

A practice drill using bottom english on cut shots is shown in figure 13-6. Place the 1-, 2-, and 3-ball near the side pocket as shown; place the cue ball such that the 1-ball must be cut into the side pocket. Using bottom english try to make the 1-ball and get shape on the 2-ball, then make the 2-ball while getting shape on the 3-ball. The cue ball may not always end up in exactly the proper position, therefore the pocket may have to be cheated occasionally to get shape on the next ball. Once the side pocket shots are perfected the exercise can continue by shooting the 4-, 5-, 6-, and 7-ball into corner pockets. If all seven balls can be run without letting the cue ball strike the cushion, you're well above average.

The same ball placement used in the bottom-english drill shown in figure 13-5 can be used for a top-english drill. Shoot the object ball such that the cue ball rolls forward as little as possible after impact; mark the cue ball position. Keep repeating the shot, each time trying to roll the cue ball just past the previous marker. Deduct a point each time the cue ball fails to go past the previous marker. Continue until you don't think you can improve your score. Keep a record of your average and best effort. A good barroom player should average about 8 points.

These top and bottom drills can be used to determine your personal maximum english. With top english one should be able to make the cue ball go to the head rail and rebound back to the foot rail. With maximum bottom english one should be able to draw the cue ball back to the foot rail and rebound between one and two diamonds away. Keep a dated record of your maximum top and bottom english. Compare your best effort with that of your friends.

Side english can be practiced using the drill shown in figure 13-7. Place the cue ball on the foot spot, place a piece of chalk under the cushion on either side of the foot string to

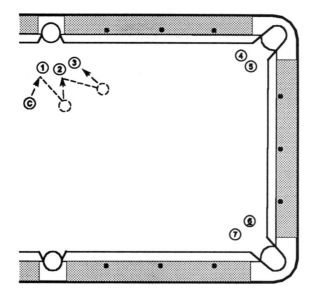

FIGURE 13-6. A position drill using bottom english.

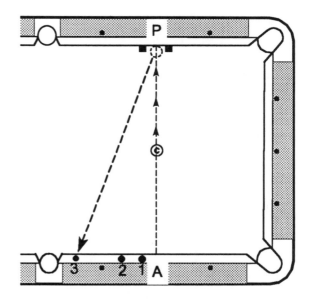

FIGURE 13-7. Side-english drill.

insure that the proper point (point P) will be struck. Shoot the cue ball into the cushion between the two pieces of chalk with as little left english as possible. The cue ball will rebound back somewhere to the left of position "A"; mark this point with a piece of chalk or coin under the cushion. Keep repeating the shot, each time using progressively more left english. If the ball fails to rebound to the left of the last marker, deduct a point. Continue until you don't think you can improve your score. Repeat the drill using right english. An excellent barroom player will average about 4 or 5 points.

A more difficult side-english drill is shown in figure 13-8. Place two pieces of chalk, about 3 inches apart, under the center of the foot cushion. Position the cue ball on the head spot. Begin by randomly positioning a target ball anywhere behind the center string. Shoot a kick shot into the target ball by striking the foot rail between the pieces of chalk. Leave the target ball where it stops and continue shooting kick shots at it. Keep a record of how often the target ball is hit and missed; express your success rate as a percentage. A good barroom player will have a success rate of about 40 percent.

Using side english on a kick shot is fairly easy. Using side english while shooting an object ball requires greater precision because of english-induced throw and possible cue ball curve. Figure 13-9 shows a practice drill requiring the pocketing of an object ball while using side english. Place an object ball (5-ball) on the center spot. Place the cue ball one diamond distance away (position "A") so that the shot is straight into the corner pocket. Shoot the object ball into the corner pocket using a little right side english. Repeat the shot using progressively more english until it can be made with maximum right side english; repeat the procedure using left side english. Then move the cue ball an additional diamond distance (position "B" then "D") from the object ball and repeat the procedure.

The shot from cue ball position "D" is difficult enough even without english, so don't despair if your success rate is low. This drill is not only intended to improve accuracy while using side english, but also to apprise you of your accuracy limits. If you can't make a long shot using side english, you should be aware of it so you can avoid these shots during competitive play. This drill will also keep you aware of your accuracy limits as your skills progress.

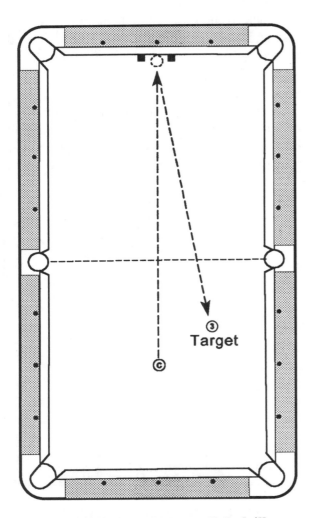

FIGURE 13-8. Side-english drill.

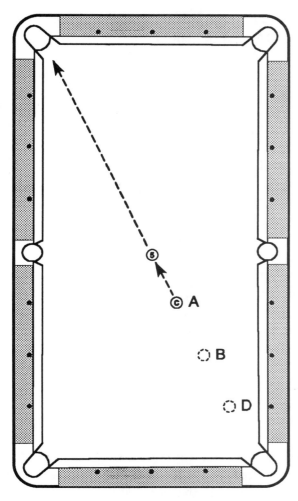

**FIGURE 13-9. Pocketing a ball
while using side english.**

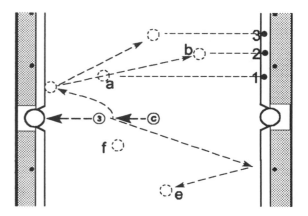

**FIGURE 13-10. A drill requiring the
use of various types of english
and cheating the pocket.**

Figure 13-10 shows a drill that requires a combination of various types of english and cheating the pocket. Place the object ball (3-ball) on the center string one diamond distance from the side pocket; place the cue ball on the center spot. The objective is to pocket the object ball, strike one cushion, and leave the cue ball progressively farther from the center string with each successive shot. An example of top right english is shown; on the first shot the cue ball stops at position "a", a marker is placed on the rail at position 1. The second shot is shot identical to the first but shot a little **harder** causing the cue ball to

stop at position "b" which is marked as position 2. The second position could also have been gotten by shooting the same speed as the first shot but with a little more right english. A point is deducted from your score if the object ball isn't pocketed, cue ball fails to strike one cushion, cue ball fails to stop farther from the center string than the previous shot, or the cue ball strikes a second cushion. Repeat the drill using top left and the cushion to the left of the center pocket. Bottom side can be used with this drill by backing the cue ball to the near cushion as demonstrated in getting to position "e". The same scoring system is used for both top and bottom-english drills. A good barroom player should average about 5 or 6 shots using top side, and 3 or 4 shots using bottom side.

The same object ball and cue ball positions can be used for another challenging test. Place a target ball at position "f" between the object ball and cue ball and to one side of the cue ball's path. Use whatever english is necessary to cause the cue ball to make contact with the target ball after pocketing the object ball. Leave the target ball where it lies for the succeeding shots. The first few shots are relatively easy but as the target ball gets pushed farther from its original position

181

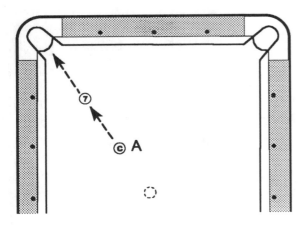

FIGURE 13-12. A stun-stroke drill.

it becomes harder to hit. A good shooter will be able to hit the target ball with regularity regardless of where it is.

Stun stroke--As previously stated, the stun stroke is the most important concept in pool, therefore it must be learned early and perfected with practice. The mechanics of the stun stroke have been discussed in detail in Chapter 7. However, because it is so important, the concept will be repeated again to refresh your memory.

The stun stroke is a shot in which the cue ball has neither forward nor backward roll at the time of impact with the object ball. This is accomplished by using just enough bottom english so that the english will completely dissipate by the time the cue ball gets to the object ball. This means that the amount of bottom must be coordinated with cue ball speed and consequent travel time. If the object ball is struck head-on when using a stun stroke, the cue ball will stop (stop shot) and remain at the point of impact. If a stun stroke is used on a cut shot, the cue ball's path will be perpendicular to the path of the object ball. This means that the stun stroke can be used as a reference in judging cue-ball carom direction for every cut shot. In knowing where the cue ball will go with a

stun stroke, a judgment can be made as to whether you want forward or backward rotation at the time of impact.

Figure 13-11 shows a drill in which a stun stroke is used on a straight-in shot. The objective is to stop the cue ball upon striking the object ball. Place an object ball (7-ball) about 1 foot from a corner pocket as shown. Place the cue ball in position "A" about 1 foot from the object ball; pocket the object ball three times using a slow, medium, and fast cue ball speed.

Progressively move the cue ball an additional foot from the object ball and repeat the procedure. As will quickly become obvious, the farther the cue ball is from the object ball, the harder it must be struck, therefore it becomes increasingly more difficult to shoot it at three different speeds.

Figure 13-12 shows a stun stroke drill that requires the cue ball to move forward or backward slightly after impact. Place the object ball (8-ball) about three diamonds away from the corner pocket and the cue ball near the center of the table (position "A"). The objective is to pocket the object ball while allowing the cue ball to roll forward about 1 foot (position "B"). From the same

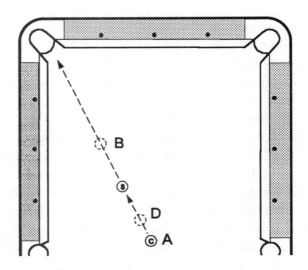

FIGURE 13-11. A stun-stroke drill.

cue ball position, again pocket the object ball but this time back the cue ball up 1 foot to position "D". With each successive shot, try to move the cue ball an additional foot from the object ball.

In order to make the cue ball roll forward to "B", a stun stroke is shot at an imaginary ball at position "D". This means that the cue ball will have no rotation when it gets to "D", but will have some forward rotation when it strikes the object ball. To make the cue ball back up just a little, a stun stroke is shot at an imaginary ball at position "B". The cue ball will have some backward rotation as it strikes the object ball causing it to back up after impact.

Figure 13-13 shows a drill in which the stun stroke is used on a cut shot. Place an object ball (1-ball) on the center string one diamond distance from the side pocket; place the cue ball at various distances and angles from the object ball as shown. The objective is to pocket the object ball and cause the cue ball to carom off perpendicular to the path of the object ball. Shoot three shots from each cue ball position, each at different speeds. Place the chalk on the rail perpendicular to the path of the object ball. This will make any error easier to detect. If the cue ball has forward roll at impact it will strike the cushion toward "A". If it has backward rotation it will strike the cushion toward "B". The cue ball can be deliberately made to strike the cushion toward "A" by imagining that the object ball is nearer to the cue ball, or strike the cushion toward "B" by imagining the object ball farther from the cue ball. As in the previous drill, using an image ball helps to control the forward or backward rotation at impact.

When the stun-stroke cut shot has been mastered, practice the stun stroke with side

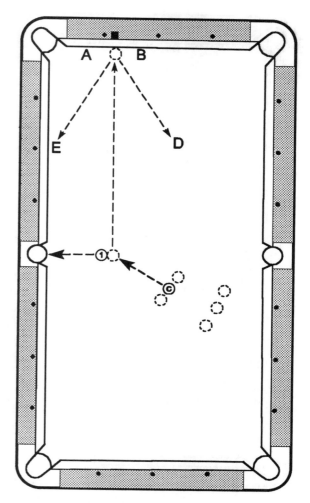

FIGURE 13-13. Practicing a stun stroke on a cut shot.

english. Using the same ball positions as shown in figure 13-13, try to make the cue ball strike the cushion at the chalk marker and rebound toward "D" with right side, and toward "E" with left side. This type of shot is used frequently in competitive play. The stun stroke avoids scratching in the corner pocket; side english is applied, as required, to get shape on the next ball.

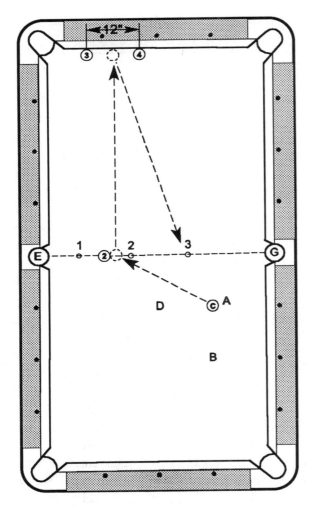

FIGURE 13-14. A stun-stroke test.

this becomes too easy, try a stun stroke with side english. Put enough side english on the cue ball to cause it to rebound across the center string as near to pocket "E" as possible without striking the side cushion. Mark the point where it crosses the center string. Keep repeating the shot, each time trying to cross the center string progressively farther toward pocket "G". Subtract a point from your score upon failure to pocket the object ball, failure to hit the end cushion between the two balls, failure to increase the distance from pocket "E", or when the side cushion is struck before the cue ball crosses the center string. The entire procedure is repeated from cue ball positions "B" and "D". With some practice a good barroom player should score an average of 3 increments from each cue ball position.

Rail shots--Many players dislike rail shots and often elect to shoot a more difficult shot just to avoid the rail shot. Actually, rail shots generally offer a larger target area than comparable shots away from the rail. Another reason a rail shot is easier is because the rail is adjacent to the object ball and can be used as an aim reference. The pocket is at the end of the rail, therefore you need not even look at the pocket while aiming.

Place an object ball (5-ball) on the side rail one diamond from the corner pocket as shown in figure 13-15. Place the cue ball in position "d". Estimate the cut angle, type and amount of side english (if any) that should be used, and where the target area is in relation to the object ball. Check your estimates with the rail-shot chart in Chapter 8, then shoot the shot. Repeat the procedure using cue ball positions "e" through "j". Move the object ball to positions "j then "k" and repeat the drill.

There will be shots where cue ball positioning requires english other than optimum rail shot english. These shots should be practiced but only after you're able to

And now, a stun stroke test drill: Place an object ball (2-ball) on the center string one diamond from the side pocket as shown in figure 13-14. Place the cue ball one diamond from the center string and one diamond from the opposite side cushion (position "A"). Place two balls (3- and 4-ball) on the end rail 12 inches apart as shown in figure 13-14. The objective is to pocket the object ball with a stun stroke and make the cue ball go to the end rail between the two balls. Repeat the shot from cue ball positions "B" and "D". Your success rate can be expressed as a percent. A good barroom player will have a success rate of about 70 or 80 percent. When

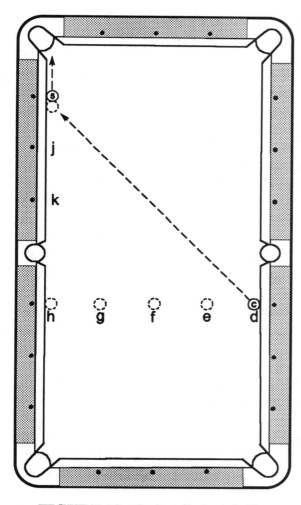

FIGURE 13-15. A rail-shot drill.

consistently make rail shots using optimum english.

Bank shots--When a bank shot is missed, it is difficult to determine specifically what was done wrong. The miss could be the result of an error in judging the proper banking point, curve caused by roll, collision-induced english, or an error in aim or speed. The miss could be caused by any one or combination of these variables. With so many possibilities the specific error may never be determined. It is difficult to correct an error if it can't be isolated and identified.

Practice drills for bank shots must be designed to minimize the variables so that the effect of each can be identified. For example, shooting head-on into the object ball eliminates collision-induced english (and aim error, to a large extent) so that concentration can be on speed control. If one were to repeat the same head-on shot several times at different speeds, one could be fairly confident that the difference in rebound angle is due to speed and not aim, banking point, or some other variable. The following are a series of drills designed to teach bank shots by progressively adding more variables.

Figure 13-16 shows a drill in which the cue ball is banked into the side or corner pockets. Place the cue ball on the long string one diamond from the center string (position "A"). Bank the cue ball into the side pocket while taking great care to strike it in the center. Striking the cue ball dead-center is so important that it may be advisable to look at the cue ball as the shot is executed rather than at the banking point. Shoot the shot at slow, medium, and fast speeds; repeat any shot that is missed. Note that when the shot is executed at a fast speed, the banking point is about half the distance to the pocket. This can be used as a reference in the future. Move the cue ball to position "B" and again bank it into the side pocket at three different speeds. Place the cue ball at position "C" and bank it into the corner pocket. Repeat this exercise from each cue ball position but this time reverse the pockets, from "C" into side pocket "P", and from "A" and "B" into the corner pocket "Z".

Not all tables are identical, therefore the banking point will vary somewhat from table to table. Different cushions on the same table may even react differently. Before playing on an unfamiliar table, its banking characteristics should be tested using this drill. If this drill is practiced often on a familiar table, it can be used as a standard by which other tables are

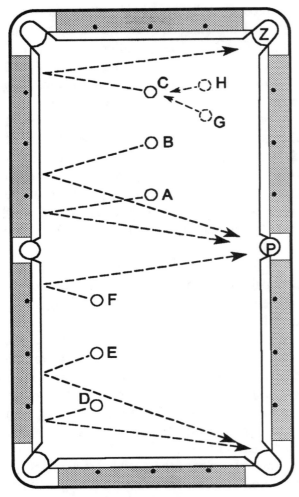

FIGURE 13-16. A bank-shot drill.

rate, the drill should be repeated using an object ball. Place an object ball at position "A", position the cue ball such that the object ball must be struck head-on (no cut angle). Use all of the positions from "A" through "F" shooting each shot at three different speeds.

As discussed in Chapter 10, a cut shot at the object ball causes it to have side english (collision-induced english) which requires a slight adjustment in banking point. Practice all of the previously described object-ball bank shots using a cut angle of about 30 degrees from both directions. This is demonstrated by cue ball positions "G" and "H" while banking an object ball at position "C". Experiment using enough side english to negate collision-induced english as described in Chapter 10.

Another good bank shot exercise is shown in figure 13-17. The object ball (7-ball) is placed on the side cushion one diamond from the end rail. The cue ball is placed in the middle of the table directly out from the object ball (position "A"). The object ball is banked into the opposite corner pocket. Note that this shot requires a half-ball hit. Having a definite aiming point makes this shot easy to remember. Move both balls an additional diamond distance from the end rail and repeat the shot from cue ball positions "B" and "D". The object ball probably won't be made very often when it's three diamonds from the end rail, but a good drill demonstrates what can't be done as well as what can be done. When the object ball is more than one diamond distance from the pocket, it is advisable to use enough side english to negate collision-induced english.

Since a half-ball hit causes the object ball to rebound one diamond away in the width of the table, it follows that it will rebound two diamonds away in the length of the table. This half-ball bank shot is illustrated by cue ball position "E" when banking the 9-ball. Practice banking the length of the table from cue ball positions "E" and "F".

compared. The better you become at this drill the easier it will be to detect differences in other tables.

The entire banking drill should be repeated from cue ball positions "D", "E", and "F" (figure 13-16). Then move the cue ball three diamonds from the banking cushion and repeat the exercise. Your score can be expressed as a percentage of successful attempts. This exercise emphasizes banking point relative to speed which is basic to all bank shots. It would be futile to practice bank shots with more variables until at least a 50 percent success rate is attained with this drill.

When all of the cue-ball bank shots can be made with a better than 50 percent success

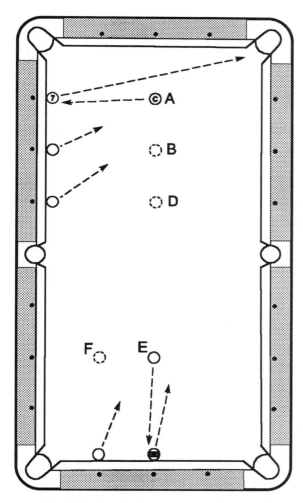

FIGURE 13-17. A bank-shot drill.

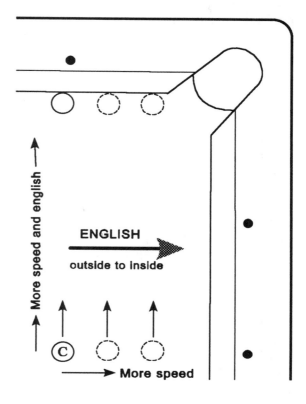

FIGURE 13-18. Half-ball bank shots.

When the object ball is less than one diamond distance from the end rail (when banking the width of the table) it would normally have to be struck fuller than a half-ball hit. However, hitting the object ball fuller than a half-ball hit could result in a double kiss (object ball rebounds back into the cue ball) which means the shot would be missed. But, these shots can still be made with a half-ball hit using <u>speed</u> and <u>english</u> to control rebound angle.

Figure 13-18 shows the proper speed and english. The cue ball can be moved closer to the object ball providing it is struck progressively **harder** and with outside english (left english in **this** case). (The outside english

is required because the angle of incidence becomes larger as the cue ball is moved closer to the object ball). Both balls can be moved closer to the pocket but the outside english must be progressively changed to no english, then to inside english. The exact speed and english will vary somewhat from table to table.

These half-ball bank shots don't seem like much on paper, but they are easy to learn and to remember. It is a near certainty that sometime in your pool career you will use one of these shots to turn a certain loss into an easy victory. You will surely enjoy the times when your opponent is missing these shots, or nudging them around, while you're making them.

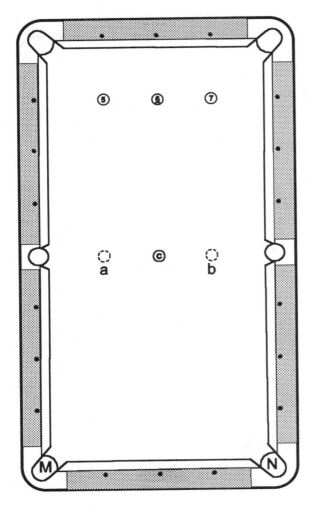

FIGURE 13-19. Long bank shots.

To facilitate learning bank shots, it is important to develop terminology that expressly describes the errors when they occur. Simply saying "I hit that ball too far to the left, or right", will not help you develop a correction for the problem. Examples of various banking errors are shown in figure 13-20. These errors can be described in several ways. They can be described in relation to the distance to the adjacent pocket; that is, "banking point "a" was <u>too far</u> from the pocket," or "banking point "b" was <u>too close</u> to the pocket." However, if the object ball is on the cushion to begin with, the error can't be described using this

Figure 13-19 shows a bank-shot drill shooting the length of the table. Place three object balls on the table as shown by the 5-, 6-, and 7-ball. With the cue ball on the center spot, bank each of the balls into pocket "M" or "N". Repeat the exercise from cue ball positions "a" and "b". A good barroom player should make an average of 4 of the 9 shots.

The main purpose of bank-shot drills is to provide a frame of reference that serves as the rudiments of a rote system. These exact drill shots may not occur often but similar shots will. When faced with a similar shot during competitive play, only a slight adjustment need be made to the familiar drill shot.

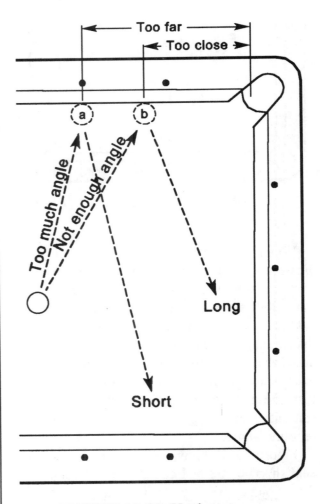

FIGURE 13-20. Various terms used to describe bank shot errors.

terminology. The error can be described in relation to the angle of incidence; striking at "a" would be "<u>too much angle</u>" (angle of incidence too high), or striking at "b" would be "<u>not enough angle</u>" But, probably the best way to describe banking errors is in relation to the intended pocket. If the ball strikes the cushion at "a" it can be described as "<u>coming up short</u>," or striking at "b" described as "<u>coming up long</u>." Whichever terminology is used, be sure that you're consistent. If you can't describe, to yourself, what you did wrong you won't be able to fix it.

Kick shots--A kick-shot drill is shown in figure 13-21. Shoot the cue ball from

positions "a" through "h", into cushion "A" to make the object ball (4-ball) into pocket "P". A good barroom player should average about 4 successes out of the 7 shots.

The same ball positions can be used to practice two-cushion kick shots. Use cushions "A" and "C" in whatever order is required to make the 4-ball.

Still another two-cushion kick shot can be practiced from these ball positions. This drill requires the use of both side cushions. Shoot the cue ball into cushion "B" such that it rebounds to cushion "A" then into the object ball (a *zee* shot). The average barroom player will initially have difficulty making more than 2 out of the 7 shots. The key to making this shot is in the proper blending of speed, incidence angle, and running english. Running english should be used in favor of approach angle in gaining the proper rebound angle off the first cushion. With some practice, the average barroom player should be able to make about 40 percent of these shots.

A similar zee shot drill can be used to develop a shot that most players won't even attempt, much less make. Instead of kicking for the object ball, place the object ball successively in positions "a" through "h". With ball-in-hand, bank the object ball two rails ("B" and "A") into pocket "P". As learned in the previous two-rail drill, it helps to have running english on the ball when it strikes the first cushion. This can be accomplished by transferring english from the cue ball to the object ball.

The short kick shot, with the object ball only a few inches off the banking cushion, comes up often enough to warrant a specific practice drill. Many players use the short kick shot only when they can't get a direct shot at the object ball. On occasions, a ball can be shot straight-in but in doing so there would be no chance of getting position on the next ball. In these cases the short kick shot can be

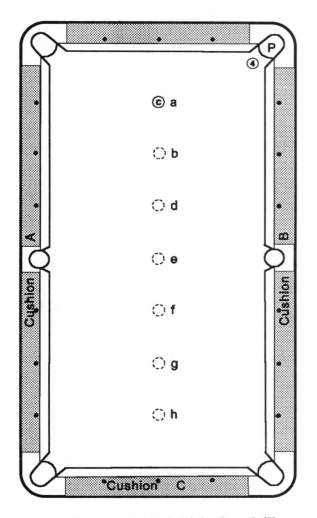

FIGURE 13-21. A kick-shot drill.

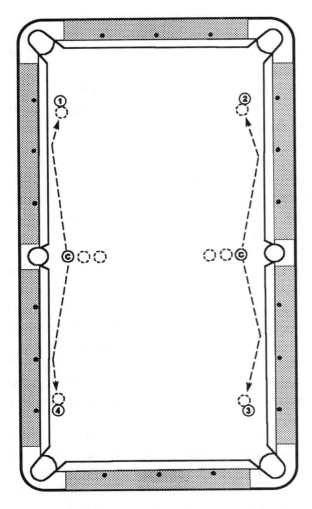

FIGURE 13-22. Short kick shots.

Carom shots--Carom shots are practiced so that they can be made during competitive play, but even more importantly, so that they are recognized and considered as an option during competitive play.

Figure 13-23 shows the ball placement for a carom-shot drill. Place a ball (8-ball) on the center spot. Place an object ball (1-ball) one diamond distance from both the side rail and center string. With ball-in-hand, shoot the 1-ball into the 8-ball such that it caroms into the side pocket. Replace the 8-ball and repeat the shot from positions 2, 3, and 4. A good barroom player should be successful about 80 percent of the time from positions 1 and 2 and about 50 percent of the time from positions 3 and 4.

Another situation that occurs occasionally requires the cue ball to be shot around another ball (to the cushion) before striking the object ball. To practice this type of shot, place a ball (2-ball) about one diamond away from the pocket and one ball diameter plus ½ inch from the cushion as shown in figure 13-24a. Practice shooting the cue ball into the cushion such that it rebounds into the 2-ball then into the pocket. Vary the cue ball

used to provide many different position possibilities.

Figure 13-22 shows a short kick-shot drill. Place an object ball one diamond distance from each corner pocket as shown. Vary the distance between the ball and cushion from about ½ inch to 2 inches. Place the cue ball about one ball diameter out from the side pocket and shoot a kick shot at each object ball. Replace the object balls and repeat the exercise with the cue ball two, three, and four ball diameters from the side pocket. Your success rate can be expressed as a percent. With some practice, a good barroom player should make about 70 percent of these shots.

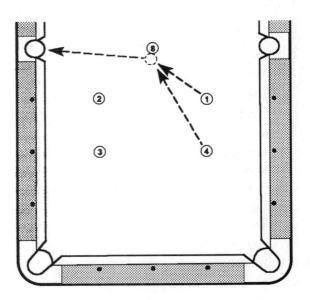

FIGURE 13-23. A carom-shot drill.

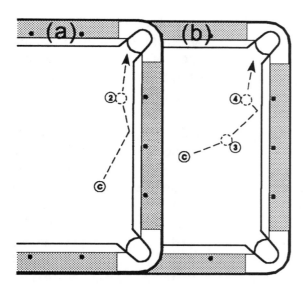

FIGURE 13-24. Carom and kick drills.

position somewhat for each shot. When this becomes easy, use an object ball struck with the cue ball for the same exercise.

Figure 13-24b shows a challenging exercise requiring a carom off two balls. Place a ball (4-ball) one ball diameter plus ½ inch from the cushion and one diamond distance from the corner pocket. Place the 3-ball and cue ball such that the cue ball will carom off the 3-ball, into the cushion, into the 4-ball, then into the pocket. This shot won't be made very often but a lot will be learned about carom shots in the process of trying to make it.

Spot shots--The spot shot should be practiced not only because it comes up frequently, but also because it offers excellent aim and execution practice. The proper ball placement for the spot shot was discussed in Chapter 11. When executing the spot shot, observe the path of the cue ball after contact with the object ball. Practice varying this path first by speed control, then with various combinations of top, bottom, and side english.

Power break shots--Most players don't practice break shots because it takes too much time to repeatedly rack the balls. Actually, most aspects of the break shot can be practiced without using a full rack of balls. At first, the coordination of forward body and arm movement should be practiced in slow motion without a cue ball. As coordination increases, the speed of the stroke can be increased and a cue ball used.

The cue ball should be shot from the center of the table directly at the center of the foot rail and allowed to rebound back and forth. If the cue ball jumps upon striking the first rail it's being struck above center, or the butt end of the stick is being held too high (causing cue ball to jump when struck). A small jump off the second rail generally occurs due to normal roll (polished balls will jump less). Any inadvertent side english will result in an altered rebound angle off the first cushion. Inadvertent side decreases power and therefore should be avoided. **The amount of power applied can be judged by how many times the cue ball rebounds back and forth.** A good player will cause the cue ball to strike five rails. The distance the cue ball rebounds is very sensitive to the power applied because it is reduced by about 60 percent each time it strikes a cushion. For example, if the cue ball is struck hard enough to roll 500 feet, it would rebound about 0.3 foot off the fifth rail; if the initial speed is increased 50 percent to the equivalent of a 750 foot roll, it would rebound 2.9 feet off the fifth rail. This calculation is not absolutely accurate because the 40 percent cushion efficiency assumes that the ball has normal roll which is not necessarily the case here. However, the point is, the rebound distance off the fifth rail should be monitored very closely in determining the relative power applied to the cue ball.

For a more advanced practice technique, place an object ball on the foot spot, shoot into it as though it were the head ball in a rack of balls. Shooting from a few inches on either side of center table helps avoid a second collision with the cue ball. This practice technique helps perfect aim and proper application of bottom english; however, inadvertent side english is more difficult to detect. The amount of power applied can be judged the same as with the cue-ball-only practice technique.

Before ending a break-shot practice session a few shots should be taken at an actual rack of balls. This allows the implementation of any improvement. If this isn't done there is a tendency to slip back to the old way of breaking when shooting into a full rack of balls.

If you're a serious player you'll have to go one step further -- muscle building. The power break, to a large extent, depends on brute strength. Brute strength can be increased by exercising the proper muscles. This exercise requires an expendable cue stick and a standard, plastic covered, bar-bell weight of 5 to 10 pounds. Force the weight as far as possible onto the stick. Figure 13-25 shows an assembled exercise stick. Using a rail bridge, thrust the stick back and forth as hard and as rapidly as possible. Continue thrusting until the muscles are about half fatigued. Rest for a while then repeat the procedure two more times.

Ideally, this power break exercise should be done at some time other than during the regular practice session. Fatiguing the shooting muscles may diminish speed control for a short time.

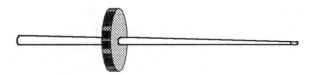

FIGURE 13-25. A power-break exercise stick.

One should use some type of flexing and stretching routine before shooting the power break under game conditions. This insures against undue strain on the muscles and allows the extraction of maximum power.

Clusters--Clusters can be more devastating than most opponents. Dealing with clusters is more of a thinking process than a shooting technique. Although clusters will always present problems, study and practice will help reduce their devastation. Much can be learned simply by experimenting with cluster shots.

When breaking up a cluster, there is a tendency to blast away with no regard for where the balls will end up. This is not the best technique; the clusters should be studied to determine which direction each ball will go, then bumped just hard enough to move the balls to the desired position. Cluster-drill practice should be conducted just as a cluster situation should be approached during game conditions. That is, they should first be examined carefully to determine if any of the balls can be pocketed. If so, one can then concentrate on getting the best shape to execute the shot. If none of the balls can be made, then the cluster must be broken up while shooting another ball.

To set up a cluster drill hold three balls in one hand, close your eyes and set them on the table in a random fashion. Start with ball-in-hand and try to make all three balls with the fewest number of shots. Obviously, making one of the balls while breaking up the cluster is the most desirable, therefore the cluster must be checked for makable balls first. If none of the balls can be made with the first shot, the second alternative must be considered; it must be determined how the cluster can be struck so that each ball will move to the most advantageous position for the succeeding shots. This drill can be made a little harder by having to carom the cue ball off another ball (key ball) before hitting the cluster. In this case both cue ball and key ball can be placed in the most advantageous position. Granted, this drill may be easier than most game-condition cluster problems, but by being relatively easy it accomplishes two things. First, confidence is built so that clusters are no longer intimidating; and second, selecting the best position for the key ball is valuable experience in helping to select a key ball during a game.

Figure 13-26 shows a two-ball cluster drill. Place two sets of frozen balls on the table as shown. Place a key ball anywhere on the table and start with ball-in-hand. Try to make all five balls in the fewest number of

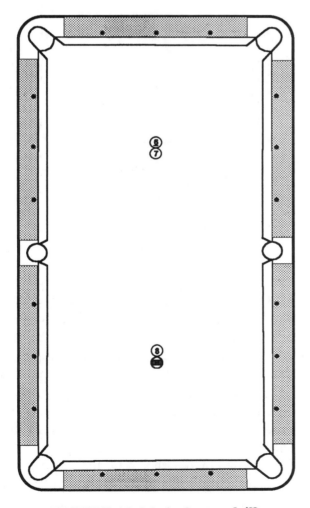

FIGURE 13-26. A cluster drill.

shots. The average barroom player will average about 8 or 9 shots when first shooting this drill; when the shooter learns to capitalize on the bank shot options, this average should drop to 6 or 6.5 shots.

Shape drills--For every shot, it is essential to know where the cue ball will end up when using medium speed and no english. This knowledge is used as a reference to determine if the shot should be shot faster, slower, or with english. Your ability to get shape will always be limited by the accuracy of your reference shots.

Figure 13-27 shows a reference-shot practice drill utilizing a cue ball target. The target can be an ordinary piece of paper or tissue paper. Place an object ball (3-ball) one diamond from the end and side cushions as shown. Begin with the cue ball at position "A". Place the target where you think the cue ball will stop when using medium speed and no english. Keep repeating the shot and moving the target until the cue ball comes to rest on the target. Move the cue ball to each of the eight other positions repeating the process at each position.

The second shape drill is similar to the first except that the target is placed randomly on the table. Using the same ball positions as in the previous drill, try to pocket the object ball and stop the cue ball on the target.

These two drills can be unified into one. First, place the target where you think the cue ball will stop when using medium speed and no english, then execute the shot. Then place the target in a random position and shoot the shot again from the same cue ball position. Use whatever speed and english that is required to make the cue ball stop on the target. This pair of shots should be shot from each of the indicated cue ball positions. This drill is beneficial in that it duplicates the mental process required for every shot. That is, guessing where the cue ball will end up

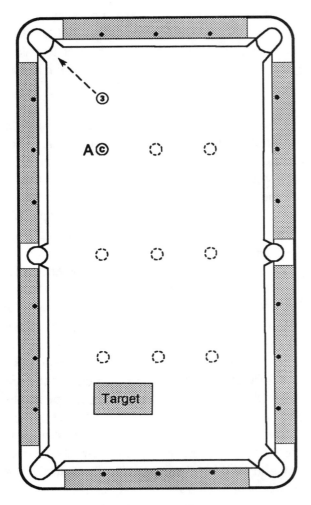

**FIGURE 13-27. A position drill.
Pocket the object ball and try to
stop the cue ball on the target.**

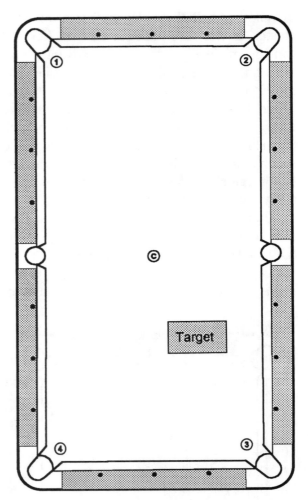

**FIGURE 13-28. A position drill.
Make each ball and try to
stop the cue ball on the
randomly placed target.**

using medium speed and no english, then shooting it with the appropriate speed and english required for shape.

For another target drill, place a ball at the edge of each corner pocket as shown in figure 13-28. Place the position target randomly on the table. Start with the cue ball on the center spot; shoot the 1-ball and try to stop the cue ball on the target. Shoot the remaining balls in numerical order, from where the cue ball lies, each time trying to stop the cue ball on the target. This drill is more difficult than it appears; the reason is that the cue ball curve,

caused by roll, is greatest just after impact with the object ball. This makes it difficult to estimate its direction at the time it strikes the cushion. Figure 13-29 shows two examples of this shot. In figure 13-29a, the cue ball caroms off the object ball then curves before striking the cushion which causes it to rebound in direction "A". Figure 13-29b shows what happens if it is shot very fast or from close range; either way, the cue ball will have very little roll and therefore won't curve

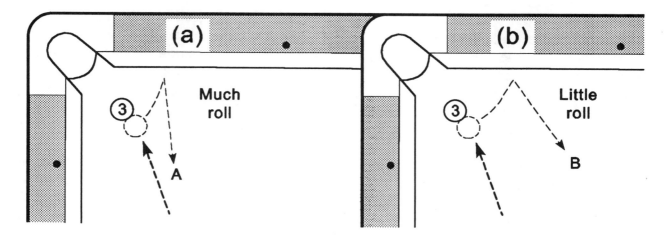

FIGURE 13-29. The cue-ball's carom path depends on its speed and state of roll.

much before striking the cushion, and will consequently rebound in direction "B".

Coin-operated tables--A coin-operated table is one in which the object balls do not return after being pocketed. The cue ball returns but coins must be inserted in order to get the other balls back. Management wants the tables to make as much money as possible so they usually don't want them used for practice drills, especially those drills that take a long time and don't consume balls. Drills on coin-operated tables usually must be done before or between regular games. Generally, the only ball available is the cue ball thereby limiting the types of drills that can be practiced. Drills conducted on a coin-operated table aren't so much for learning but rather for loosening up before a competitive game and for familiarization with the table's characteristics.

Banking characteristics can be tested using the cue-ball banking drill shown in figure 13-16. Each cushion should be tested; sometimes they react differently because they're loose, out of alignment, or set too high or too low.

Cushion efficiency (resiliency) can be tested using the speed drills shown in figure

13-1. These drills are effective in testing the speed of the table as well as cushion efficiency. Determine how level the table is by dropping a ball from about 2 inches onto the inside edge of the cushion (this assures that the ball is propelled perpendicular to the cushion with no english) and observe how straight its path is. Be sure to test all parts of the table. One side could be level while the other side is not; this is usually due to improper shimming of the slates.

The side-english drill shown in figure 13-7 can be used to determine how efficiently the cushions convert side english into change of rebound angle. This is a function of friction between ball and cushion; if the cloth is old and worn the rebound angle will not be affected as much by side english.

Effective pocket size can be tested by shooting the cue ball farther and farther to the edge of the pocket until it fails to go in. At least one corner pocket and one side pocket should be tested.

If there are any object balls available, use them for stun stroke practice at different speeds and distances.

DRILL GAMES

Practice drills, although beneficial, can become boring. Some drills can be made into a game so that practice becomes more enjoyable. The following drill games can be scored and recorded which helps kindle a person's competitive nature and encourages practice.

Figure 13-30 shows the ball placement for a bank-shot drill game. Position six object balls on the table as shown; start with ball-in-hand, thereafter shoot from where the cue ball stops. The objective is to bank each of the balls into a pocket; a point is scored for each ball that is pocketed. If an object ball is shot at and missed it is taken off the table; balls that are accidentally moved are also taken off the table; if no ball is struck, an object ball is taken off the table. Obviously, a perfect score is six; an average barroom player should average about three points per game.

Figure 13-31 shows the ball placement for a rail-shot drill game. Six balls are evenly spaced on the cushions as shown. Start with the cue ball on the center spot (position "A"). Thereafter shoot from where it stops. The objective is to make all the balls in the fewest number of shots. If a ball is shot and missed, or if it is accidentally moved, it is returned to its original position; scratches are penalized

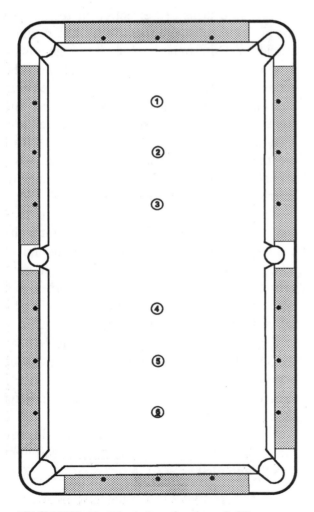

FIGURE 13-30. A bank-shot drill game.

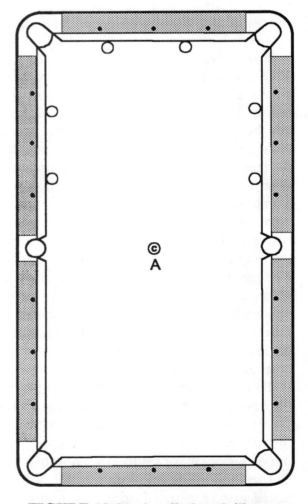

FIGURE 13-31. A rail-shot drill game.

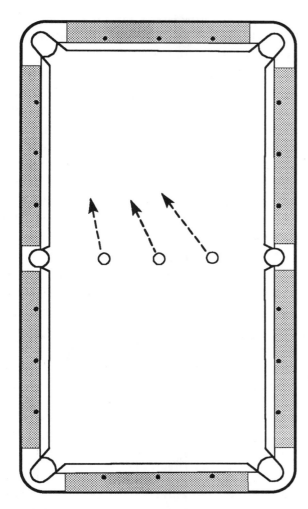

FIGURE 13-32. A position drill game.

Figure 13-33 shows an exercise in cue ball direction control. Place four object balls on the long string as shown. Begin with the cue ball on the center spot. The objective is to hit one of the object balls and pocket the cue ball. When the cue ball is successfully pocketed it is scored as a point and is replaced on the center spot for the next shot. Each time a shot does <u>not</u> score, one of the object balls (shooter's choice) is removed from the table and the next shot is made from where the cue ball stopped. The object balls stay where they stop, and if one is pocketed accidentally it stays down. Points can continue to be scored as long as an object ball

one point. A perfect score is six, the average barroom player should average about 9 shots per game.

Figure 13-32 shows an exercise in getting shape on long shots. Three object balls are evenly spaced on the center string. Start with ball-in-hand and thereafter shoot from where it stops. The objective is to pocket all three balls into the same corner pocket (any corner pocket) in the fewest number of shots. If a ball is shot at and missed, or accidentally moved, it is returned to its original position. After some practice the average barroom player should score a perfect three about 50 percent of the time.

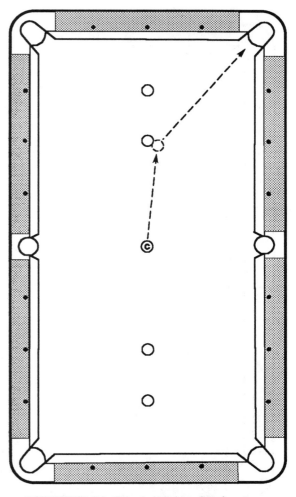

FIGURE 13-33. An exercise in cue ball direction control.

remains on the table. With some practice the average barroom player will score an average of about 5 points per game; with a lot of stun stroke practice this average can be raised considerably.

Figure 13-34 shows a kick-shot exercise. There are seven different cue ball starting positions. Start at position 1 and proceed through position 7. The cue ball must be banked into a pocket. The number of points scored depends on how many and which cushions are struck. The side cushions are worth one point and the end cushions are worth two points. The object is to score as many points as possible in seven shots. For example, the shot diagrammed in figure 13-34

is worth 4 points: side (1) end (2) side (1). No points are scored if the cue ball is not pocketed or goes into the wrong pocket. The beginner may elect to start with one-cushion bank shots scoring a conservative one or two points each shot. With some practice, one should be able to make some six point shots with a success rate of 25 to 50 percent. A good barroom player should average about 10 points for the seven shots. This is an excellent late night exercise because there is no noise from ball collisions to disturb the neighbors.

Selecting proper shot sequence can be practiced by trying to run three randomly positioned object balls. Balls can be randomly positioned by rolling them, by hand, into the cue ball at a fast speed. It is difficult to predict how they will carom off the cue ball, therefore final ball positions will be fairly random. Begin with ball-in-hand and try to run all three balls in three shots. A good barroom player will be successful about 75 percent of the time.

This drill can be made harder by changing the rules. Require that the cue ball strike a cushion between shots. That is, the cue ball must go to a cushion after pocketing an object ball for shape on the next ball.

PRACTICE PLAY

Playing pool can be classified into three categories; *competitive play, casual play,* and *practice play.* In competitive play the prime objective is to <u>win</u>; in casual play the prime objective is to have <u>fun</u>; and in practice play the prime objective is to <u>learn</u> and improve. Practice play can be done alone or with another player. During practice play one should experiment with new shots, techniques, and strategies. People subconsciously condition themselves to react a certain way under a certain set of

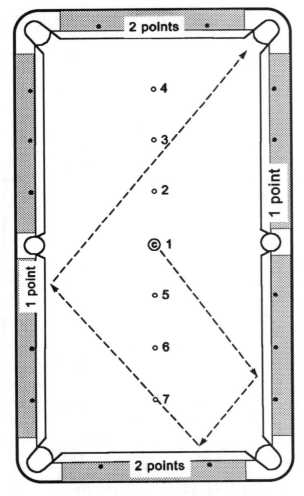

FIGURE 13-34. A kick-shot drill.

conditions. In most respects this is good, however it prevents experimenting with alternative solutions that may actually be better solutions. During practice play alternative solutions should be searched for and occasionally tried. For example, a person may always attempt a bank shot rather than shoot a long cut shot. In practice play, the long cut shot should be tried occasionally.

Habit makes it difficult to recognize, much less try, alternative solutions. A good way to be assured of doing things differently is to force yourself to play the entire game differently. Play a few games without using english (wipe the chalk off the tip). This will help force concentration on speed control for getting shape. Play a few games using nothing but bottom, then top english. Shape will suffer but occasionally a viable alternative to your normal playing technique will be recognized. Occasionally, shoot an entire game with your opposite hand. It is surprising how fast a person can learn to shoot reasonably well with the opposite hand. Shoot entire games with the mechanical bridge. The more it is used the better it will be used. Every player must occasionally use a finger tip bridge in order to shoot over another ball, and the chance of making these shots drops substantially. The odds can be improved considerably by practicing with this bridge; force the use of the finger tip bridge by placing another ball behind the cue ball for each shot during an entire game.

The position spot technique discussed in Chapter 7 must be learned and refined during practice play. To facilitate, cut out a one-inch diameter circle of cloth or paper to represent your desired position spot. Before each shot, place the position spot on the table exactly where you intend to make the cue ball come to rest. Be aware, your psyche will try to prevent you from using the position spot just to avoid embarrassment. However, if you intend to improve your cue ball positioning

skills, you must suffer the agony of embarrassment each time you fail to get good position. Eventually your position errors will become progressively smaller and embarrassment will give way to elation.

When players with unequal pool skill practice together, there's a tendency for the lesser player to get discouraged and the better player to get sloppy. To avoid this tendency, the game should be handicapped to make it easier and more encouraging for the lesser player and more challenging for the better player. The following are some examples of how to handicap a game of EIGHT-BALL.

1. Limit the eligible pockets for the better player.
2. Require that the better player shoot balls in numerical order.
3. Require that the better player cause the cue ball to strike a rail after striking the object ball.
4. Remove some of the lesser player's balls from the table.
5. Assign some of the balls belonging to the lesser player to the better player.
6. Require that the better player call shots one or more balls in advance.
7. Require the better player to bank a specific number of balls.
8. Require the better player to shoot with the opposite hand.
9. Give the lesser player the break shot.

If you're fortunate enough to obtain tutoring from an expert, you should think out loud while playing. In so doing, the expert can detect any flaws in your analytical processes. Conversely, be sure to ask the expert to also think out loud. This may reveal some strategy options that you have never even considered. You may eventually start thinking and acting like the expert.

The rules of a game can be changed to facilitate practicing certain shots. For example, two people can play EIGHT-BALL banking every ball. Be cautioned, inexperienced players may miss so many shots that the game becomes a frustrating rather than a learning process. In this case the game can be made easier by allowing ball-in-hand for each bank shot. The players will make more shots thus avoiding frustration while still getting valuable bank shot practice.

Any time you miss a shot stop and think about it; determine exactly why it was missed. If the problem can't be isolated and examined it can't be corrected. If you're playing alone, the balls should be replaced in their original position and shot again. The last experience is remembered best by the mind and muscles, therefore the shot should be repeated until it is executed properly.

On many occasions during competitive play, it is difficult to decide which ball to shoot or which is the easiest way to get shape. A decision is made and the shot is executed. If everything works out fine it is assumed that the proper decision was made. If the shot is missed then the decision is questioned. Whether the shot is made or missed offers some evidence as to the correctness of the decision, but it is not proof positive. When these situations are encountered during practice play, the position of the involved balls should be marked before the shot is executed. The various alternatives should be tried several times by replacing the balls in their original position after each shot. With the results of these test shots, a valid judgment can then be made as to the best of the alternatives. Being reasonably certain of the best solution will help improve judgment the next time a dilemma is faced.

Competitive play can be a significant part of the learning process. Specific skills are not learned efficiently during competitive play but skill and knowledge deficiencies may be revealed. The mind must be conditioned to employ the skills already acquired; frequently, the stressful conditions caused by competitive play tend to temporarily obliterate one's established repertoire of skills. One must learn to apply one's knowledge under competitive conditions by <u>exposure</u> to competitive conditions. Being able to employ one's skills in a serious competitive situation is what it's all about.

PRACTICING WITHOUT A POOL TABLE

For many reasons, some people don't have easy access to a pool table. Many of the required skills can be learned, at least to some extent, without a pool table. In some respects it may be better to learn some of the fundamentals without a table. The lure of shooting balls can distract one's concentration.

Stance, stroke, and bridge--It would be foolhardy for an aspiring golfer to pick up a golf club, for the first time, on the golf course. The fundamentals of grip, stance, and swing must first be practiced in the backyard, on the driving range, or on the practice putting green. The same is true for pool -- the pool table is not the best place to learn many of the fundamentals.

Stance, stroke, and making a bridge can be practiced on any surface that is about 29 inches above the floor. The stroke can be perfected by stroking through a wire loop. Make the loop by wrapping a piece of wire around the middle of an old cue stick (it may leave a mark so don't use a good stick) as shown in figure 13-35. Move about three inches toward the tip and make a slightly smaller loop. Make several loops each progressively smaller. Stand the loop up by sticking the long end into an eraser or similar piece of rubber as shown in figure 13-36.

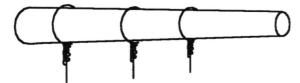

FIGURE 13-35. Making practice loops.

Practice stroking through the largest loop first then advance to progressively smaller loops. Start with the cue tip about 4 or 5 inches from the loop, then stroke forward 3 or 4 inches through the loop as shown in figure 13-36. Initially, the eye should focus on the loop; as the stick is being stroked back and forth, focus should change to some point beyond the loop to an imaginary object ball. A person should eventually be able to stroke through a loop that is only a few millimeters larger than the cue shaft.

Just as the golfer goes back to the driving range occasionally, so should the pool player practice stroking through the loops occasionally. This will insure that no unwanted pumping or sloppiness will creep into the stroke. Stroking with the opposite hand can also be learned with the wire loops. In this way a reasonable proficiency can be attained without ever missing a shot.

Cue-ball deflection--It usually takes a long time for a new player to be able to

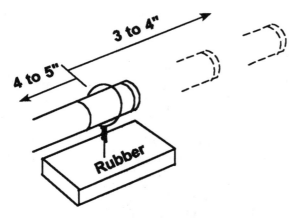

FIGURE 13-36. Use of practice loops.

predict where the cue ball will go after contact with the object ball. The learning process can be accelerated by practicing on paper. Draw a rectangle representing a pool table as shown in figure 13-37. Draw a cue ball at the center of the table and several object balls randomly positioned on the table. Simulate shooting each of the balls into a pocket. Calculate the cue-ball deflection path for three different conditions: (1) normal roll, (2) stun stroke, and (3) center ball medium speed. Using the 1-ball in figure 13-37 as an example, proceed as follows:

1. Draw the path of the object ball.
2. Draw the initial path of the cue ball.
3. Measure the cut angle (30 degrees).
4. Determine cue-ball deflection angle assuming normal roll (37 degrees -- from figure 5-5).
5. Draw the deflection path of the cue ball with normal roll.
6. Draw the deflection path assuming that a stun stroke is used.
7. Draw the deflection path with a center-ball hit. This path will depend on the distance between the cue ball and the object ball and also on how hard the cue ball is struck.

The more shots that are diagrammed, the easier it will be to estimate the cue-ball deflection path at different speeds, normal roll, stun stroke, and center-ball hit. Doing the analysis on paper forces one to consider of all the variables. Knowing how the variables affect the cue-ball deflection angle facilitates the proper execution of actual shots.

Bank shots--Unless they are done by rote, bank shots are about 80 percent knowledge and 20 percent shooting ability. The analysis can be done on paper which makes the bank shot an ideal candidate for practicing without

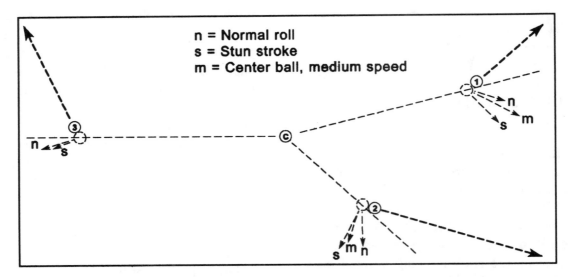

FIGURE 13-37. Practice calculating cue-ball's deflection path on paper.

a table. A review of Chapter 10 is advised before attempting the paper practice.

Draw a rectangle representing a pool table; draw a cue ball and an object ball that is to be banked. Calculate the geometric banking point using each of the banking systems. Calculate the error caused by cushion distortion, roll, and collision-induced english. Determine how much correction must be applied to the angle of incidence.

As with the cue-ball deflection angle, this exercise forces one to become aware of all the variables and how each affects the rebound angle. The more bank shots that are analyzed on paper, the more the brain becomes conditioned to consider all the variables. When shooting a bank shot on a real table, the brain will have some basis from which to reason and resolve.

Rail shots-- Rail shots are excellent candidates for paper practice. Draw a table with several balls along the rail at different distances from the pockets and with different cut angles. First estimate the required cut angle, point of aim, and type of english (if any) that should be used. Measure the cut angle and the distance between object ball

and pocket. Determine the optimum target point and english from figure 8-9. This exercise offers good training in estimating angles and distances. With this capability one need only memorize the rail-shot chart to be a rail shot expert.

Strategy--Strategy encompasses many aspects of the game. But, in games like EIGHT-BALL, the most important aspect of strategy is selecting the proper sequence of shots. Practicing strategy on paper conditions one to plan three shots in advance. In order to select the proper sequence one must be aware of all the possibilities. When playing, there is a tendency to shoot as soon as one of the possibilities is recognized. With paper practice a shot does not follow the analysis, therefore more time can be given to analysis. Proper training conditions the mind to allow more time for analysis and for exploring more possibilities.

Draw a pool table on a large piece of paper. Use a paper punch to punch disks out of cardboard or heavy paper. Number the disks to represent balls. Place three simulated object balls and a cue ball randomly on the simulated table. After identifying all the probable sequences, select the easiest one using the probability technique discussed in Chapter 12. Take your time, remember you're trying to expand your recognition of probable shots and sequences. Randomly rearrange the four balls and repeat the analysis. This exercise can be made more difficult by using more than three object balls. This way, the proper balls as well as the sequence must be determined.

PRACTICE OVERVIEW

Good days bad days--When practicing or playing pool you will undoubtedly have good days and bad days. When you're having a good day, stay with it because you're doing things right and staying with it will reinforce good habits. When you're having a bad day, quit practicing. You're doing something wrong and the longer you play the more you'll reinforce the bad habits. The more you reinforce bad habits, the harder they are to correct.

On those occasional bad days, practice something different; shoot with your opposite hand or with the mechanical bridge; practice massé shots, jump shots, or curve shots. Some people find practicing trick shots relaxing and therapeutic.

Several bad days in succession is considered to be a "slump." When you're having a slump the fundamentals should be reviewed. Carefully check your stance, arm positions, bridge hand and distance, and most importantly, your <u>head position</u>. The most common problem is inadvertently tilting the head, or moving it to one side, which distorts visual perception and in turn causes aim errors. The best way to avoid a slump is to carefully and deliberately <u>review the fundamentals each time you start shooting</u>. If some quirk is introduced during the first few

shots, it tends to remain the entire shooting session and perhaps longer.

Playing plateau--Most players continue to improve until they reach a plateau. They may spend the rest of their pool careers at this plateau even if they shoot regularly. Failure to improve could either be the failure to gain new knowledge or failure to improve ability. The best way to determine what the deficiency is, is to test yourself. Find an expert player to advise you on every shot while you're playing a third person. If expert advice improves your game, you're deficient in the knowledge department. If expert advice doesn't improve your game, your ability is deficient. Remember, the expert can only give you knowledge, not ability.

Knowing that you missed a shot before the cue ball gets to the object ball is an indication of an ability deficiency. You know where to aim, therefore knowledge and judgment are not deficient; immediately recognizing the error is evidence of this. If ability is the problem, work on stance and stroke. Concentrate on those drills that emphasize aim accuracy, speed control, and english. If the problem is a knowledge deficiency you should seek the advice of a more knowledgeable player. Many players suffer from (if I may be permitted to coin a term) *"solitary syndrome."* They simply will not accept advice from others. Indeed, they may even become angry when given unsolicited advice even when they know they are in desperate need of advice. Unfortunately, solitary syndrome prevents many pool players from gaining new knowledge and improving their game. A good way to avoid solitary syndrome, while still gaining knowledge, is to discuss the game of a third party. That is, two players can exchange ideas about a game that they are only observing. Each can indicate what they would do under the prevailing circumstances. In this way knowledge is gained without a hint of criticism.

If you have a bad habit and know it, solicit the help of your friends to help you overcome it. For example, if you lift the stick off your bridge hand and end every shot with the stick in the air -- have a friend ring a bell, blow a whistle, or yell at you each time you do it. Your game will suffer during the retraining process but your long term gain will more than compensate for the short-term loss.

Practice equipment and conditions-- When practicing, use the same equipment that you use for competitive play. Don't save the good stick and don't put on a new tip just before the big game. The same is true for clothing. Make sure that every article of clothing is tested under practice conditions. Never play, or even practice, with leather soled shoes. They have a propensity for slipping. If a necktie is required during the competitive game, practice with a necktie. The tie may not have any direct effect on your aim, stroke, etc., but your subconscious mind will be preoccupied by it until it becomes familiar.

If your competitive games are played under noisy conditions, try to practice under noisy conditions. Turn on several radios, televisions, etc. If you play under barroom conditions, there's a possibility that you may dull your senses with alcohol. Some people can play under the influence and some can't. The trick is being able to focus concentration; if a person consciously tries, concentration can be focused for short periods even while under the influence. Use maximum concentration effort the moment the shot is executed.

Practice time-- How much practice time is required? The answer varies depending on the individual's ability, motivation, and expectations. Generally, the better one wants

to become the more time that must be spent practicing. A person who desires to become an expert will probably have to practice 4 or 5 hours a day. Probably the most critical time in a person's pool career is when he/she first begins to play. Most neophytes have high expectations of progress. If they don't progress as fast as expected, they become disillusioned and may lose their desire to practice. The beginner must concentrate on stance and stroke. It is frustrating to struggle to form a proper bridge; even when one manages to get it right, it's not very fulfilling. The initial struggle to master the basics with such little reward is frustrating. For this reason the beginner's practice sessions should be kept short but frequent. The neophyte can practice making a bridge while watching television or while doing some other casual activity. Stroke can also be practiced for short periods throughout the day. A few minutes every hour devoted to these fundamentals is more beneficial than an extended period at the table.

As a player's skill increases, more table time is required. The joy of watching the balls fall into the pockets is rewarding and is a source of perpetual motivation. At this point the required practice time depends on the individual player. Some players have a natural aptitude for the game, their mind and muscle memories are superior to others. These people require less practice time than do others to attain the same competence. In any case, practice time should be controlled by motivation. While you're motivated and shooting well keep on practicing, but quit before you become bored and sloppy.

Once a player becomes an expert, practice can be slanted toward reinforcement and refining rather than learning. Practice can be reduced to a few hours a day while still maintaining a high degree of proficiency. Practice time should be increased somewhat for a few weeks prior to an important tournament. Those players that have an unorthodox stance, or stroke, usually must practice more than others to maintain proficiency.

Just prior to an important tournament (a few hours), practice should be limited to easy warm-up shots that can be made 95 percent of the time. Shooting only easy shots keeps the confidence level up.

Practice time varies in quality. Casually shooting balls is not quality practice time, but shooting drill shots is. The rate at which one advances is determined by quality practice time. The average player gains more from one hour of drill shots than from ten hours of casual shooting.

Ideally, to be of greatest benefit, practice should be done at the end of the day just before going to sleep. Both mind and muscle memory fade faster when more information is heaped upon them. Going to sleep while pool is fresh in the mind allows it to be imprinted better and retained longer. The ability to learn and retain are much better before eating than after; try to schedule your practice sessions before rather than after meals.

CHAPTER 14
OVERSIZE CUE BALL

There is probably more pool played on coin-operated pool tables than any other type of table. When an object ball is pocketed on a coin-operated table, it can't be retrieved without inserting more coins. The table must be able to differentiate between object balls and cue ball so that it can return the cue ball when it is accidentally pocketed. Some tables use a magnetic separator; the cue ball is embedded with metal fillings so that a permanent magnet inside the table can route it to a separate exit. Other tables use a size separator and a cue ball that is about 1/8 inch larger than the object balls.

The magnetic cue ball is a little heavier than the normal cue ball and therefor has slightly different playing characteristics. Both the size and weight difference of the *oversize* cue ball cause it to react considerably different than the normal cue ball. Players must be aware of, and compensate for, these differences.

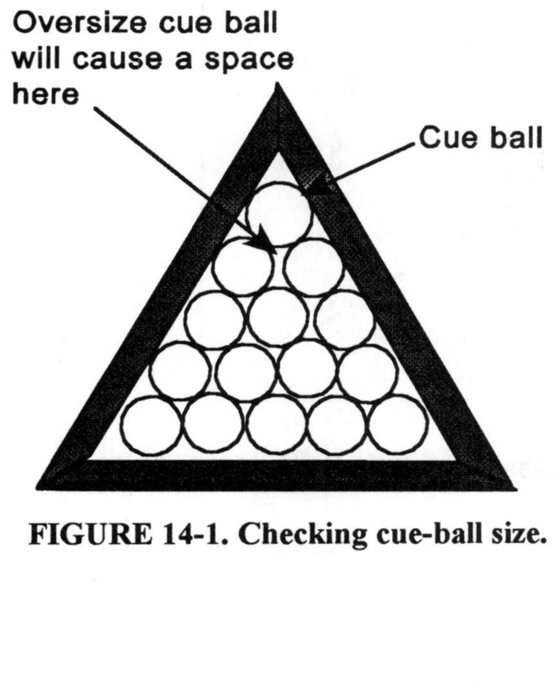

To determine if the cue ball is oversize, rack all the balls then replace the front ball with the cue ball as shown in figure 14-1. If there is a space between the balls in the second row, it's an oversize cue ball.

RESISTANCE TO MOVEMENT

An oversize cue ball is about one ounce heavier than a normal cue ball, therefore it has greater inertia and thus requires more energy to make it move. It has to be struck harder than a normal ball in order to propel it at a given speed.

RESISTANCE TO STOPPING

The oversize cue ball travels farther than the normal cue ball after colliding with an object ball. This difference decreases as the cue ball's speed increases. Assume the cue ball has normal roll and collides head-on into an object ball; the oversize cue ball moves 60 percent farther at very slow speed; 55 percent farther at slow speed; and only 35 percent farther at medium speed. As speed increases

Oversize cue ball will cause a space here

Cue ball

FIGURE 14-1. Checking cue-ball size.

roll energy is converted into linear energy less efficiently due to slippage between ball and cloth.

⚫   ⚫   ⚫

CUE BALL DEFLECTION

The oversize cue ball is deflected less than a normal cue ball after colliding with an object ball at an angle. Figure 14-2 shows the deflection angle for both cue balls at different cut angles (assuming normal roll). This difference in deflection angle is probably the most significant difference between the two balls and is probably the most difficult to adjust to.

⚫   ⚫   ⚫

CUSHION EFFICIENCY

Figure 14-3 shows the direction of the rebound force for two different size balls. The centers of both balls are below the cushion. The ball is forced backward and down into the table. A portion of the downward force component is lost to friction. The center of

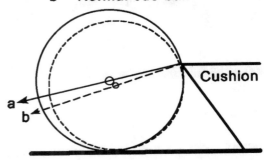

REBOUND FORCE

a = Oversize cue ball
b = Normal cue ball

FIGURE 14-3. Direction of rebound force, off the cushion, for normal and oversize cue balls.

the oversize cue ball is higher. Therefore, the downward force is smaller and thus less energy is lost to friction. Since less energy is lost to friction the oversize cue ball should rebound more efficiently and consequently farther. This reasoning does not take roll into account. If both balls have normal roll they actually rebound about the same distance. This is due to a balancing of forces. The

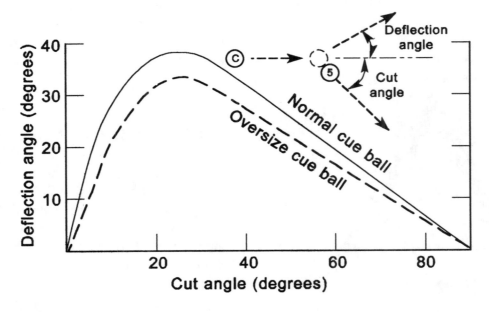

FIGURE 14-2. Deflection angle for normal and oversize cue balls.

oversize cue ball maintains more forward roll after contacting the cushion; consequently it takes more linear energy to attain normal roll in the opposite direction. The loss of linear energy causes it to rebound less efficiently.

EFFECTS OF ENGLISH

Side english is more effective in changing the rebound angle of an oversize cue ball. There are two reasons for this: First, there is less friction between ball and table surface when the ball strikes the cushion (due to less downward force) which allows its direction to be changed easier. And second, there is more surface area in contact with the cushion which increases friction causing spin to be converted into change of direction more efficiently. In any case, the difference in rebound angles is small and will probably go unnoticed by all but the expert players.

The effect of top and bottom english are considerably different between the two balls. As previously stated, with normal roll the deflection angle, after contact with the object ball, is significantly smaller for the oversize cue ball. Generally, the oversize cue ball requires only about half as much top english as would be required with a normal cue ball. Bottom is just the opposite. The oversize cue ball requires about twice as much bottom to get the same reaction.

Because of the significant differences in cue-ball reaction caused by size (and weight), it is important to practice with the same size cue ball that will be used during competitive play.

AIM ADJUSTMENT

An aim adjustment must be made when using an oversize cue ball. Figure 14-4 shows a half-ball hit with two different size cue balls

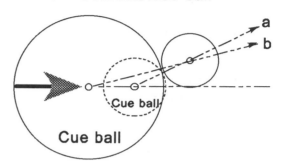

PATH OF OBJECT BALL
a = Normal cue ball
b = Oversize cue ball

FIGURE 14-4. Top view showing the difference in cut angle for a half-ball hit with normal and oversize cue balls.

(size difference exaggerated). With the normal cue ball the cut angle is 30 degrees (direction "a"). If an oversize cue ball is shot along the same path the cut angle is smaller (direction "b"). The difference in cut angles increases as the cut angle increases. For example, the difference in cut angle is 1 degree for a 30-degree cut shot, and 2.5 degrees for a 60-degree cut shot. One must allow for this difference when aiming. Keep in mind; when switching from a normal cue ball to an oversize cue ball, the cut angle must be increased slightly.

RAIL SHOT COMPENSATION

Rail shots are more difficult with the oversize cue ball. Figure 14-5a shows a normal cue ball striking the cushion and object ball at the same time. The alignment of centers is parallel to the cushion. With an oversize cue ball the alignment of centers is 1.9 degrees into the cushion as shown in figure 14-5b (exaggerated). This difference in

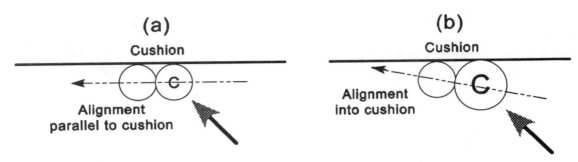

FIGURE 14-5. On a rail shot, the alignment of object ball and cue ball are not parallel to the cushion when an oversize cue ball is used.

alignment angles must be compensated for in order to pocket the object ball.

Figure 14-6 shows two methods that can be used to compensate for the alignment angle. The shot can be made using cushion-side english as shown in figure 14-6a. English-induced throw throws the object ball away from the cushion. Another option is shown in figure 14-6b. The cue ball is shot hard and aimed to strike the cushion first; it sinks into the cushion before making contact with the object ball, thus alignment is parallel to the cushion.

When the cut angle is small, english should be used to throw the object ball. As cut angle increases, english-induced throw becomes smaller, therefore speed must be used to compensate for alignment. Even when the

proper compensation is made, rail shots with the oversize cue ball have a smaller permissible error. Therefore, rail shots with the oversize cue ball should be avoided whenever possible, especially those shots with very small or very large cut angles.

Because the oversized cue ball strikes the cushion at a higher point on its circumference, it has a greater tendency to clime up the cushion or even jump over the cushion. This is especially true if the ball has topspin either from normal roll or top english. The application of bottom english is advisable when there is a chance that the cue ball will jump off or over the cushion.

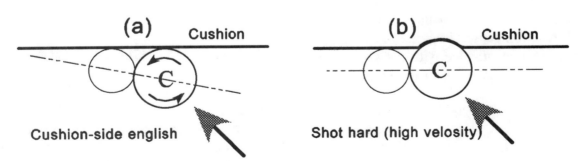

FIGURE 14-6. To compensate for the oversize cue ball, cushion-side english can be used (throws the object ball) or it can be shot using more speed.

CUE STICK

As previously stated, the oversize cue ball has greater inertia and therefore has greater resistance to movement when at rest. To compensate for the resistance to movement, the cue stick must have greater inertia. The additional stick inertia can be gotten by stroking it faster or by using a heavier stick. It is easier to use a heavier stick than to modify one's stroke. When an oversize cue ball is used, a stick weighing one or two ounces more than your regular stick should be used. The increased stick weight won't compensate for all the differences but it will help.

If one plays exclusively with the oversize cue ball, its size won't present much of a problem. If one alternates between using an oversize cue ball and a normal cue ball, there will be a problem adjusting to each. At the moment of execution the mind may not remember which ball is being used and consequently the shot may be missed or shape won't be gotten. Using a heavier stick serves as a reminder as to which ball is being used. It is even better if a visual reminder is also used. This can be done by using a stick with a different shaft thickness, or better yet, one with a different colored ferrule. If your normal stick has a white ferrule, then use one with a black ferrule when an oversize cue ball is used. If you can't find a stick with a black ferrule you may be able to die one black with an indelible felt-tip pen. If you don't play with an oversize cue ball often enough to justify having a second stick (or shaft), you can temporarily modify your regular stick by wrapping a piece of black tape around the ferrule.

CHAPTER 15

MIND AND BODY

The mind has complete and total control over the body. It has the power to cause a burn blister at the touch of an ice cube, or pleasure at the prick of a needle. If the mind says a shot will be missed, it *will* be missed, if the mind says the shot will be made, it *will* be made. Consider this example of the mind's dictatorial power; imagine two lines 8 inches apart on the kitchen floor, most people would have no problem staying between these lines while walking across the room. Now imagine walking the length of an 8-inch plank elevated 500 feet above the ground; most people would fall off and be killed. Obviously, one needs more than knowledge and ability to successfully perform a task, and so it is with pool.

MOTIVATION FOR PLAYING

Why do people play pool? Answers vary between individuals, the following are some common reasons:

1. Emotional stimulation--The highs when performance is excellent and the lows when performance is poor; neither can exist without the other.
2. The challenge--Competition to determine who has superior ability.
3. Self gratification--The feelings generated by being able to dictate an orderly, controlled response; in this case the movement of billiard balls.

4. Peer recognition--Praise, admiration, and the elevation in pecking order.
5. Tangible reward--Yes, some people play for money or other valuables.

Most pool players are motivated by all of these reasons but to varying degrees. Motivation and proficiency work in unison; the greater the motivation, the greater the proficiency and vice versa. Success or failure at pool (or anything else) is largely due to motivation. Therefore, if high aspirations are to be fulfilled, motivation must be deliberately nurtured. Self reward can be motivating; congratulate yourself when you make a good shot or shoot a good game. At times you may shoot a good game and still lose. Recognize these occasions and give yourself appropriate credit.

PSYCHOLOGICAL LIMITATIONS OF PERFORMANCE

A shot can be practiced over and over until all the muscles function in perfect coordination - you now have the physical ability; whether the shot is made or missed from that time on depends on your mind. Our mind determines whether we function at maximum physical capacity or at some lesser level.

We practice all conceivable types of shots in order to program our minds. When all is well, the mind maintains its programming and we perform at peak efficiency. However, under stressful conditions the programming is sometimes short circuited, garbled messages are sent to the muscles and performance suffers. Psychological pressure influences total game performance; analytical judgments concerning strategy, tactics, etc. may be impaired along with muscle control and coordination.

Psychological pressure is generally not an influencing factor in a casual game among friends. As the importance of the contest increases, psychological pressure becomes increasingly more prevalent. Identical conditions may cause varying degrees of stress in different individuals. An individual may be able to play under tournament conditions with little or no effects of stress, but the same person may suffer stress effects in a money game; other individuals may be just the opposite.

CHOKING

The term choking is loosely used for a variety of situations where an error is committed. As used here *choking* refers to severe anxiety that manifests itself in physical and emotional symptoms. The physical symptoms are characterized by rapid heart rate, rapid shallow breathing, upset stomach, involuntary muscle contractions, general nervousness, and clammy skin. The mind becomes overactive processing input at a faster than normal speed which prevents sustained concentration.

Anyone from the neophyte to the seasoned professional athlete can become a victim of choking. The degree of impairment depends mostly on the type of activity being performed. Unfortunately, pool players suffer more than most others from the symptoms of choking. Every shot requires finesse; just the

exact amount of coordinated muscle power. If the mind sends vague or contradictory messages to the muscles the required coordination is lost and the shot is missed. The inability to concentrate causes strategy and tactical errors as well. The incapacitating effects of choking can cause a *cycle of frustration*. Choking can cause a shot to be missed, the frustration of missing the shot causes more anxiety, more anxiety cause more choking and around it goes.

Choking can be treated from two directions; by reducing the underlying anxiety and by treating the symptoms thus breaking the cycle of frustration.

Anxiety is much like a phobia and can be treated in a similar manner. Progressive exposure to the anxiety producing situation will desensitize the emotional reaction to it. For example, if playing for money causes anxiety, start small, play frequently for small amounts, then increase the stakes in small increments. Talk to yourself. There will be moments when you tend to relax. When this occurs, purposefully compliment yourself. The reward (compliment) will help perpetuate the relaxation.

One of the most anxiety producing situations is waiting while your opponent is shooting. By the time it's your turn to shoot, you're so rattled by anxiety that you *can't* shoot. Anxiety, in these situations, can be minimized by mentally critiquing your opponent's play. Assume an arrogant attitude, concentrate on everything that your opponent does wrong. This will minimize your insecurities and keep your mind actively involved in the game.

Some people cause themselves to choke by overemphasizing the importance of winning. To reduce this tendency, priorities must be shifted. Instead of making winning the first priority, make staying calm your first priority. Just saying that you're shifting priorities doesn't make it so. In fact, there is a compelling tendency to say it just so you <u>can</u> win. To actually shift priorities you must be prepared to lose a few games, or tournaments, in the process. Eventually, remaining calm will become easier and the balls will start to fall even with the low priority.

Treating the symptoms of choking can fool your subconscious into thinking that the stressful situation no longer exists. Start by deliberately breathing slower and deeper. This will normalize the oxygen - carbon dioxide balance in your blood. Yawning occasionally will help relieve tension. We are preconditioned to associate yawning with calmness, drowsiness, or otherwise low emotional state. The *sigh*, as in "sigh of relief" works in the same manner as the yawn. But, be sure you don't disturb your opponent; reserve the sigh for when you're at the table or such time that your opponent won't be distracted.

Tense muscles cannot function with the finesse required in pool. Muscle tension can be relieved by exertion (making it work). Select a muscle (or muscle group) and flex it, hold the flexing until it becomes uncomfortable, then let it relax. Repeat the flex-relax exercise two or three times, then move on to another muscle group and repeat the exercise. The muscles can be conditioned to relax on command by saying "relax" (or substitute any word you like) as you let the muscle relax. This conditioned-response training can be performed at any time regardless of what your doing. However, the best time is when you're in bed where the relaxation can be total. Once the conditioned response is established, you won't have to go through the flexing part while playing pool -- all you need do is command your muscles to relax. This conditioned-response technique can be used for any of life's traumatic situations, not necessarily only in pool.

Occasionally, a mild case of muscle tension can be alleviated by walking it off. Take a stroll before showing up for the game, even a short walk to the rest-room can be relaxing. During your turn at the table, walk around the table between shots. Even without muscle tension it is good practice to walk the long way around the table to get to your next shot.

❶   ❷   ❸

CONCENTRATION

Webster's definition of concentration is "to collect or focus one's thoughts, efforts, etc." The focusing can be done at several levels. You can focus on a pool cue, on a pool cue tip, or on the chalk on the tip. Concentration, in pool, is used at several levels focusing on various aspects of the game.

When first learning to play pool, concentration must be on the basic physical things like foot position, bridge, head position, stroke, etc. As one advances, these basic functions will be done automatically without conscious thought. The conscious mind is then free to focus on other aspects of the game. This is an important concept for beginners and pool instructors to realize. **"IF THE BASICS ARE NOT AUTOMATIC, LEARNING BEYOND THAT STAGE WILL BE SLOW AND CONFUSING BECAUSE <u>CONCENTRATION IS DIVIDED AND DILUTED</u>."**

Physical distractions-- Physical distractions are usually *visual* or *aural*; that is, concentration is disrupted by consciously or subconsciously seeing or hearing something extraneous. Most visual distractions are the perception of movement such as a person walking by, a television set, or a blinking advertisement. Concentration can also be disrupted by static objects such as a cue rack, chalk marks, wall paper, or anything else within visual range. Aural distractions can be a radio, television, traffic noises, etc., but most commonly, conversations.

Visual and aural stimuli are distractions only because the mind is curious. It wants to look and listen so as to identify and categorize all sights and sounds. The mind is particularly curious about unfamiliar things. While your conscious mind is dealing with what you have your eyes and ears focused on, the subconscious mind is busy checking out the peripheral sights and sounds. The moment the subconscious mind detects anything unusual or unfamiliar, it tries to get the conscious mind to check it out (distraction). Familiar things are less distractive; a person that lives near a railroad won't even notice the passing train while the visitor is totally distracted by the noise and vibration.

Physical distractions can be minimized by desensitizing yourself to them. For example, if you're going to play in unfamiliar surroundings, go there in advance and expose yourself to the unfamiliar sights and sounds. Look around, read all the advertisements; study the decor, pool table, etc. Close your eyes and try to describe everything within visual range. Repeat this procedure until you can describe everything without looking. If this is done until it becomes boring, your mind will cease to be curious because the stimuli will be familiar. Try to anticipate distractions; imagine where the cocktail waitress will be walking; where people will be walking to the rest-room, juke box, etc. By the time you have to play pool your subconscious mind will be desensitized to the surroundings and will allow you to concentrate on pool.

Keep in mind: **IF YOU ARE DISTRACTED BY SOMETHING OR SOMEONE, IT'S YOUR OWN FAULT, NOT THE FAULT OF THE**

DISTRACTION. Thinking this way will keep you in control of the situation. Relinquishing control is only an excuse to lose.

Mental distractions--Mental distractions are thoughts that are not related to playing pool. Extraneous thoughts may be about winning or losing the game, what other people think of your performance, or simply second guessing and self doubt. One may be preoccupied with thoughts unrelated to pool, an argument, how to make the house payment, or even sex.

Each time the mind wanders from pool it must be brought back. The longer it is allowed to wander the more difficult it is to bring it back. Try to saturate your mind with pool. Repeat your analysis or calculate the relative odds of alternate sequences of shots. Try to keep your mind on pool even when your opponent is shooting. Compare your strategy scheme with that of your opponent. Conversing, joking, and kibitzing during the game is permissible when shooting a casual game but not when you're involved in serious competition.

Missing a shot can be devastating, especially if it is an easy shot and/or an important shot. These situations must be treated with "balanced objectivity." If missing the shot doesn't bother you, you're probably not a serious player and you can expect to repeat the error in the future. This is not all bad because immediate performance will not be diminished and the game will probably be as fulfilling as you expect it to be. At the other end of the spectrum, a player may be totally devastated by missing a shot, and the devastation can completely destroy performance. The occasion may precipitate statements like "that was stupid" or "how could I be that dumb?" Actually, knowledge or intelligence probably had nothing to do with missing the shot -- it is usually simply a lack of concentration. Be realistic, you're going to miss some shots and lose some games. When a shot is missed, review your thought process just prior to executing the shot; what were you thinking about when you should have been concentrating on the shot? If this analysis is made often enough you may discover a recurring problem with your thought process which can then be corrected.

The ball that determines the winner is often referred to as the *money ball*. The money ball is the most difficult ball to make because it has its own unique set of associated mental distractions. Some people have a tendency to think beyond the money ball to the thrill of victory. The thrill of victory is an emotional high associated with psychological and material rewards. The mind may find it very pleasant to think about and anticipate these rewards, so much so that it has difficulty concentrating on the shot. However, in most cases, it's the fear of losing these rewards that disrupts concentration. The best way to avoid allowing the mind to think about the rewards is to pretend that it's not the money ball. Technically you're not concerned about where the cue ball ends up (except to avoid a scratch) because there is no need for shape. However, imagine that there is another ball that must be made, then execute the shot while trying to stop the cue ball at a predetermined position spot. This makes the money ball more like any other ball and minimizes the unique emotional characteristics associated with it.

Dead stroke--*Dead stroke* is a term used to depict a euphoric state of mind in which concentration is so thorough that maximum performance is attained seemingly without effort. In dead stroke, there is practically no conscious effort. Everything seems to happen by itself. Unfortunately, you can't command yourself to get into dead stroke, but since it is a state of perfect concentration, your best

shot is to train yourself to concentrate. The better your concentration, the closer you will come to attaining and sustaining dead stroke.

PSYCH-OUT

Psych-out is defined as the use of psychological methods to influence or confuse the thinking of an opponent. Psych-out techniques are used, to some degree, in practically every sport. The effectiveness of psych-out techniques depends primarily on the type of sport. Those sports that require precise muscle coordination and great concentration are the most susceptible; pool is at the top of the list in this category.

The psych-out can either be unintentional or intentional. It is permissible to unintentionally psych-out your opponent by demonstrating superior knowledge and ability.

The intentional psych-out (also called *sharking*) is caused by taunting, deliberate intimidation, guilt provocation, delaying play, or visual and aural distractions. To be more specific about intentional psych-out techniques would only create greater awareness of them which would make them more effective. **Those people who employ deliberate psyching techniques are the dregs of the sport and the species.** They sacrifice their self-esteem for a momentary advantage. The advantage is short lived. The loss of self-esteem lingers on. *Never* dilute your own concentration by employing intentional psych-out techniques.

How can you defend against a psych-job? Psyching-out can only occur when you allow it to. The best defense against the psych-out is to psych yourself <u>in</u>. Intensify your concentration by focusing all your senses on the game. If the distraction is aural, focus on the click of the balls as they collide; try thinking louder. If the distractions are visual, focus on the balls, carom angles, ball locations, etc. Intense concentration can be like looking at things through a microscope -- you may discover things you have never known before.

Players can psych *themselves* out; this is usually the result of entertaining negative thoughts. Every negative thought has a positive flip side. As soon as a negative thought is recognized one must change it to its positive flip side. For example, one may have the negative thought "I don't deserve to win this game," immediately think, "I do deserve to win this game, I'm a better player than my opponent." The last thought that the mind harbors, in this case the positive thought, has the most influence on the subconscious mind.

After making a very good or very lucky shot, it is not uncommon for a person to miss the following shot. This is because the person has a guilty conscience and inwardly feels that the opponent should be shooting. In these cases the person should take extra time before shooting the next shot. During the interim you can rationalize, "the Pool God wouldn't have given you the shot if you were not deserving."

A person can be psyched-out by missing an easy shot. One should feel bad about missing a shot but it shouldn't be carried too far. If the disappointment lasts into the next shot it can disrupt the entire remaining game. After a little agony the missed shot should rationally be considered a learning experience. The miss may indicate a skill deficiency. Identifying a skill deficiency is the first step in the learning process.

The best way to play with confidence and maintain a state of concentration is to "**pretend**." Pretend that you're an actor playing the part of the greatest pool player that ever lived. Make believe the cameras are rolling and that your actions and mannerisms must exemplify supreme confidence and

playing excellence. Good actors pretend so thoroughly that they are consumed by, and figuratively become, the characters that they are portraying. When this happens you will play to the best of your ability with confidence and composure.

MENTAL PROCESSES

The human brain consists of two hemispheres separated in the vertical plane. Each hemisphere operates in a specific manner and performs specific functions. Data is stored in the left brain in objective form such as words, numbers, etc. These data are processed in a logical sequential manner like in a computer. The right brain stores, retrieves, and processes subjective information. The subjective information is in the form of sounds, smells, tastes, images, and emotions. The right brain does not understand language; it has no concept of words, numbers etc.

The left brain - right brain concept is extremely important in pool because analysis and execution each require different brain processes. Separating these processes is essential; any overlapping or intermingling causes errors.

Shot analysis--Shot analysis is done exclusively by the left hemisphere of the brain. The analytical process includes identifying problem balls, determining how they will be dealt with, selecting shot sequence, and in short, conducting all the elements of strategy, tactics, etc. The analytical processes will become easier with practice but will never be done automatically. Conscious effort will always be required to conduct the analysis. Reading this book is a left brain programming process. Getting advice from a professional pool player is likewise a programming process.

Shot execution--Just as analysis is the exclusive domain of the left brain, shot execution is the exclusive domain of the right brain. If analysis continues during the execution phase, the shot will more than likely be missed. Once analysis is completed, concentration must be shifted to the right brain. After years of practice, execution will become automatic. Then one need only instruct the right brain as to what is desired and it will do it. The right brain gives the orders to the nerves and muscles and causes them to work in unison to accomplish a specific physical task.

The concept of *positive thinking* has been around for a long time. Positive thinking works reasonably well with abstract thoughts (thoughts that cannot be pictured) but it is not the best technique for substantive thoughts (thoughts that can be depicted by pictures). Thoughts such as "I <u>will</u> make this shot" or "I <u>will</u> win this game," even if said repeatedly and with great conviction, will probably not help your game. Indeed, these thoughts usually do more harm than good because they can precipitate a cycle of frustration when a shot is missed or a game is lost.

Positive thinking is a left brain activity. If the concept were changed to *positive imagery*, which is a right brain activity, it would be a valuable tool in dealing with substantive issues. Positive imagery, or simply imaging, is the process of visualizing the desired action or result prior to execution. **IMAGERY IS THE ONLY WAY THE RIGHT BRAIN CAN BE INSTRUCTED TO PERFORM.**

Imaging is the process of visualizing the entire shot in every detail; the path of the cue ball, the collision with the object ball, the path of the object ball into the pocket, the path of cue ball after collision, and the cue ball coming to rest at a predetermined spot.

Imaging techniques must be employed in all sports that require muscle control and coordination. The high diver hesitates and visualizes every aspect of the dive before jumping. The same is true for the high jumper, pole vaulter, and so on.

Be aware of and <u>avoid</u> <u>negative</u> <u>imagery</u>. For example, consider the golf ball that must be hit over a pond to the green. What you absolutely do not want to do is hit the ball into the pond. If you instruct your right brain not to hit the ball into the pond, you conger up an image similar to that shown in figure 15-1. The caption says "do not hit the ball into the pond." But, all the right brain sees is the ball going into the pond it doesn't understand language so it can't read the caption. With this image to guide it, the right brain causes the ball to be hit into the pond; it is very happy because it feels that it has done exactly what it was instructed to do. And indeed it did; it made reality match the image that it was given.

Next time you miss a shot, immediately think back to the moment just before striking

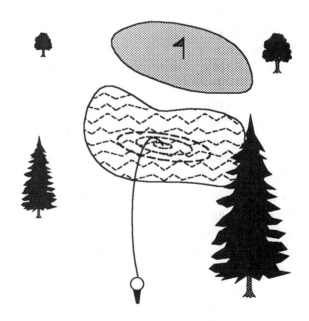

FIGURE 15-1. Dnop eht otni llab eht tih ton od.

the cue ball. Did you have a negative image in your mind? Recall how often players have remarked after missing a shot, "I knew I was going to miss that shot!" It was probably missed just as it was imagined before execution.

The consequence of hitting the golf ball into the pond must be considered as part of the analysis done by the left brain. In pool, all the negative aspects must also be considered; "If I don't hit my ball I will be charged with a foul;" "If I shoot that object ball the cue ball will scratch." These are negative thoughts that are true and valid and therefore must be considered; *but*, only as part of the analysis made by the left brain. Once the left brain has completed the analysis, preparation for execution must begin with no negative thoughts or images.

Proper positive imaging cannot be done using generalities. For example, you may imagine that the cue ball will end up somewhere in a particular area. But, the cue ball can't be pictured in more than one place at a time, therefore the exact *spot* must be pictured. If you had a photograph of the table after the shot you would see the cue ball in a specific place. It would be impossible to see it in a *general area*. The same applies to every other aspect of the shot; everything must be imagined with precision.

Even when the proper imaging technique is used, the right brain cannot duplicate anything that it has not been programmed to do. Programming is done by practicing. Successful shots have to be made during practice so that the right brain can store the proper images. When it is called upon to execute a shot, it searches through its memory bank of shots; when it finds the exact same shot, it executes by using the exact same muscle stimulation it used the previous time. This is why it is important to observe every aspect of a shot, including where the cue ball goes and its exact path. If only vague images are stored, that is how the shot will be executed on retrieval. Remember, good shooting technique requires that the body remain in shooting position until the balls stop moving. A person that moves up and out of shooting position as soon as the cue ball is struck, never observes a complete shot from the shooting position. If shots are never observed from the shooting position, they can't be accurately imagined from that position. When a shot is made exactly as planned, it should be repeated in the mind. Visualize the total shot again exactly as it occurred. This will reinforce the right brain image of the shot making it easy to retrieve the next time it is required.

Keep in mind that the shots that are missed are also stored in the right brain. They must somehow be negatively labeled so that they won't be retrieved by mistake. Since the right brain doesn't understand language the missed shots can't be labeled with words. The only way they can be labeled is with an **emotion**, and the proper emotion is **agony**. **YOU MUST AGONIZE OVER A MISSED SHOT**, at least for a short time while it's being filed. It's easy to agonize over a shot that is missed during a tournament or other important game. It is equally important to agonize over shots that are missed during practice. The best way to agonize during practice is to keep records. Wanting to maintain a good record induces agony when a shot is missed. Conversely, when a shot is executed perfectly, its image must be labeled with a positive emotion. Feel happy about the good shots, repeat them in your mind while you're feeling good. The more difficult the shot, the more it must be savored when made.

Imaging must also be done on a larger scale which encompasses the total game. Imagine your victory in detail prior to the game, the successful break shot, the balls going into the pockets, and the congratulatory hand shake with your defeated opponent. Imagine all of the positive emotions that you will feel as each ball goes into a pocket. Imagine the joy and adulation of your friends when you win. Imagine all of these things as though they have already happened. This process programs the right brain as to the desired final result.

PHYSICAL CONDITION

Pool is not as physically demanding as many other sports, however, mental stress is physically exhausting; in this respect, the mental stress of competitive pool is tolerated better if a person is in good physical condition.

Exercise--Probably the greatest benefit one attains from exercising is cardiovascular conditioning (heart and lung). Simply walking or jogging will satisfy this objective. However, the pool player wants more out of exercising - namely, timing, rhythm, general muscle coordination, and hand-eye coordination. Jogging provides cardiovascular conditioning but little else. Skipping rope or working-out on a speed bag provides cardiovascular conditioning and also helps timing and rhythm.

<u>Juggling</u> is the best pool-specific activity. Juggling promotes timing, rhythm, hand-eye coordination, and most importantly, hand-speed control. Juggling may even provide cardiovascular stimulation by adding some spins, dips, jumps, kicks, etc. When learning to juggle, one should avoid juggling with hard or heavy objects because they may cause injury or damage. Also, avoid balls that bounce or you'll spend most of your time chasing them.

Exercise on the day of the tournament or important game should be limited to between 10 and 25 percent of your normal daily exercise. If your normal exercise is very strenuous (like weight lifting), reduce it to about 10 percent; if your normal exercise is mild (like walking), reduce it to about 25 percent.

Eating--All serious athletes should have a regimented diet and eating schedule prior to the big game. Anxiety causes the stomach to constrict and produce excess acid. If too much food is eaten, anxiety may cause the stomach to throw it back up. Even a mild case of stomach upset can be distracting and may trigger a cycle of frustration. Before the big game eat only light, easily digestible food; this means carbohydrates like fruits and vegetables. Avoid fat and protein, this means **no** hamburgers or hot dogs.

Allow at least two hours for digestion before the game. If you get hungry during the event, snack on some fruit like an apple or pear. If you are even the least bit prone to choking, take an antacid as soon as you start to feel the anxiety.

Vitamin and mineral supplements-- Vitamins and minerals are essential for the proper function of the brain, nerves, and muscles. These are the exact things that we want to function at maximum efficiency during the big game. It follows that we should take special care to insure that our bodies have sufficient quantities of each of the vitamins and minerals.

The U. S. Government has published "Recommended Daily Allowances" for the essential vitamins and minerals. The recommended intake is that which keeps a person from getting sick. More and more researchers are discovering that optimum intake (for best health) is generally more than the recommended intake. Therefore, to be on the safe side, one should take vitamin and mineral supplements daily.

Stress tends to deplete the body of some of the critical vitamins and minerals; therefore an extra dosage should be taken with the last meal before the big event. Note: If you are already taking megadoses daily, don't take any more with the last meal.

The extra dose of vitamins and minerals should be taken under any tournament conditions and especially under barroom tournament conditions when alcohol is to be consumed. Alcohol is known to deplete the system of several critical vitamins and minerals. The cerebral cortex area of the brain is responsible for the manifestation of thoughts and associating ideas. Alcohol decreases the function of the cerebral cortex while caffeine stimulates it. Therefore, the effects of alcohol can be diminished by drinking coffee or other caffeine containing beverage. The effects of alcohol and caffeine differs between individuals. Each individual should experiment to determine the proper caffeine intake to negate the effects of alcohol. The dosage of caffeine varies with the source. An average cup of brewed coffee contains 100 to 150 milligrams of caffeine; a cup of instant coffee contains 80 to 90 milligrams. If a caffeine containing beverage is not available, the caffeine can be taken in pill form. Caffeine pills are available anywhere vitamins are sold. Note: Be cautioned, caffeine tends to increase anxiety, if nervous tension is a bigger problem than the effects of alcohol -- don't take caffeine.

Rest and relaxation--One should strive to get one's normal amount of sleep the night before the big event. More or less than the normal amount may be detrimental to your game.

It takes some time after awakening before all the muscles begin to function at peak efficiency. One should allow a minimum of two hours between waking and the playing of an important game. Walking or other mild form of exercise helps to speed up muscle coordination.

The eyes should be rested prior to the big game. Avoid reading, television, and even driving if possible.

222

CHAPTER 16
TOURNAMENT POOL

Anyone that is serious about pool will eventually shoot in some type of pool tournament. When it happens, don't be surprised if someone starts arguing about who plays who and when. There are several different types of tournaments; each can be conducted several different ways with different charts, rules, etc. Probably no tournament can be completely fair and impartial. Weak players may be matched against strong players and some players will have to play more matches than others; but, such is life.

Three of the more common types of tournaments are examined here. They include the ROUND ROBIN, SINGLE ELIMINATION, and DOUBLE ELIMINATION. The following are some common tournament terms:

Game--A single contest between two players.

Set--Two or more consecutive games between the same players.

Match--One or more games or sets between two players to decide the individual winner.

Race-to-X--A predetermined number (X) of wins which constitutes a set. For example, a set consisting of a "race-to-5" means whoever wins 5 games first wins the set.

◑　　　◐　　　◑

ROUND ROBIN TOURNAMENT

A *round robin* tournament is a contest in which each participant is matched against every other participant. The basic concept is to determine the player's ability relative to the entire group rather than the individuals. It eliminates the inequities of some players having to play against stronger players by virtue of a chance drawing. The number of participants is limited only by the time available. The number of matches required, to determine the winner, can be calculated using the formula (x) (x-1) / 2 = number of matches (x represents the number of participants) The required number of matches increases faster than the number of participants; for example, with five participants 10 matches are required, with ten participants 45 matches are required.

Figure 16-1 shows a round robin tournament chart. In this example, the players are represented by the letters A, B, C, and D. The players names are listed both horizontally and vertically to indicate who plays whom.

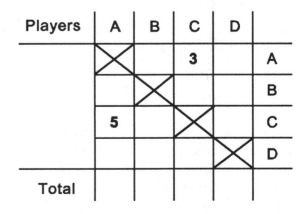

Players	A	B	C	D	
	✕		3		A
		✕			B
	5		✕		C
				✕	D
Total					

FIGURE 16-1. A round robin tournament chart.

Match scoring is recorded in the boxes below the player's name. For example, player A wins 5 games while playing player C who wins 3 games. The numbers in the vertical column, below each player's name, are added to determine the total for each player.

Scoring system--Several different scoring systems can be used; it's imperative that the type of scoring system be specified before the tournament begins. Three types of scoring systems are examined here:

1. The winner of each match gets one point and the loser gets zero. This system tends to emphasize the individual against individual concept rather than the individual against the group. This system produces more ties than the other systems because of the low scores. Figure 16-2 shows an example of this system in which each of three participants wins one match and loses one, and all three are tied. If each match consists of several games, ties can sometimes be resolved by resorting to the number of wins between the tied individuals.

2. Each match can consist of a specified number of games. This system can be

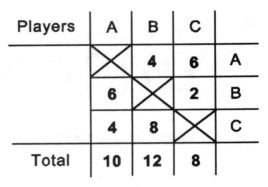

FIGURE 16-3. Each match consist of 10 games, each player receives one point for each game won.

called "best of X" where X represents the number of games to be played in each match. X is generally an odd number so the match won't end in a tie; however, it's really not important who wins the match because each player gets credit for every game won. Figure 16-3 shows an example of a round robin tournament using a "best of 10" scoring system. Note that there is a definite first, second, and third place; using the previous scoring system all three players would be tied. The major problem with this system is that at some point some players may, statistically, not have a chance to win. They may then concede the remaining games to their opponent because there is no incentive to win. The persons receiving the conceded games will have their totals unfairly increased. The best thing about this system is that the time required can be estimated more accurately then with the other scoring systems because you know in advance that each match will be X number of games.

3. This system is similar to the previous scoring system except that each match consists of a specified number of wins rather than a specified number of games. For example, assume it's a "race-to-10" as shown in figure 16-4. The winner of each match will always have the specified

Players	A	B	C	
	✕	1	0	A
	0	✕	1	B
	1	0	✕	C
Total	1	1	1	

FIGURE 16-2. A scoring system in which the winner of the match receives a point for each win.

Players	A	B	C	D	
	╳	7	10	4	A
	10	╳	10	8	B
	9	5	╳	10	C
	10	10	5	╳	D
Total	29	22	25	22	

FIGURE 16-4. A race-to-10; the winner of each match gets 10 points, the loser gets a point for each game won.

number of wins (score of 10) and the loser will score anywhere from zero to 9. This system has an advantage over the previous system in that losing players cannot increase their opponent's score by conceding; the winner of a match gets a specific score regardless of what the loser does. With this system, as with the previous system, a player can win the tournament while losing every match (providing there are more than three players). This concept is difficult for some people to comprehend, especially if they are accustomed to playing tournaments where all game wins are voided if the match is lost. With this scoring system it's difficult to estimate the time required for the tournament. In the example given, the total number of games could vary from 60 to 114.

There is less likelihood of ties with the second and third scoring systems because the numbers are larger which offers a greater scoring diversity. In case of ties, the person that wins the match between the tied individuals should be given the victory.

Playing order--Playing order, in the first round, is dictated by the player's position on the chart which is determined by some random method. In all succeeding rounds, the players with the lowest number of wins should play first. This accomplishes two things: First, the players that are most likely to win will play last; this keeps spectators interested to the very end. And second, the weaker player is less likely to concede games because the mathematical probability of losing the tournament is not known.

Assume a random technique was used to position the players on the chart in figure 16-4. The playing order would be as follows:

Game
1. A plays B - by virtue of chart position.
2. C plays D - by virtue of chart position.
3. B plays C - lowest scores.
4. A plays D - to complete the second round.
5. B plays D - lowest scores.
6. A plays C - to complete the third round and tournament.

Player A wins with a total score of 29, player C is second with 25 wins, and players B and D are tied with 22 wins. However, in the match between players B and D, B won by a score of 10 to 8. Therefore player B takes third place and player D takes fourth.

Handicapping--When there is a known disparity of playing skills, the weaker players may be given an advantage before the tournament begins; this is called handicapping. Handicapping helps equalize everyone's chance of winning and encourages players of all skill levels to participate. It is relatively easy to handicap a round robin tournament; the weaker player or players are given some wins before the tournament begins. Figure 16-5 shows an example of handicapping. Players A and D are both very

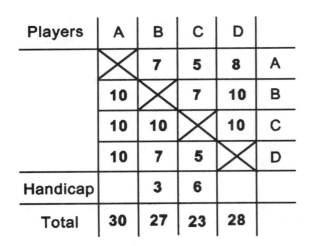

Players	A	B	C	D	
	✕	7	5	8	A
	10	✕	7	10	B
	10	10	✕	10	C
	10	7	5	✕	D
Handicap		3	6		
Total	30	27	23	28	

FIGURE 16-5. An example of handicapping.

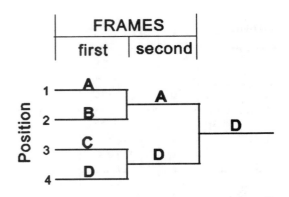

FIGURE 16-6. An example of a single-elimination flow chart.

skilled players and don't receive a handicap. Player B doesn't shoot much and usually only wins about 6 games against A or D in a race-to-10; therefore player B is given a 3-game handicap. Player C hardly ever plays, hasn't even read this book and is consequently a poor player; player C is given a handicap of 6 games. The amount of the handicap is generally decided by mutual agreement, if detailed records are kept, a more scientific determination of the appropriate handicap can be made. Ideally, the best players should maintain a slight statistical advantage even after handicapping. This serves to reward superior skill.

SINGLE ELIMINATION TOURNAMENT

A *single elimination* tournament means that a player who loses one match is eliminated from the tournament. The winner of each frame advances to the succeeding frame and is matched with another player with an identical record. Play continues until only one player is without a loss, and he or she is the tournament winner.

Figure 16-6 shows a typical 4-position single-elimination flow chart. Any type of random technique can be used to assign the players their initial position on the chart. The player in position 1 plays the person in position 2 and so on. In this example, A beats B and advances to the second frame, D beats C and also advances to the second frame. Player D beats player A and wins the tournament.

Scoring system--In the single elimination tournament each match can consist of one single game or a "race-to-X" (X being any specified number of wins). With the race-to-X scoring system in a round robin tournament, the individual players can maintain credit for the games won even if the match is lost. This is not the case with the single elimination format -- the match can be lost by a score of 10 to 0 and it records the same as a 10 to 9 loss.

Bye positions--Two players are required to play a match and when there's an odd number of players in a frame, someone must get a *bye*. The player that is matched with the bye gets an automatic win and advances to the next frame.

226

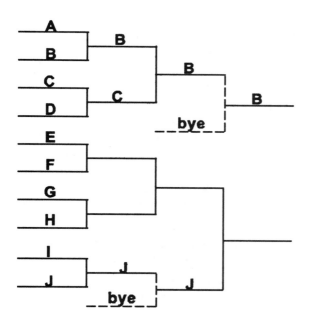

FIGURE 16-7. An example of assigning byes in any frame that has an odd number of players.

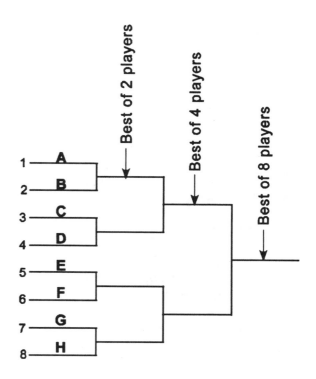

FIGURE 16-8. The value of a bye doubles with each succeeding frame.

When there are 2 players, or multiples thereof (4, 8, 16, etc.) there are no byes and the tournament chart is said to be symmetrical. With any other number of players, there must be one or more byes. Figure 16-7 shows a 10-position flow chart. There is an even number of players in the first frame so there are no byes. However, only 5 players advance to the second frame thereby requiring a bye. Another bye is required in the third frame because there are only 3 players.

The bye has a different value depending on the frame in which it occurs. Figure 16-8 shows an 8-position chart; a win in the first frame technically means that the winner is the best of two players, a win in the second frame signifies the best of four players, and a win in the third frame signifies the best of eight players. In essence, the value of a win <u>doubles</u> with each succeeding frame. The same is true for the bye, it doubles in value with each succeeding frame. In figure 16-7 players B and J both receive a bye, but the bye given to player B has twice the value because it occurs one frame later.

The significance, or value, of the bye should ideally be kept to a minimum so that advancing on the flow chart reflects the skill of the player rather than random chance **The value of the byes are minimized when they are confined to the first frame**. In order to confine the byes to the first frame the smallest symmetrical flow chart, that will accommodate all the participants, <u>**must**</u> be used. For example, assume there are 5 players. That's too many players for a 4-position chart so an 8-position chart <u>**must**</u> be used. With 8 positions and only 5 players, 3 byes must be used in the first frame. Thereafter no byes will be required. The byes must be uniformly distributed on the flow chart *before* the player positions are selected. Figure 16-9 shows what happens if the byes

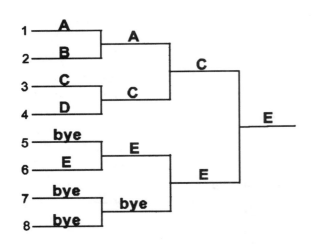

FIGURE 16-9. When two byes are positioned together, one of them must be advanced to the next frame.

are positioned together. One bye advances to the second frame thereby making it more valuable. In this example, player E advances all the way to the third frame without playing a single game.

Buy-in positions--There is another solution to the problem of not filling out a symmetrical flow chart. It is called a *buy-in*. This means that an individual is allowed to enter the tournament more than once and plays in more than one position. A buy-in can be substituted for a bye thereby avoiding the injustice of giving someone an automatic win. Figure 16-10a shows a 4-position chart with only three participants. By random selection, player C gets a bye in the first frame. Assuming all players are of equal ability, player C has a 50 percent chance of winning the tournament while players A and B each

ENTRY FEE $10

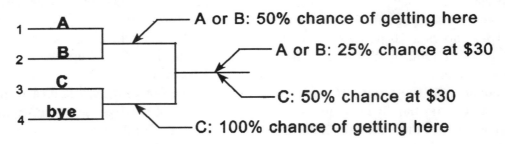

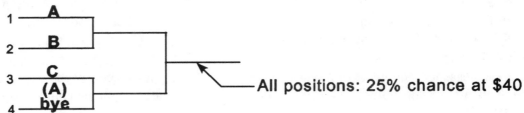

FIGURE 16-10. A player can be allowed to play in more than one position to minimize the injustice of the bye.

have only a 25 percent chance of winning. If player A is allowed to buy-in, as shown in figure 16-10b, each position will have an equal 25 percent chance of winning.

The buy-in, versus the bye, is easier to evaluate when the entry fee is also considered. Assume a $10 entry fee: Using a bye there will be $30 in the pot, and with the buy-in there will be $40 in the pot. Player B, who has a 25 percent chance either way, will obviously prefer to shoot for $40 rather than for $30. Therefore he is in favor of the buy-in. With the buy-in, player A will have twice the chance of winning but has paid twice the entry fee, and therefore has no proportional advantage. In summary, the bye gives one or more players a disproportionate advantage while the buy-in doesn't.

Skill level should be considered when deciding whether to allow a player to buy-in. A player with average skill will not affect the statistical chances of the other players (assuming they too are average). A player with less than average skill will cause the statistical chances of the other positions to go up. Conversely, a player with more than average skill will cause the statistical chances of all other positions to go down. But keep in mind, if the good player isn't allowed a buy-in, somebody will get a free game (caused by the bye), and the prize money will be less.

There is another consideration when the person that is buying-in is not of average skill. Assume that a particular player usually wins 60 percent of his games. If he is made to play himself, his chance of winning in the first frame, in each position, is effectively reduced to 50 percent; conversely, the 40 percent player will raise his chance to 50 percent in the first frame. In effect, having to play one's self acts as a handicapping system since it lessens the better players chances and increases the lesser players chances. In figure 16-10b, if player A beats both B and C, he will have to play himself in the second frame

which will mean an automatic win. If he is made to play himself in the first frame, that will not happen. Because of the automatic built-in handicapping, the person that is buying-in should be made to play himself in the first frame.

Probably the best way to treat vacant positions on the single elimination chart is by a combination of byes and buy-ins. This system is referred to as the *loser eligible buy-in* or *buy-back*. With this system the vacant positions are initially assigned byes, and after each first frame match, the loser is given the option of buying back into the tournament at the last assigned bye position. For example, in figure 16-10a the bye is initially assigned to the fourth position. If player B wins the first match he advances to the second frame and player A is given the option to buy back in at position 4. If player A does not want the buy-back, the fourth position remains a bye and player C gets a free win. If there were more players and bye positions, they would each be given a chance to buy-back upon losing. However, they should only be given the option to buy-back at the last assigned bye position. This prevents them from picking and choosing who they will play.

❂   ❂   ❂

DOUBLE ELIMINATION TOURNAMENT

A *double elimination* tournament means that each participant must lose twice before being eliminated from the tournament. The double elimination tournament is simply an extension of the single elimination tournament. An additional flow chart is used for the players that suffer one loss. This chart is called the *loser's chart* or *bracket, one loss bracket*, or *second-chance bracket*. It will be referred to here as the second-chance bracket. The winner of the second-chance bracket must beat the winner of the winner's bracket twice in order to win the tournament.

Figures 16-11 through 16-15 show the standard symmetrical double elimination charts having 4 through 32 positions. The letter that appears in the winner's bracket between matched players is assigned to the loser of that match, and the loser is moved to the corresponding letter position in the second-chance bracket. For example, in figure 16-16, the letter between Neal and Valerie in the first frame of the winner's bracket is B, so the loser of that match (Neal) is moved to the B position in the first frame of the second-chance bracket. The letters are arranged such that a player will statistically have the least chance of being matched with the same person twice.

Scoring system--The scoring system for the double elimination tournament is essentially the same as for the single elimination tournament. The match can consist of a single game or a race-to-X. In either case each match is scored simply as a win or a loss.

Bye positions--As in the single elimination

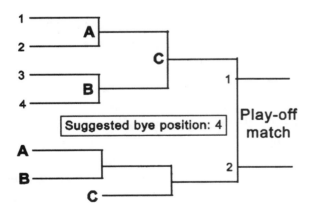

FIGURE 16-11. A standard 4-position double elimination flow chart.

tournament, the smallest possible symmetrical flow chart must be used, and the vacant positions are assigned byes. The byes must be separated and confined to the first frame of the winner's bracket. The bye is treated as a loser and thus is moved to the appropriate position in the second-chance bracket. If more than one quarter of the positions are initially occupied by byes, they will extend into the second frame of the second-chance bracket. There are more frames in the second-chance bracket, therefore the bye in the second frame is not critical. The suggested bye positions shown on figures 16-11 through 16-15 will statistically have the least influence on the outcome of the tournament. The bye order can be changed somewhat while still maintaining statistical integrity. However, if the suggested bye positions are used, any appearance of bias by the tournament director will be avoided. The bye positions must be entered on the chart before player positions are randomly selected.

Buy-in positions--Buy-in positions are treated the same as in the single elimination format. Persons that buy-in should be made to play themselves in the first frame of the winner's bracket. The loser eligible buy-in should be confined to the first frame of the winner's bracket. As in the single elimination tournament, the loser in the first frame should only be given the option to buy-back at the last assigned bye position. Players that opt to buy-in will initially be playing in two positions which may cause some delays if both positions are scheduled to play at the same time. Usually, playing order can be manipulated somewhat to avoid delays.

Example tournament--Assume twelve people want to have a double elimination tournament with loser eligible buy-in. The smallest symmetrical chart that can be used is the 16-position chart. With twelve players four byes are required, and they are tentatively assigned to positions 16, 1, 9, and 8 (figure 16-16). Neal plays Valerie and loses; Valerie moves to the second frame and Neal moves to the B position in the second-chance bracket. Neal elects to buy-back and is assigned bye position 8 (last assigned bye position). Danny loses to Paulette and is moved to the C position in the second-chance bracket. He elects not to buy-back. The next match is between positions 7 and 8. Neal loses to Alice, and he is not given the option to buy-back because he has already bought-in

once. Linda loses and elects to buy-back and is assigned to position 9. Mikie loses to Kaycee and elects not to buy-back. At this point the only match remaining in the first frame is between positions 9 and 10. Linda loses but is not given the option to buy-back because she has already done so. Since there are no more players eligible for a buy-back, the byes from positions 1 and 16 are moved to the appropriate position in the second-chance bracket. Note that there is no entry for the second match in the final frame. If Linda had won the first match it would have gone to a second match. Linda, having lost, has two loses and is therefore eliminated from the tournament.

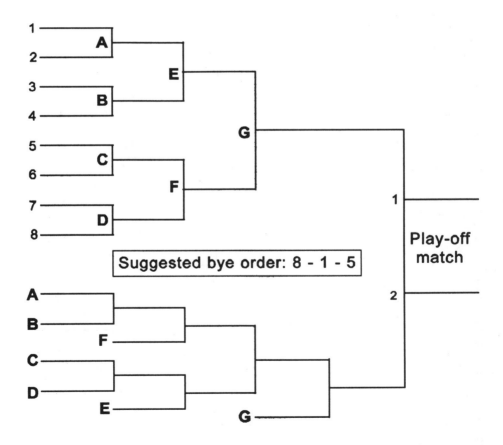

FIGURE 16-12. A standard 8-position double elimination chart.

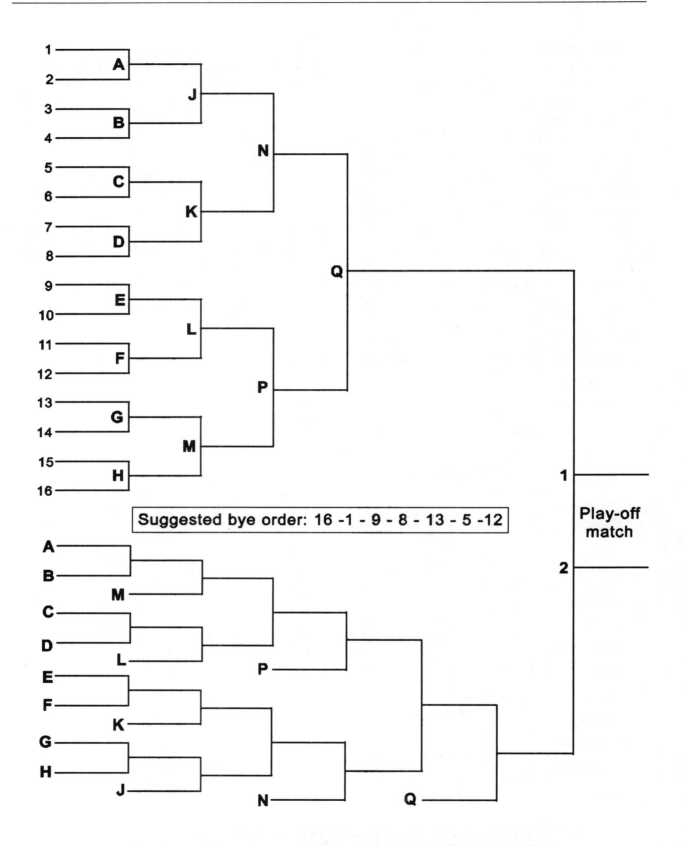

Suggested bye order: 16 -1 - 9 - 8 - 13 - 5 -12

FIGURE 16-13. A standard 16-position double elimination chart.

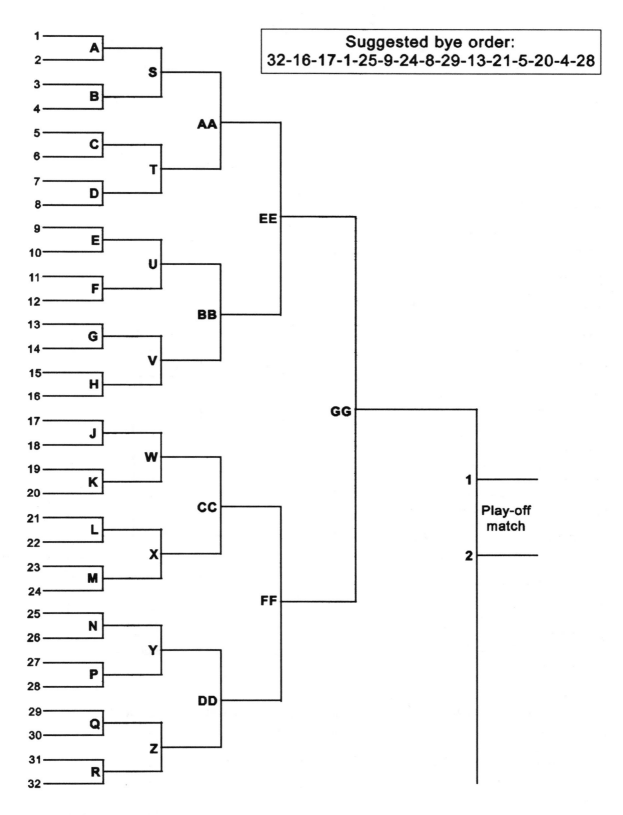

FIGURE 16-14. The winner's bracket of a standard 32-position double elimination chart.

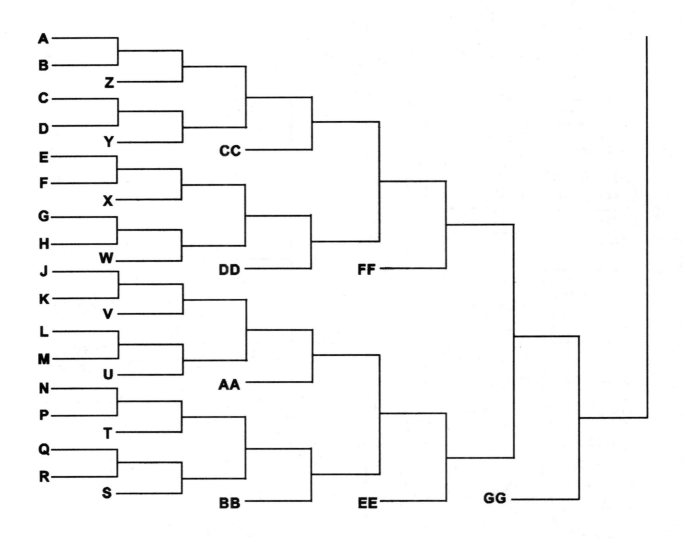

**FIGURE 16-15. The second-chance bracket of a standard
32-position double elimination chart.**

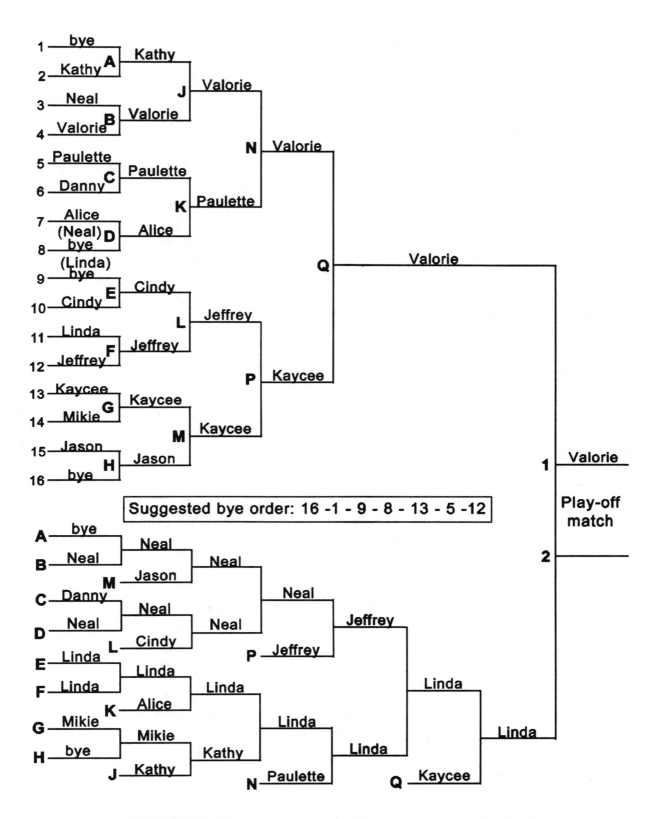

FIGURE 16-16. An example of a 12-person double elimination tournament using a 16-position chart.

Frame grouping charts--There is another type of double elimination chart that is called the *frame grouping chart*. Figure 16-17 shows an 8-position frame grouping chart The winner's bracket is the same as in the standard chart, the difference is in the second-chance bracket. With the standard chart, players in the second-chance bracket alternately play someone from the second-chance bracket then someone who has just come from the winner's bracket. With the frame grouping chart, losers in each frame continue to play as a group in the second-chance bracket until there is only one person left. The remaining person then plays the winner of another group in the second-chance

bracket, this continues until there is only one person left in the second-chance bracket. Figures 16-18 and 16-19 show the second-chance bracket for 16-and 32-position charts respectively.

Comparative analysis--The winner's bracket is identical for both the standard and frame grouping charts. The byes and bye-ins are selected and positioned the same for each chart.

There are some inequities in using the frame grouping chart when there are a large percentage of byes. Figure 16-20 shows an example; with five players and an 8-position

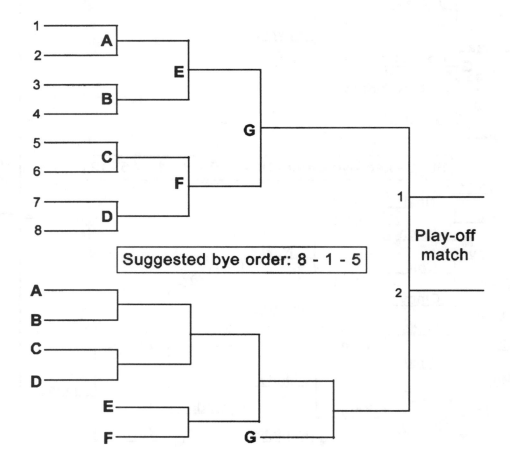

FIGURE 16-17. An 8-position frame grouping flow chart.

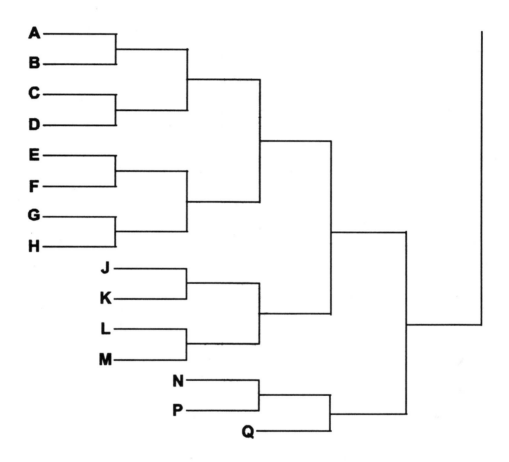

FIGURE 16-18. Second-chance bracket of a 16-position frame grouping flow chart.

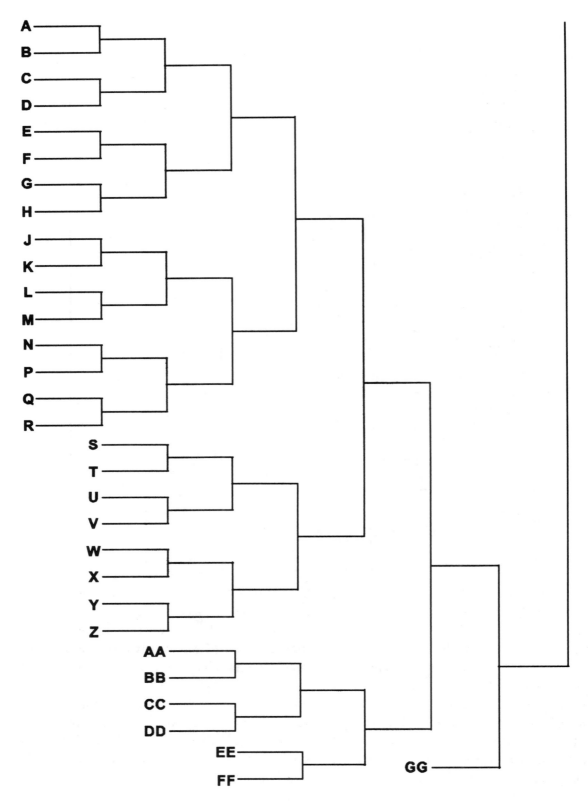

FIGURE 16-19. Second-chance bracket of a 32-position frame grouping flow chart.

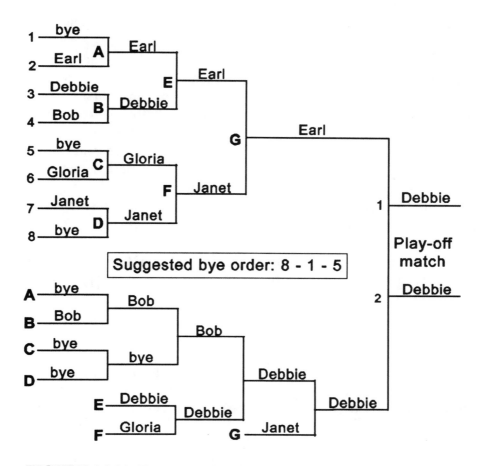

FIGURE 16-20. Example of a 5-person tournament using an 8-position frame grouping flow chart.

chart, there is only one match and consequently one loser (Bob) in the first frame of the winner's bracket. Bob is moved to the first frame of the second-chance bracket along with 3 byes and is subsequently given the next two matches by virtue of the byes. In essence, Bob gets all the way to the third frame of the second-chance bracket without winning a game. Debbie had to play three matches and win two in order to get to the same position. With the standard chart,

both Bob and Debbie would get only one bye in the second-chance bracket.

The probability of repeat matches (playing the same person twice) is about the same for each type of chart. For example, with both 16-position charts, it is impossible to have a repeat match until the fourth frame of the second-chance bracket. At this point the statistical probability of repeat matches varies somewhat but is small enough to be insignificant.

In any double elimination tournament, the player that stays in the winner's bracket plays fewer matches than the others. For example, with a 16-position standard chart, the winner can play as few as 5 matches or as many as 9 matches. The number of matches required, when coming through the second-chance bracket, varies with the type of chart and when the first loss occurs. Table 16-1 shows all of the possibilities with both types of symmetrical charts having 4 through 32 positions. The 4- and 8-position charts are the same. On charts with 16 or more positions, more matches are generally required with the standard chart if the first loss occurs in the early frames. Since the penalty for losing in an early frame is so severe (requiring more matches) some consider it more equitable to play only one match in the final frame regardless of who wins. However, when only wins are considered, the discrepancy is not so great.

The frame grouping chart contains an inherent handicapping system; that is, it tends to match players according to ability. For example, with the 16-position chart, the losers of the first frame matches are statistically the weaker players. These players play among themselves for the next three frames in the second-chance bracket. This virtually guarantees that someone from this group (weakest players) will make it to the fourth frame of the second-chance bracket.

◗   ◖   ◗

COMBINATION TOURNAMENTS

Under some circumstances it may be best

Number of positions on chart	Minimum matches to win	First loss (frame)	Total matches to win standard chart	frame grouping
4	3	1	5	5
		2	5	5
8	4	1	7	7
		2	7	7
		3	6	6
16	5	1	9	8
		2	9	8
		3	8	8
		4	7	8
32	6	1	11	10
		2	11	10
		3	10	10
		4	9	10
		5	8	8

TABLE 16-1. Comparison between the standard flow chart and the frame grouping flow chart.

to have a combination tournament which combines a single or double elimination tournament with a round robin tournament. Generally, the motivation for the combination tournament is to reduce the number of byes that are required. For example, if there are 12 players, a single elimination tournament will require 4 byes, and in effect, will give 4 of the 12 players an unfair advantage. Using a combination format, no byes will be required; they will play two frames with no byes and end up with 3 players remaining. These 3 players will then play a round robin to determine finishing order. In this format no player has an advantage. A 12-person double elimination tournament will work equally well. The initial 12 players will be split into three 4-person double elimination tournaments. The 3 winners of the double elimination tournaments will then play a round robin.

Table 16-2 shows the number of positions required to have a combination tournament with no byes. Combination tournaments may require some byes but generally substantially fewer than the single or double elimination tournaments. For example, if there are 24 players, a single or double elimination tournament will require 8 byes. Table 16-2 shows that no byes are required if they play a single or double elimination tournament then a 3-person round robin. Table 16-2 can be used to determine the various options for any given number of players For example, with 20 players the options are: 12 byes for a single or double elimination tournament; 4 byes for a 3-position round robin combination tournament; or no byes for a 5-position round robin combination tournament.

SEEDED TOURNAMENTS

In a *seeded tournament* the player's ranking is taken into consideration in the assignment of opponents in the early frames. It is structured to insure that those players that have the greatest skill are not matched against each other in the early rounds. The lowest ranked players play among themselves in the early rounds. As the tournament advances, progressively higher ranked players begin to participate.

The entry fee is generally higher for the better players. A seeded, 64-position single elimination tournament, could be structured as follows: The 32 lowest ranked players ($300 entry fee) play in the first frame; the 16 victorious players are matched with players ranked 17 through 32 ($400 entry fee); the 16 victorious players from this group are matched with players ranked 1 through 16 ($500 entry fee); the remaining frames are played in the normal manner.

The seeded format has desirable features for both the low ranked players and the high ranked players. The low ranked players like it because they don't have to play a high ranked player in the early rounds, and their entry fee is less. The high ranked players like it because they play fewer matches before getting into the money.

Number of players	Remain for Round Robin
4-8-16-32-64-128	0
6-12-24-48-96	3
10-20-40-80	5

TABLE 16-2. Number of positions required for a combination tournament with no byes.

EPILOGUE

After reading this book you have a good start with regard to pool knowledge, but don't stop here. Read other books and stay current by subscribing to pool periodicals; invest in instructional video tapes. Excellence germinates in the mind; feed and nurture your mind. Introduce your friends and relatives to the game -- some of them will fall in love with pool and be forever grateful. Share your knowledge, half the pleasure of knowing is being able to share it with others. People tend to remember where they get critical bits of knowledge -- be remembered. Tell your friends and colleagues that you're a pool player; let them know you have a unique multifarious talent. Show off your talents; confound your friends by explaining the complicated interaction of variables in a simple rail shot. If you can't confound your friends, go back to page one and start all over again.

INDEX

AND

GLOSSARY OF

SELECTED TERMS

BEHIND THE HEAD STRING: The area between the head string and the head cushion. Also called the "kitchen." 148, 151-52, 175-76

BIG BALL: A kick shot in which the object ball is near the cushion. The cue ball can either strike the object ball directly or strike the cushion first then the object ball, thus offering a "big" target.

BILLIARDS: Frequently used as a synonym for pool; in its strictest sense, a game played with a cue ball and two object balls. 1, 16, 31, 37, 53, 119-20, 155, 174, 213

BILLIARD SHOT: In pool, a shot in which the cue ball caroms off an incidental ball before striking the object ball. Also referred to as a "cue-ball carom shot."

BOTTOM ENGLISH: The reverse rotation of a cue ball caused by striking it below center. Also called "draw." 59-65, 69, 79-84, 89-90, 93, 95, 107, 113, 114, 133, 149, 159, 162, 167, 177-79, 182, 192, 209-10

BREAK BALL: A ball that can be pocketed while using the cue ball to break out additional balls.

BREAK OUT: To scatter or move balls into a more advantageous position. Same as "bust out".

BREAK SHOT: The first shot of a game. 8, 28, 147-50, 191, 199, 221

BRIDGE: The support for the cue shaft as it slides back and forth during aim and execution. 15, 23-24, 29-31, 34, 148, 150, 199-200, 204

BRIDGE HAND: The hand that is used to form the bridge; the left hand for right-handed players. 10, 15, 21, 23, 28-31, 33-34, 61, 148, 203-04

BUST OUT: To scatter or move balls into a more advantageous position. Same as "break out."

BUTT OF CUE: The large end of a cue stick. 6, 12, 14-15, 26, 61, 65, 76, 125, 127, 130, 142, 150, 153-55, 191

BUY-BACK: A player is allowed to reenter a tournament at a bye position. 229-31

BUY-IN POSITION: A vacant position on a tournament chart that a participant is allowed to purchase thus facilitating a multiple entry. 228-30

BYE POSITION: A vacant position on a tournament chart; the person paired with the bye gets an automatic win and advances to the next frame. 226, 229-31

CALLED BALL: The ball that the shooter indicates will be pocketed with the ensuing shot.

CALL POCKET: A game rule requiring the shooter to indicate the ball to be pocketed and the pocket in which it is to be made.

CALL SHOT: A game rule requiring the shooter to indicate the ball to be pocketed, the pocket it is to be made in, and all caroms and cushions in-between.

CAROM: A ball striking or glancing off another ball; also called a "kiss." 20, 22, 53, 82-2, 98, 107, 113-17, 154, 164-67, 170, 182-83, 190-92, 194, 198, 218

CASE GAME: The final game of a match or tournament.

CASUAL PLAY: A casual game of pool in which the prime objective is to have fun. 14, 18, 198

CENTER SPOT: An imaginary point directly between the center pockets on the center string. 17-18, 69, 92-93, 177-78, 180-81, 188, 190, 194, 196-97

CENTER STRING: An imaginary line connecting the center pockets. 17-18, 93, 154, 180-81, 183-85, 190, 197

CHALK: A gritty substance that is applied to the cue tip to keep it from slipping off the cue ball. 8-9, 11, 18-21, 39-40, 54, 59, 72, 84, 105, 111, 117, 145, 147, 174, 180, 183, 199, 215-16

CHEATING THE POCKET: The object ball is made but is deliberately shot to the side of center-pocket in order to get better shape. 90, 92-93, 181

JUMP STICK: A cue stick that is designed specifically for jump shots. It is generally shorter and stiffer than a regular cue stick. 153

KEY BALL: A ball that can be pocketed while accomplishing a second objective. 161-62, 166, 193

KICK SHOT: A bank shot in which the cue ball strikes a cushion before striking the object ball. 35, 85, 119, 128-30, 133-34, 138-39, 168-69, 180, 189-90

KISS: A collision of two balls; also called a "carom." 187

KITCHEN: The area, on the table surface, between the head string and the head rail. 17

LAG FOR BREAK: A procedure used to determine which player has the option of taking the first shot. A ball is shot from behind the head string to the foot cushion; the player whose ball comes to rest nearest the head cushion wins the lag. 147, 152

LEAVE: A term used to express the difficulty of the shot that is left for one's opponent. Usually used qualitatively; for example, "good leave" means that the cue ball was left in a difficult position for the opponent's first shot. 87, 168

LIGHT HIT: Cue ball strikes an object ball at a high cut angle. Same as "thin hit" or "thin cut."

LIP OF POCKET: The corner of the cushion at the pocket. 43, 45-46

LONG STRING: An imaginary line dividing the table in half lengthwise. 17, 185, 197

MASSÉ SHOT: A shot in which the cue ball curves substantially (usually more than 90 degrees). 147, 155, 203

MECHANICAL BRIDGE: An implement used as a bridge when a shot can't be reached in the normal manner. Also called a "crutch" or "rake." 23-24, 31, 199, 203

MISCUE: Cue tip slips off the cue ball. 8, 20-21, 59-65, 70, 81, 150

MONEY BALL: The ball that determines the winner. 217

NAP: The downy surface of the cloth formed by short fibers. 18-19, 23, 97

NINE-BALL: A game in which balls numbered one through nine are shot in numerical order. The player that makes the 9-ball wins the game. 22, 33, 87, 147, 157, 168-69, 171

NIP STROKE: A stroke with little or no follow-through. Usually employed to avoid striking the cue ball twice.

NORMAL ROLL: A state of roll in which there is no slippage between the ball and cloth. 53-59, 66-67, 78, 81, 83, 94-95, 107, 116, 132-33, 143-44, 152, 191, 201, 207-10

OBJECT BALL: The ball, other than the cue ball, that is principally involved in the shot. 3-4, 22, 28, 34-40, 43, 45, 47, + other

OBJECT-BALL CAROM SHOT: A shot in which the cue ball strikes an object ball which in turn caroms off another ball before going into a pocket. 115-16, 170

ONE-POCKET: A game in which each player has only one designated pocket in which to make balls; the game is won when a player pockets more than half the object balls.

ON THE RAIL: A ball resting against a cushion. Same as "on the cushion." 177

OPEN BRIDGE: A hand bridge in which there is no finger over the top of the cue shaft. Also called a "vee bridge." 12, 15, 29, 31

OPENING BREAK SHOT: The first shot of a game. 8, 28, 147-50, 191, 199, 221

OPEN TABLE: A situation in which neither player has a designated group of balls.

OUTSIDE ENGLISH: Striking the cue ball on the side opposite to which the object ball is cut; for example, cutting the object ball to the left while striking the cue ball to the right of center. 72, 74-75, 187

RAIL TRACK: A line, parallel to the rail, 1/2 ball diameter from the cushion. The rail track is usually a lighter color than the rest of the cloth. 97, 105, 119, 123-30, 137, 142

RAIL TRACK SYSTEM: A banking system in which the geometric banking point is determined. 119, 129

RAKE: An implement used as a bridge when the shot can't be reached in the normal manner. Also called a "crutch" or "mechanical bridge." 23

REVERSE ENGLISH: Side english which causes the cue ball's rebound angle, off a cushion, to be larger than it would normally be. 77, 79, 136

RIDE THE BALLS: Hitting the balls hard hoping to accidentally pocket one or more balls. Also referred to as "giving the balls a ride."

ROTATION: A game in which all fifteen balls must be pocketed in numerical order. 87, 147

ROTE SYSTEM: A banking system whereby a particular bank shot is repeated until the banking point is committed to memory. 130, 145, 188

ROUND ROBIN TOURNAMENT: A tournament in which each participant is matched against every other participant. 223-26, 241

RUN: A series of balls made in succession. 147, 164, 168-71, 179, 198

RUNNING ENGLISH: Side english which causes the cue ball rebound angle, off a cushion, to be smaller than it would normally be. 77-79, 119, 135, 138, 189

RUN THE RACK: Starting from the break shot and pocketing all of one's balls.

RUN THE TABLE: Pocketing all of one's remaining balls. 171

SAFETY: A shot in which the objective is to leave a difficult shot for the incoming player. 167-69

SCRATCH: Cue ball accidentally goes into a pocket. 9, 148, 183, 196, 217, 220

SEEDED TOURNAMENT: A tournament in which the player's ranking is taken into consideration in determining the paring for matches. 241

SET: Two or more consecutive games between two individuals. 223

SHAFT: The front half (narrow portion) of a cue stick. 5, 8-11, 15, 21-22, 28-33, 61, 70-71, 201, 211

SHAPE: Refers to the position of the cue ball relative to the difficulty of the next shot. Generally used qualitatively; for example, "good shape" means that the cue ball is in a good position for the next shot. Similar to "position." 67, 77, 79, 81-83, 87-96, 106, 149, 157-66, 170-71, 175, 179, 183, 192-94, 197-200, 211, 217

SHAPE ZONE: A zone on the table from which the next ball can be pocketed without difficulty. 88-89

SHARKING: The use of devious tactics to psych-out an opponent. 217

SHOT MAKER: A player that is good at pocketing the object ball but not necessarily good at getting shape.

SIDE CUSHIONS: The two longest cushions which contain the side pockets. Also referred to as the "long rails." 17, 80, 92, 95, 151, 169, 184, 186, 189, 198

SIDE ENGLISH: That component of a ball's rotation (spin) relative to its vertical axis. Side english is imparted to the cue ball by striking it to the left or right of center with the cue stick. 59, 69-86, 90, 94, 98-107, 110-113, 133-39, 155, 176, 179-80, 183-87, 191-95, 209-10

SIGHTS: Inlays (diamond or circular shaped) on the rails that serve as reference points. Also referred to as "diamonds."

SINGLE ELIMINATION TOURNAMENT: A tournament in which a player is eliminated after losing one match. 223, 226, 229-30, 241